The Lasting Honour

The Lasting Honour

The Fall of Hong Kong, 1941

Oliver Lindsay

'. . . Every day that you are able to maintain your resistance you and your men can win the lasting
honour which we are sure will be your due.'
Winston S. Churchill. *21 December, 1941*

HAMISH HAMILTON: London

First published in Great Britain 1978
by Hamish Hamilton Limited
90 Great Russell Street London WC1B 3PT

Copyright © 1978 by Oliver Lindsay

British Library Cataloguing in Publication Data

Lindsay, Oliver
    The lasting honour.
    1. Hongkong – Seige, 1941
    I. Title
    940.54′25   D767.3

Photoset, printed and bound in Great Britain by
Redwood Burn Ltd, Trowbridge and Esher

To Clare

Contents

Illustrations

between pages 82 and 83

between pages 114 and 115

*Illustrations 1a, 2a, 6b, 6c, 6d, 7b and 8a are reproduced by kind
permission of The Public Archives of Canada (reference numbers:
C 49742, C 49740, PR 643, PR 642, PR 628, PR 552, PR 482); 1b,
5b and 8b by kind permission of the Imperial War Museum, London
(reference numbers K 1668, HU 2766, SE 5016); and 2c, 3a, 3b, 4a,
4b and 6a by kind permission of National Defence HQ Ottawa.*

Maps

(drawn by Denys Baker)

(Place names shown on maps 2–3 are indicated by grid references in index.)

Acknowledgements

Old soldiers are said to fade away. This certainly is not so, judging by the enthusiasm and massive correspondence from those Hong Kong veterans who have contributed to this story. Thirty-seven years after the fall of Hong Kong, most of those who survived the war are flourishing.

I express my grateful thanks to them for giving me both their reminiscences and their time.

I was very fortunate in meeting in Hong Kong British, Portuguese and Chinese who explained to me what had happened on the precise ground over which they had fought. Among them were Brigadier Sir Lindsay Ride, CBE, ED, and Alf Taylor, who has contributed much to this story. (The ground has changed: some of the hills north-west of Kowloon, where the Royal Scots fought so desperately, have now been flattened for land reclamation projects, and the Colony's sedate cricket pitch is now adjacent to the Wong Nei Chong Gap.)

More recently I have met many throughout Canada who have added their personal accounts, as have others in England, Scotland and Australia. I should particularly like to thank: The Rev. Gordon Bennett, H. A. de B. Botelho MBE, ED, D. C. Bowie OBE, R. R. Chaplin, Brigadier J. N. Crawford MBE, MD, Brigadier J. P. Crowe, F. H. Fairclough, John Harris, T. D. Hunter, Iain MacGregor, Doctor Isaac Newton, Eric Potts, E. J. Soden, Wing-Commander H. G. Sullivan OBE and J. S. R. Thomson.

Special thanks are due to those who commented on appropriate passages and explained essential detail. They include: Lieutenant – Colonel H. A. Bush, J. A. Ford MC, Colonel A. G. Hewitt MBE, MC, Major-General and Mrs. C. M. M. Man, Brigadier J. H. Price OBE, MC, ED, B. A. Proulx MBE, Brigadier C. R. Templer DSO, Brigadier C. Wallis MC, and Mrs Barbara Anslow who also permitted me to quote from the diaries of her mother, Mrs. M. Redwood.

Others who very kindly helped me include Mr. and Mrs.

Fergus Kyle, Roger Lamble, Mrs. J. K. Lawson, Brigadier Sir
John Smyth Bt, vc, pc, mc, Augustus Muir, Major N. P. Pavri,
Colonel C. P. Stacey obe and John Stroud. I am grateful to
L. W. Bush mbe for permission to quote from his book *Road to
Inamura*; to George G. Harrap for permission to quote from
Through Japanese Barbed Wire by G. Priestwood and to Laurence
Pollinger Ltd for permission to quote from *Hong Kong Incident* by
Phyllis Harrop.

I obtained valuable assistance from Colonel B. A. Fargus
obe, the Regimental Secretary of the Royal Scots, and Major
A. E. F. Waldron mbe, Secretary of the Regimental Association
of the Middlesex Regiment, and I am grateful for permission to
quote from their Regimental Histories. Major R. G. Bartelot,
of the Royal Artillery Institution, also proved helpful, and
Major-General C. M. Maltby's encouragement was much appreciated.

The Department of Documents of the Imperial War
Museum and the Library of the Royal United Service Institute
were both immensely efficient. My warm thanks are also extended to the Public Records Office, and to Sheena Barber and
Kathy Witt for their typing.

I must also record the extensive courtesy and help of the
Directorate of History at National Defence Headquarters,
Ottawa, who over two years gave me unlimited access at all
hours to their Hong Kong files.

Finally I thank my father, Sir Martin Lindsay of Dowhill, Bt,
cbe, dso, without whose advice and encouragement this book
might never have been completed, and also my wife, Clare. She
typed most of the drafts, and provided me with innumerable
cups of black coffee at strange hours during three enthralling
years of research in Hong Kong, Canada and Great Britain.

Brookwood House,   *Oliver Lindsay*
Brookwood, Surrey
July 1978

Prologue

The Peninsula Hotel, Hong Kong. It was nearly midnight on Saturday, 6 December, 1941. Both Ballrooms were packed. The orchestra started to play the current favourite 'The Best Things in Life are Free', when suddenly the music stopped. The President of the American Steamships Line appeared on a balcony above the dance floor. Urgently waving a megaphone for silence, he shouted: 'Any men connected with any ships in the harbour – report aboard for duty.' After a second's pause he added menacingly: 'At once.' The dance was forgotten. Men hurriedly said 'Goodbye.' Others drifted down into the lobby and outside to waiting rickshaws.

* * *

Beyond Kowloon, up in the mountains manning the Shingmun Redoubt, the men of the Royal Scots watched the rapidly-changing shadows as the clouds raced across the moon. To their right were the Rajputs and Punjabis. The digging of trenches continued. Patrols groped forward to check that the perimeter wire was still in place.

At Shamshuipo, Sydney Skelton of the Royal Rifles of Canada tucked the diary which he was writing for his fiancée into his large pack. His battalion was to move to battle stations at first light. Covered by the massive guns of Stanley Fort, His Majesty's Motor Torpedo Boats patrolled far out into the South China Sea to give early warning of the enemy's approach. In the musty, heavily-camouflaged pill-boxes of Hong Kong Island the machine-gun battalion of the Middlesex Regiment stood-to. The Hong Kong garrison was ready for war.

* * *

Thirty miles to the north, the officers of Colonel Doi Teihichi's 228 Imperial Japanese Regiment studied markings in crimson ink upon their maps. Their objective was the Shingmun Redoubt, and then the British Crown Colony of Hong Kong itself.

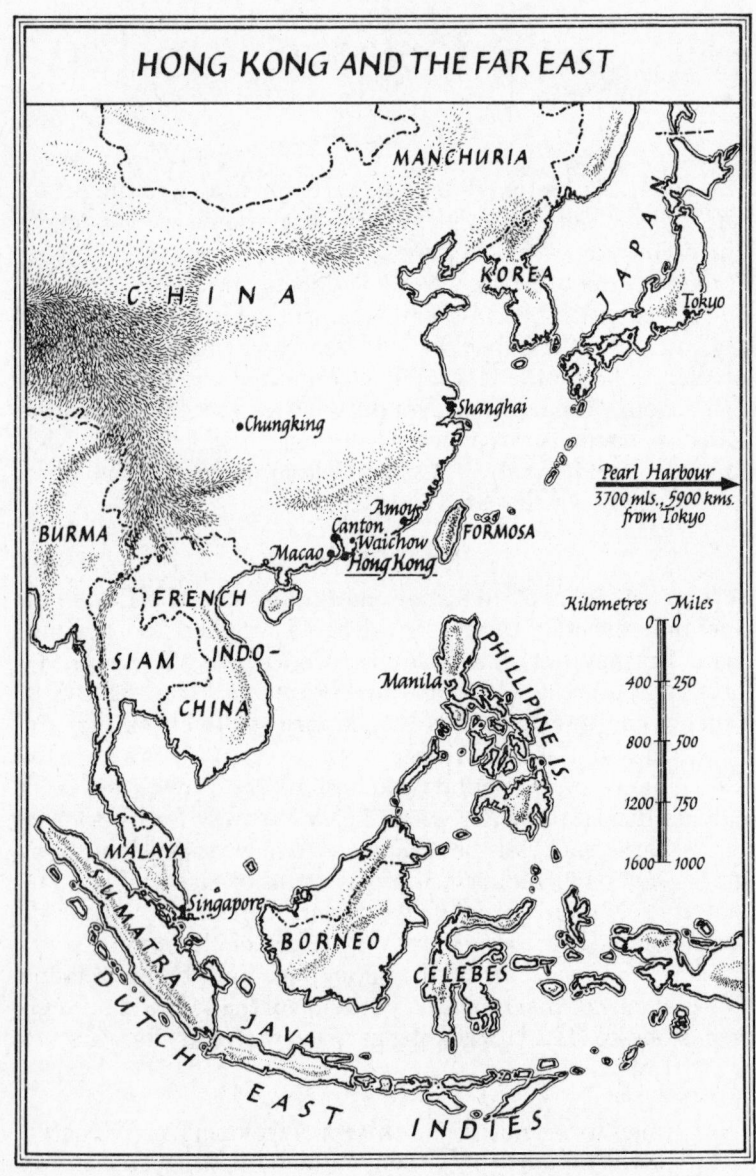

HONG KONG AND THE FAR EAST

MANCHURIA

CHINA

KOREA

JAPAN

Tokyo

Chungking

Shanghai

Pearl Harbour
3700 mls., 5900 kms.
from Tokyo

BURMA

Amoy
Canton
Macao · Waichow · FORMOSA
Hong Kong

FRENCH

INDO-

SIAM

CHINA

Manila

PHILLIPINE IS.

Kilometres   Miles
0   0

400   250

800   500

1200   750

1600   1000

MALAYA

Singapore

BORNEO

CELEBES

SUMATRA

DUTCH

JAVA

EAST   INDIES

1
The Strategic Liability

By the Spring of 1941 Winston Churchill regarded war with Japan as inevitable. As Japanese armies bit deeper into China, he was to advocate that the isolated garrison in Hong Kong of less than ten thousand regulars, reservists and local volunteers should be reduced to a symbolic scale: 'We must avoid frittering away our resources on untenable positions.'[1]

Major General A. W. Bartholomew, the General Officer Commanding in Hong Kong until 1938, had no confidence in any plan with which it was hoped to defend Hong Kong without massive reinforcements, and in his view to put less than a full division along the border would be foolhardy, for he considered that the ground favoured the attacker. He even wondered if the enemy should be resisted at all in the event of a mass attack.[2]

* * *

Japan's ambitions for an Empire had not been satisfied by the capture of Korea in 1890 and of Manchuria in 1931. The Japanese claimed that by 1935 seventy per cent of their Empire still lay within Japan, whereas nine out of ten members of the British Empire lived beyond the British Isles.

The good relationship which had existed between the two nations in the First World War, when they had been allies, had been quickly eroded afterwards. Both Britain and America had forced Japan to modify her arbitrary demands for a predominant position in China. In 1922, at an international conference in Washington, Japan grudgingly agreed that her capital ships would be less than a third the tonnage of the combined British and American fleets. A third humiliation for Japan at the same time was caused by Britain abrogating the Anglo-Japanese Alliance, seeking instead to develop her special relationship with America.

Japan was condemned by the League of Nations as an

aggressor, due to her refusal to withdraw her army of occupation from Manchuria. She responded by withdrawing from the League, and in 1933 crossed the Great Wall, invading northern China.

In 1937, the defence of Hong Kong was discussed in detail by the Chiefs of Staff in London. They debated whether to reinforce immediately the normal establishment of four battalions. A more attractive but less practical proposition was to leave the garrison at its existing strength, and rely on speedily reinforcing the Colony should a threat arise. It was concluded that in the event of war Hong Kong would be untenable without reinforcements, and it might be necessary to fight in the Colony regardless of the fate of the garrison, in order to encourage the Chinese resistance against Japan. The loss of the port facilities to the Japanese would also be a grievous blow to China, since sixty per cent of their arms were imported through Hong Kong. Furthermore, the loss of the Colony would have a grave effect on Britain's prestige. For these reasons the Chiefs of Staff decided not to evacuate or reduce the garrison. Instead they regarded Hong Kong as important and useful but not vital, and decided that the existing garrison, unreinforced, should defend the outpost as long as possible.

In April, 1938, General Bartholomew told the War Office: 'I still regard the building of defences as unnecessary. I have also made it clear that troops must resist with arms any sudden attack on themselves or their charge, but this is not to apply to any properly-organized and authoritative request by a military command to enter the concessions. . . .'[3]

To ensure that the virtual hopelessness of the position was understood in London, General Bartholomew signalled the War Office again on 13th April 1938: 'In event of wanton attack on Hong Kong, the garrison would have no option but to fight . . . the chances however of effecting a prolonged resistance even in the best circumstances seem slight.'

The War Office needed no convincing. The vulnerability of the outpost was well understood. It was uncertain whether a fleet could be despatched to the Pacific in the event of a second war with Germany, nor could reinforcements necessarily be spared from Singapore. It was again confirmed that the Hong Kong garrison would have to do the best it could with what it had.

However Major-General A. E. Grasett, who took over from General Bartholomew in November, 1938, was to take a much more optimistic view. He quickly became well-known in Hong Kong for his personal charm, good humour and social popularity. He was a tall, slim, elegant officer who had spent most of his service with the Royal Engineers although he was Canadian-born. General Grasett believed the Japanese forces to be vastly inferior in training, equipment and leadership. They fought well against third-rate Chinese, he argued, but they had yet to meet first class troops such as his battalions, which would give them a bloody nose.

By May, 1938, Japan had extended the war to South China and landed troops at Amoy, some 300 miles north-east of Hong Kong. In July the Chiefs of Staff once more reviewed the position of Hong Kong. They considered that Japan might widen her grip on South China, and move close up to the Hong Kong frontier before the outbreak of war, and so be able to bring the port under air and artillery bombardment. They concluded that the denial of the port to the Japanese for as long as possible was the sole military reason for Hong Kong's defence.

The outbreak of war with Germany in September, 1939, compelled the Admiralty to withdraw the major units of the China Squadron either for use in the Indian Ocean or to reinforce the Home and Mediterranean Fleets.

Japan adopted a waiting policy, while her armies bit deeper into China. In October a Japanese expeditionary force landed at Bias Bay, only thirty-five miles north-east of Hong Kong, and Canton was captured. The Colony's isolation was now almost complete.

Yet the British Foreign Office took heart from Japan's seemingly interminable struggle with China, and optimistically concluded that she was in no position to attack British or Dutch possessions. However, in June, 1940, the picture underwent a startling change with the collapse of France. Until then Britain had always relied on a French fleet in the Mediterranean to contain the Italian Navy, leaving some British warships to patrol Far Eastern waters. Now Britain was dramatically faced with the need to keep a powerful fleet in the Mediterranean, leaving virtually no ships for the defence of Hong Kong and Malaya.

Japan also rejoiced in the defeat of Holland, which so greatly increased the possibility of seizing by force, or by belligerent diplomacy, the Dutch East Indies' abundant quantities of oil, rubber, tin, bauxite and other raw materials. Within five days of the move of the Dutch Government to London, the Japanese arrogantly demanded that the Governor-General of the Netherlands should meet their claims for all the materials they needed. The Japanese demands were rejected.

With the British Commonwealth standing alone against the combined strength of Germany and Italy, a general settlement with the Japanese was essential. The British Ambassador in Tokyo reported that there was a real danger of Japanese entry into the war.

The British Government was doubtful whether, by giving in to Japanese demands, a general settlement could be reached. Nevertheless, in view of the lack of American support, it was reluctantly agreed that the Burma road, by which Nationalist China received up to 5,000 tons of supplies a month, was to be closed. The great importance to the Chinese of the Burma road was that it was their only practicable supply line for petrol. About 20,000 tons had reached them by this route in the seventeen months ending in May, 1940.

Japan saw only weakness in this concession. On 23 September, 1940, she invaded northern Indo-China. (The US Army's Signal Intelligence service had broken the Japanese codes and accurately predicted an invasion. Unfortunately a cipher clerk had muddled the code names, and Churchill was told by President Roosevelt that England was to be invaded by Germany at 3.00 pm 23 September.[4])

Four days later Japan signed the Tripartite pact with Germany and Italy, thereby recognizing the 'new order' in Europe, and gaining encouragement in turn for her aggressive policy in the Far East. Japan hoped to discourage America, who would be faced with a two-ocean war should she throw in her lot with Britain.

The Naval Affairs Committee of the United States Senate had already decided, in June, 1940, that their Navy would not fight Japan in the Pacific without the co-operation of the British and Dutch fleets. Since there was no immediate hope of either country producing an effective fleet in the Pacific, it was evident that no United States naval help could be expected.

Entreaties to the French Naval Commander in Indo-China

to transfer his squadron to Singapore were rejected, which was hardly surprising in view of the Vichy French collaboration with Germany. There was no advantage in holding staff conversations with the Dutch, since Holland had fallen and the Dutch forces in the East Indies were totally inadequate to withstand any Japanese onslaught.

If the Hong Kong garrison could expect no support from a British Fleet, the Americans, French or Dutch, the only hopeful possibility seemed to be Chinese diversionary attacks upon the Japanese, if Hong Kong were attacked.

However China had her own problems. She was divided not only by the Japanese, but also by the political struggle between the Nationalists and Communists, which continued in a desultory manner. In 1937 both had joined in a 'United Front' to defeat the Japanese. Ostensibly integrated with the Nationalist Army, the Communists concentrated on winning over the people, and setting up base areas from which to mount guerrilla operations. The Communists were to be accused of conserving their strength and avoiding decisive engagements while consolidating political power, and the Nationalists were later to be criticised for corruption and inefficiency.

General Grasett had been ordered in July, 1940, on no account to become involved in negotiations with General Chiang Kai-Shek, since nothing could have been more provocative to Japan. Nevertheless there were 750,000 Chinese living in Hong Kong Island, in addition to which hundreds of thousands of refugees had fled to the Colony to escape the barbarities of the Japanese advancing armies. Who would be responsible for them should the Colony be besieged? Twelve months later Major-General L. E. Dennys, the British Military Adviser with Chiang Kai-Shek in Chungking, was at last authorised to hold staff discussions on a joint plan.

On 30 July, 1941, during an eight-hour alarm while the Japanese bombed Chungking four times, General Dennys asked Chiang Kai-Shek for diversionary attacks on the flanks and rear of the Japanese in the event of a full scale attack upon Hong Kong; also to send supplies into the Colony and to assist in evacuating the civil population should the Japanese blockade Hong Kong to starve out the garrison.

The talks, in which Madame Chiang Kai-Shek played a notable part, promised well, for the Chinese were as anxious as the

British to have a joint plan. They in their turn asked for air support – in particular for fighter aircraft, but none could be spared.

The urgency for joint planning had dramatically increased two months earlier when Japan had signed a neutrality pact with her traditional foe, Russia, thereby giving the world an indication of her intention to safeguard her vulnerable northern flank as a preliminary to further action in China and the southwest.

Whitehall decided that an effective deterrent would be a joint announcement that the British Commonwealth, the Netherlands East Indies and the United States had prepared a combined strategic plan with which to meet any further act of Japanese aggression. The Americans were not yet prepared to make such a declaration, as they were about to start discussions in Washington with a newly-arrived and more conciliatory Japanese ambassador. Nevertheless, at an inter-service conference of American, Dutch and British Commanders at Singapore from 22 to 26 April, 1941, ambitious plans were made to contain the Japanese. It was considered that the Japanese would probably make an attack on Hong Kong and the Philippines simultaneously. Before attacking Malaya and North Borneo, Japan could be expected to secure political and military domination of Southern Indo-China.

The Commanders decided that the United States Asiatic Fleet should make use of Hong Kong as an advanced base, and that the Dutch military forces should mainly be retained for the defence of the Dutch East Indies. The Australians had offered troops, and these were earmarked to support the Dutch garrisons. However the Chiefs of Staff in London did not agree that Hong Kong should be regarded as an advanced base, for they still thought of it more as a strategic liability than an asset. And the American Chiefs of Staff did not agree with many of the decisions made at Singapore, so there was no joint plan in the event of war.

                              *   *   *

General Grasett, the Hong Kong GOC, was posted home leaving a reputation for being rather too easy-going; it was felt that he could have done more to strengthen and reinforce the garrison defences. His critics would have been surprised to learn of the skill and persistence with which he persuaded the initially-sceptical Chiefs of Staff in London, on 5 September, 1941, to reverse their policy and recommend to the Prime Minister that significant reinforcements be provided.

The existing force in Hong Kong, he argued, was quite insufficient to deter an attack, or even delay the enemy sufficiently to destroy the port and installations, while the addition of two battalions would enable a full brigade of three battalions to deploy on the mainland, with a second brigade defending the Island from a seaward assault. In addition, the Chinese would be encouraged by confirmation that Britain and her Empire were determined to fight for their possessions in the Far East.

'The Chiefs of Staff heard an interesting account on the present situation in Hong Kong from General Grasett,' read the memorandum to Winston Churchill. 'He pointed out the great advantages to be derived from the addition of one or two battalions, and suggested that these might be supplied by Canada. The Chiefs of Staff have previously advised against despatch of more reinforcements to Hong Kong because they considered that it would only have been to throw good money after bad, but the position in the Far East has now changed. Our defences in Malaya have been improved and Japan has latterly shown a certain weakness in her attitude towards Great Britain and the United States. . . . The Chiefs of Staff are in favour of the suggestion that Canada should be asked to send one or two battalions. . . .'[5]

Initially, Churchill did not seem too sure whether to agree or not. 'It is a question of timing,' he replied on 15 September, 1941. 'There is no objection to the approach being made [to the Canadians for two battalions] as proposed; but a further decision should be taken before the battalions actually sail.'[6]

*   *   *

In Tokyo, Colonel Tosaka was putting the finishing touches to his plans for the invasion of Hong Kong. By early November he could be certain of two things: first, the forward British defensive lines close to the border lay undefended: the British were not apparently planning to fight with a brigade forward on the mainland. Secondly, the isolated garrison was not to be reinforced.

Tosaka was wrong on both counts. The Canadians were coming.

2

'The Canadians are Coming'

Since the announcement on 10 September, 1939, that a state of war existed with the German Reich, not a single Canadian Army unit had met the Germans in battle. Meanwhile Australians, New Zealanders and South Africans were heavily engaged in Libya, and reports of their exploits also in Crete and Abyssinia had nettled the Canadian brigades in England. To Canadian disappointment, hazardous plans to commit them first in Norway and then at Dunkirk had been cancelled at the eleventh hour.

Britain's request to Canada for two battalions and a brigade headquarters to add to the defence of Hong Kong came as no surprise; General Grasett had already briefed the Canadian Chief of the General Staff in Ottawa while en route to London from Hong Kong.

On 29 September, 1941, Canada agreed in principle to send the battalions. Five days earlier Colonel J. K. Lawson, the Director of Military Training, was asked to prepare a list of infantry battalions in order of their state of combat readiness. Nine battalions were relegated to List C – insufficiently trained at that time, and so not recommended for operational consideration. Colonel Lawson within a week found himself promoted to command the Canadian Brigade, which was to consist of only a small HQ and two battalions – both of which had been on List C.

The Royal Rifles of Canada and the Winnipeg Grenadiers were chosen for Hong Kong because they represented both the East and West, the French and the English-speaking Canadians. Until recently, they had been on garrison duties in Newfoundland and Jamaica respectively, and it was assumed that they would have time to train in Hong Kong.[1] The War Office in London had not precisely indicated the role there, and in National Defence Headquarters in Ottawa there was neither a map of Hong Kong nor any accurate information to provide the basis for decisions. Combat-ready Canadian battalions were not chosen for Hong Kong because they were in formed brigades which were already earmarked for Europe.

Both the Royal Rifles and the Winnipeg Grenadiers were distinguished Regiments despite their recent stagnation on undemanding garrison duties.

In 1862, six independent companies were grouped together at Quebec, and ultimately became the Royal Rifles. Some Riflemen fought in the North-West Rebellion of 1885, during the South African war, and on the battlefield of France and Flanders in the First World War as reinforcements to the Canadian Corps. Between the two World Wars, the battalion routine was two nights' drill per week, spring training at their HQ, and courses during the summer. In spite of the Regiment's long history, through no fault of its own the Hong Kong campaign proved to be the first active service that it saw, fighting as a formed body. Hitherto the Battalion had always been broken up to provide reinforcements to others. After mobilization in May, 1940, and amalgamation with 7/11 Hussars, the Regiment was posted to Newfoundland. The Commanding Officer, Lieutenant-Colonel W. J. Home MC, had among his senior officers no less than three Lieutenant-Colonels who all eagerly reverted to the rank of Major in order to serve with the Regiment: J. H. Price MC, C. A. Young MC, and T. G. MacAuley DCM. Many of the soldiers came from the Gaspé and Maritime Provinces of Canada.

The Winnipeg Grenadiers, also a Militia (Volunteer) Battalion, was formed in 1908 in Manitoba. After the First World War, the Regiment was allied to the Scots Guards, and King George VI had become their Colonel-in-Chief by the time they mobilized in September, 1939. The Regiment wore the same cap badge as the Grenadier Guards, with whom they also shared the Regimental Quick March, 'The British Grenadiers'. The Battalion served in Bermuda and Jamaica for seventeen months before being warned for special service.

'We were told we were going somewhere where it was hot, but where we would see no action and never get a medal' recalls one Canadian volunteer. Brigadier Lawson had won the Military Cross fighting with the Canadians at Passchendaele. A regular officer of the Royal Canadian Regiment, he had long distinguished himself as an exceptional leader and able staff officer. Colonel P. Hennessy was made responsible for the ad-

ministration of the Brigade. He had been awarded the DSO and
MC in the First World War.

The first problem Brigadier Lawson faced was finding additional officers and men for each battalion; first line reinforcements, the War Office had stated on 11 October, should
accompany each battalion to Hong Kong. To make matters
worse, the Winnipeg Grenadiers were already well below their
war establishment of 807. It was evident that 436 extra officers
and men were required immediately.

Yet the *Awatea*, the ship which the British Government had
provided, was to sail within a fortnight. The additional men
were to be found only by combing the training establishments;
over one hundred had not completed their sixteen weeks basic
training.

The Canadian CGS, General H. D. G. Crerar, who later
greatly distinguished himself in North-West Europe, was confident that deficiencies in training, and particularly in platoon
weapons such as the mortar and anti-tank rifle (which nobody
had fired), could be made good before the battalions fought the
Japanese.

'Information at my disposal during the latter part of September, 1941,' General Crerar was to state to the Royal Commission which was subsequently to examine the selection of the
Force, 'indicated that the outbreak of hostilities with Japan was
not imminent and that time would, in all probability, be available to carry out adequate and possibly extensive training of
Canadian forces at Hong Kong after their arrival.'[2]

At last, on 25 October, 1941, two days before the force
sailed, a brief reached them from the War Office:

'The task of the Hong Kong garrison is to defend the Colony
against external attack and to deny the use of the harbour and
dry dock to the enemy.

'The Threat: The Japanese are established on the mainland,
are carrying out operations in the vicinity of the frontier, and
are in possession of a number of air bases within easy reach of
the Colony. They also hold command of the sea and are therefore in a position to occupy the surrounding islands at
will. . . .'[3]

The War Office was unable to give specific guidance on the
new defence plan which was now to take account of the two additional battalions and the Brigade HQ. But, the brief con-

tinued, it was still based on a delaying action on the mainland – 'a position of great natural strength' – to be followed by a withdrawal to the Island.

By now Churchill was warmly welcoming the move of the two additional battalions to Hong Kong. He was influenced by the political and strategic repercussions which could be expected from showing both the Chinese and Japanese that the allies were determined to fight there, come what may. The reinforcements might also impress the Americans with our growing strength which had enabled us to strengthen this outpost.

Brigadier Lawson realized that transport would be essential for the movement of troops and supplies, and the collection of wounded if war broke out. Two hundred and twelve vehicles were allotted. There was room for twenty in the hold of the *Awatea*. The remainder were to follow in the *Don José*, which was being slowly loaded on the other side of Vancouver harbour. He was assured that all the vehicles would arrive in Hong Kong within five or six days of the battalions.

On 27 October, the first trainload of Winnipeg Grenadiers arrived at Vancouver and they immediately embarked.

Lawson was immensely irritated that none of his transport had arrived to fill *Awatea*'s holds. However there could be no delay. At 8.30 pm on the 27th, on a cool, slightly foggy evening, the ship sailed with an armed merchant cruiser as escort, H. M. C. S. *Prince Rupert*. The ship was crowded and there was some confusion at first. The long voyage had begun.

The following day, Lawson ordered unit training to be carried out as intensively as the limits of the ship would allow. This was particularly important since many of the reinforcements were totally untrained. Fifteen officers of the Winnipeg Grenadiers had only joined their battalion the previous day. The weather was excellent and the men wore summer drill. Complete blackout for both ships was enforced.

On 2 November, they entered Honolulu harbour and moored alongside a Japanese ship. Above them soared American patrol planes, and coast guard cutters fussed around. The strictest security was observed. Nobody was allowed ashore and the soldiers were warned not to disclose their identity. A concert by Hawaiian singers and dancers on the wharf below, arranged by the British Consul, was much enjoyed. A cascade of cigarettes descended upon the glamorous girls, and more than one Canadian found himself upon the wharf among them.

The ship sailed at 5.00 pm. That evening Lawson told his officers their destination. 'The first thing we heard this morning,' Rifleman Sydney Skelton of the Royal Rifles wrote in his diary on 3 November, 'was the news that we had been waiting to hear. Our officers announced we were going to China – Hong Kong to be exact. The Japanese are expected to declare war on the 15th and we are due to arrive on the 14th.'[4]

Not all the Canadians were quite so pessimistic. Others joked that there was at least some advantage in missing the battles going so badly in Libya. Some of the officers of the Royal Rifles were mystified in the choice of their destination, for they had attended a lecture at Kingston in August where a senior British staff officer from Singapore had assured them that Hong Kong was not to be defended.

'The Brigade Major (Major C. A. Lyndon) gave us a very stern talk,' continued Rifleman Skelton on 10 November, 'he told us to expect almost anything at any time, and he told us if we landed we might have to go right into action. Also he told us we might have the chance of being the first Canadians to go into action in this war. The talk gave us a very grim picture. We were told everything hard about the place and never once did they emphasize anything pleasing. This is no pleasure cruise. It might be another Dunkirk.'

On 16 November, reveille was at 5.00 am, followed by much cleaning of equipment. Gradually the rolling hills of Hong Kong appeared on the skyline and the three ships hugged the Hong Kong coast line as a pilot led them through the extensive minefields, which were covered by the great guns at Stanley. Sentries' eyes watched them through the camouflage nets of the hidden machine-gun posts along the shore. More than one soldier in the dark and musty pill-box asked his comrade who they could be. They were soon to learn.

Awatea turned into harbour. The Canadians watched, fascinated, as Chinese junks floated by. On the hills stately white houses stood out against the sparse scrub and grey towering mountains. A Chinese woman in bare feet and black flapping trousers worked hard on the rudder of a grey junk which slipped past them, while at her feet a child played contentedly. Suddenly the calm slapping of the water against the hull of the ship was broken by the deep roar of engines from some Royal

Air Force planes which flew ceremoniously above them. A sharp crescendo of ships' whistles from Royal Navy craft bade the Canadians welcome.

Awatea docked at Holt's wharf, Kowloon, and the Governor, Sir Mark Young, the Army and Royal Navy Commanders, Major-General C. M. Maltby MC and Captain A. C. Collinson, came aboard. Brigadier Lawson had refreshments served in the lounge while disembarkation proceeded quickly and smoothly.

The Canadian troops formed up on waste ground alongside the Peninsula Hotel. Led by the bands of the Royal Scots and Middlesex battalions, they marched to their quarters at Shamshuipo through welcoming crowds. General Maltby took the salute en route.

News of the Canadians' arrival spread rapidly. Among those who watched them disembark was Captain C. M. M. Man of the Middlesex Regiment with his wife: 'Our joint impression was firstly one of relief that at long last we had some reinforcements for what was a pathetically under-strength garrison,' he wrote later. 'Our second reaction was that the Canadians appeared fit, over-confident, and unusually well-equipped by our standards. I remember overhearing one Canadian just off the ship saying "When do we get to grips with the Goddamned little yellow bastards?"'⁵

The arrival of the two additional battalions and Brigade HQ now necessitated a totally different defence plan.

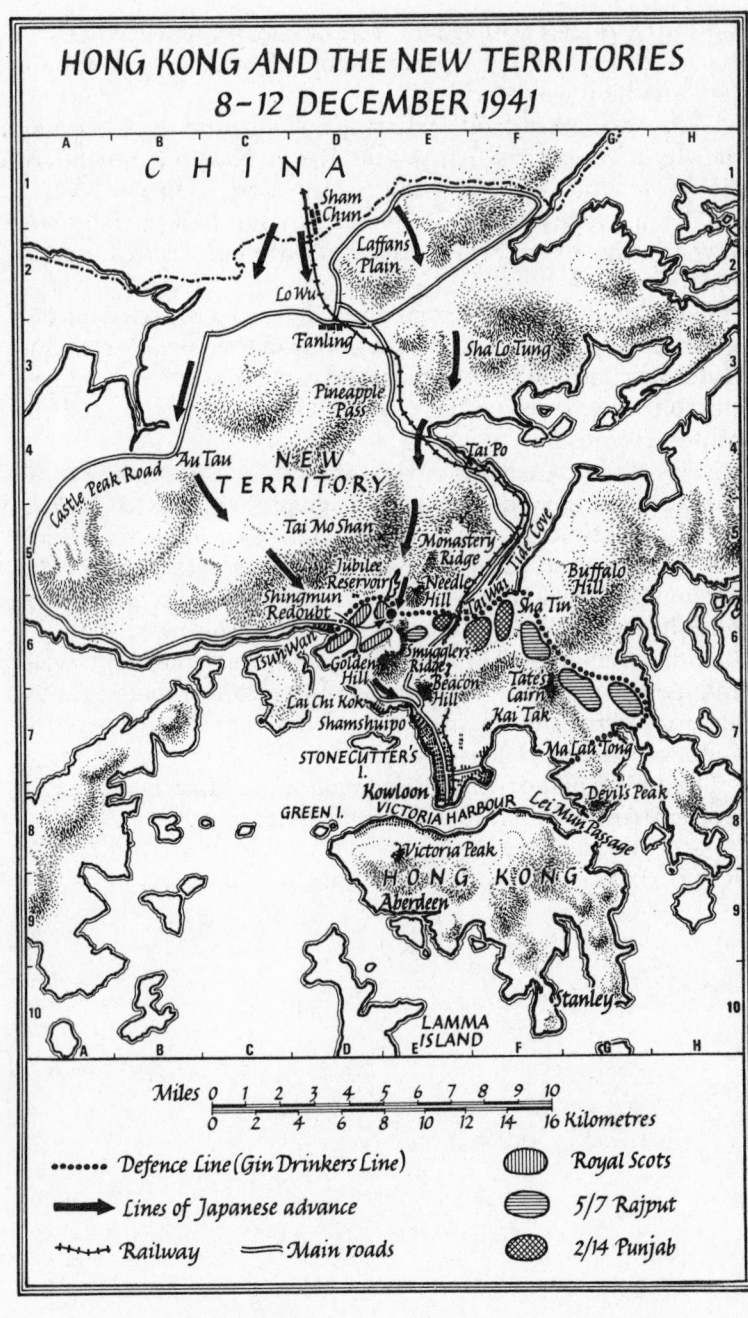

HONG KONG AND THE NEW TERRITORIES
8–12 DECEMBER 1941

C H I N A

Sham Chun

Laffans Plain

Lo Wu

Fanling

Sha Lo Tung

Pineapple Pass

Tai Po

Castle Peak Road

Au Tau

NEW TERRITORY

Tai Mo Shan

Monastery Ridge

Tai Wai

Tide Cove

Buffalo Hill

Jubilee Reservoir

Needle Hill

Sha Tin

Shingmun Redoubt

Tsun Wan

Golden Hill

Smugglers Ridge

Beacon Hill

Tate's Cairn

Kai Tak

Lai Chi Kok

Shamshuipo

Ma Lau Tong

STONECUTTER'S I.

Kowloon

Devil's Peak

GREEN I.

VICTORIA HARBOUR

Lei Mun Passage

Victoria Peak

HONG KONG

Aberdeen

Stanley

LAMMA ISLAND

Miles 0 1 2 3 4 5 6 7 8 9 10

0 2 4 6 8 10 12 14 16 Kilometres

········· Defence Line (Gin Drinkers Line)   Royal Scots

➤ Lines of Japanese advance   5/7 Rajput

+++++ Railway   —— Main roads   2/14 Punjab

3

Hong Kong

The Crown Colony of Hong Kong consists of the Island, usually referred to simply as Hong Kong, and, to the north, across a narrow channel, the Hong Kong mainland, which borders China. In 1941 the Japanese were in occupation beyond the frontier.

The Island of Hong Kong was ceded to Great Britain in 1841. It was then a desolate place inhabited by a few Chinese fishermen. The peninsula of Kowloon with the surrounding islands were ceded to Britain nineteen years later. In 1898, an agreement with the Chinese Government was concluded for an extension to the area adjoining Kowloon and this area, of about 360 square miles and known as the New Territories, was leased to Britain for a period of ninety-nine years.

The Island covers 32 square miles with a chain of mountainous ridges which extend throughout its length of 11 miles. The highest point, Victoria Peak, is often in cloud. The mountains are broken at intervals by tortuous valleys; precipitous slopes are covered by dense vegetation, almost semi-tropical in parts. A narrow, twisting road hugs most of the coast line.

In the north-west of the Island, below Victoria Peak, lies the capital, Victoria, which stretches in a narrow strip along the northern shore for about four miles. The Royal Navy dockyards in the centre lie between imposing buildings with wide balconies to the west, and the narrow, smelly, noisy slums of the Chinese area, the Wanchai, to the east. Beyond the Wanchai and the go-downs (warehouses), the land rises to Lyemun Fort which governs the approaches to the harbour from the east.

The mainland, to the north of the Island, consisted in 1941 of sparsely-populated, humble villages buried amidst mountainous, uncultivated and inaccessible ground, largely covered by forests of fir trees. Most of the population lived in Kowloon, the bustling and prosperous town opposite Victoria.

Only two good roads then connected the frontier with Kowloon: the Castle Peak road to the west and the Taipo road to the east. Both started near Fanling. The only aerodrome was at Kai Tak to the east of Kowloon, used for both commercial and military purposes. To the south-east of the airport the land tapered down towards the island, forming the Devil's Peak peninsula overlooking Lei Mun Strait.

The Governor of Hong Kong, Sir Mark Young, had arrived two months before the Canadians, in September, 1941. Few got to know him well, for he was considered by several as being an unapproachable man. He was very able, tough, courageous, unflappable, and did not suffer fools gladly. Sir Mark was of medium height, slim, and always immaculately dressed befitting perhaps his background of Eton, the Rifle Brigade and a distinguished record in the Colonial Service, which he had served in the West Indies, Middle East, Ceylon and East Africa. Although the Governor also had the title of Commander-in-Chief, the Garrison was commanded by the GOC, Major General C. M. Maltby MC, who had taken over from General Grasett in July, 1941.

General Maltby was fit, wiry and lightly-built, rather bow-legged with a slightly rolling gait. His blue eyes could be very kindly or very frosty, always betraying the mood he was in. His hair, cut very short, was sandy tinged with grey. He had a trim moustache and a complexion like the mellowed red brick of an Elizabethan English country house. He was not amused by caustic or esoteric wit; never by smut. He was almost a British caricature in some ways. The only time the staff officer who probably got to know him best ever saw him lose his temper was in the middle of a Sunday curry lunch, which he was thoroughly enjoying until the staff officer mentioned that he had instructed the cook to lace it with garlic. General Maltby threw down his fork and refused to eat any more: 'Don't you dare put any of that foreign muck in my food again,' he growled. 'I knew there was something wrong with that curry as soon as I tasted it.'[1]

General Maltby's idea of a peaceful Sunday afternoon in the hot weather was 'a stroll round the Island.' Taking up to half-a-dozen staff officers, most of whom would rather be playing golf, or sleeping, he would clamber along the most inaccessible hillsides and the roughest paths, nullahs and catch-waters for three hours, studying the possible battlefields.

General Maltby hated all forms of protocol and detested

snobbery, pretentiousness, boasters and pomposity. He had strong likes and dislikes; he was very loyal to his friends and equally intolerant of those he regarded with ill-favour. It was no secret in some military circles of Hong Kong that his relationship with the Commanding Officer of the Royal Scots was, at the best, strained. One platoon commander, who was to distinguish himself in the fighting ahead, believed him 'to be the kind of Englishman who does not understand the contrary Scots, with their mixture of pride and passion, their alternatives between rowdiness (of a kind that must sometimes have strained the nerves of policemen in the Wanchai) and the fierce dignity that is often found in small nations.'[2]

There was no doubting General Maltby's military competence. He was typical of the best of those who served with the Indian Army. He had distinguished himself as Commandant of the Indian Staff College, then as a District Commander in India, and had been warned on posting to Hong Kong that he should be ready to assume even higher responsibility.

Before the arrival of the Canadians, the GOC had only four Regular Army battalions: 2nd Battalion Royal Scots, 1st Battalion the Middlesex Regiment, 5/7 Rajputs and 2/14 Punjabis.

The Royal Scots enjoy the prestige and privilege of being the oldest and senior British infantry regiment of the Line, tracing their unbroken service to the charter given them by King Charles I in 1633. Their soldiers came mainly from the Lowlands of Scotland, from Edinburgh and the Lothians. The Battalion had arrived in Hong Kong from India in 1936. By 1941 they had been assured by General Grasett that 'he was moving Heaven and Earth to get them transferred to some other theatre of war, as they had been far too long in Hong Kong.'

No barracks were large enough to house the Battalion, which was split between three different locations on Hong Kong Island. There was some field training 'but the periods in which the Battalion could train as a unit were too short for the liking of experienced senior officers.'[3]

The 1st Battalion The Middlesex Regiment had been overseas for ten years, having left England for Palestine in 1931. In Egypt, which was their next posting, their training in desert warfare had reached a high standard; but little had been possible in Singapore, from where they had been posted to Hong

Kong in 1937.

'Despite the closeness of the Japanese along the frontier, with
whom we were in contact, we were bored,' recalls the Adjutant
of the Battalion, Captain A. G. Hewitt. 'Many of us had been
too long overseas, and as Regular soldiers we were envious of
the Army fighting Italians and Germans in the Middle East.
There was a sense of lassitude among us. Air Chief Marshal Sir
Robert Brooke-Popham, the C-in-C Far East in Singapore,
visited us in 1941 and tried to boost our morale by belittling the
Japanese. Their night work was said to be poor; their few light
automatics out-of-date and their Air Force of a low standard.'[4]

The Middlesex, nevertheless, did their best to enjoy themselves, and many of the young officers were entirely happy,
taking a great interest in life in the Far East and in sports.
'Looking back on our preparation for war,' recalls one of them,
'I am afraid we were woefully lacking in some things, except
courage and a tremendous team spirit and determination to see
things through.'[5]

'The months passed rapidly, with the Colony very much as it
was in the days of peace,' wrote the historian of the Middlesex
Regiment. 'A great deal of work was done on preparation of
fixed defences and in wiring the mainland, but here also a
shortage of material hampered efforts to make Hong Kong into
a really strong base. All this – the general state of unprepared-
ness and the widespread belief in the Colony that there was no
great danger of war in the Far East – made it more than ever difficult to maintain the Battalion at the highest pitch of readiness for
action.'[6] The Middlesex had been converted into a machine-
gun battalion and was trained to fight from static defences.

The Battalion owed their enviable nickname, 'the Diehards',
to the encouragement of a former Commanding Officer, who
lay mortally wounded on the battlefield of Albuhera in 1811,
during the Peninsular War. 'Die hard, my men, die hard!' he
was heard to shout. Their courage was such that Wellington
exclaimed: 'Cockneys make the best Troopers.'

The British and Indian Army battalions were constantly
losing their more experienced officers and NCOs to instruct at
training camps in India and Britain, and receiving in their
place barely-trained reservists.

The 5/7 Rajputs had arrived in Hong Kong from India in
October, 1940. In August, 1941, they received their vehicles

and mortars, and a forty per cent increase in strength was authorized. The reinforcements arrived in October. While they were a welcome addition, they were also an anxiety as they had had very little training, and as the Battalion had twice been 'milked' of British and Indian Army Officers and NCOs for other battalions, it was extremely hard to find experienced instructors for them.

The Regiment, formed in 1825, had fought in the Sikh wars of 1849, and proved loyal to the British Crown in the Indian Mutiny. They had since fought in China, on the north-west frontier of India, in Flanders and Iraq. Just before the outbreak of war with Germany the 5/7 Rajputs were in Central India, and had been intensively trained for mountain warfare. They were then regarded as a well-trained, crack Regiment, and had been one of the five battalions selected for 'Indianization' of which they were proud. The majority of the British officers had been replaced by Indians, but this transition was interrupted by the outbreak of war.

The 2/14 Punjabis also enjoyed a similarly long and proud history. Their Commanding Officer, Lieutenant-Colonel G. R. Kidd, was a very able and dedicated officer and had trained his battalion well in spite of it being 'milked' to a similar extent as the Rajputs. They, too, possessed a high proportion of recently arrived and partially trained reservists, and a deficiency of mortars and training ammunition.

Conscription for British residents had been introduced in Hong Kong in 1941. Most had joined the Hong Kong Volunteer Defence Corps, referred to hereafter as 'the Volunteers'. They had become something very special, for they alone were training to fight for their families and homes. They came from many professions: humble clerks and dockyard artisans to prosperous bankers and the taipans of the big trading firms. All parts of the British Isles were represented in their ranks, which included Chinese, Free French, Russians, and Portuguese, Scandinavians and Americans who can even more truly have been considered Volunteers since their nation at this time were neutral.

Some who were over 55, and so outside the normal terms of service, insisted upon forming their own Volunteer Company.

Others, such as some of those in the Colonial Government, saw no need to heed alarmist rumours. For years the bogey of

Jap invasion had been dangled in front of them, and gradually they developed an attitude of indifference to this incessant cry of 'Wolf! Wolf!' Some of the civil servants were thought to have served too long in the Colony, and had not only developed a very narrow outlook on life, but had allowed good living to affect them mentally and physically. Even appalling scandals in administration, on which public enquiries were held during the year, could not shake the lethargy with which the administration was impregnated.

One officer recalls the extraordinary optimism of some members of the Hong Kong Defence Council: 'It was not so much fatuous complacency as a determined unwillingness to have the pleasant routine of their lives disturbed by those "short-arsed yellow bastards" who were over-running China. Those of us who had seen the Japanese at first-hand in Shanghai felt very differently and were left with few illusions.'[7]

The plan for the defence of Hong Kong had so often changed. In 1937, when consideration was given to a division from Singapore reinforcing the garrison, work had started on building a chain of pill-boxes on the mainland. It was to zig-zag eleven miles along the rocky and precipitous hillside, and was called appropriately the Gin Drinkers' Line – so named because its left sector began at the scene of presumably alcoholic picnics in those happy days. Some trenches, particularly those on the west at the Shingmun Redoubt, were laboriously dug, cement overhead-protection added and fields of fire studied. However, since the garrison could expect no reinforcements, the concept of fighting well forward was stillborn, and the positions were allowed to decay. Until the arrival of the Canadians, the plan envisaged the defence of the Island only, with but two companies carrying out a delaying action on the mainland while demolitions destroyed the port installations.

The promise of the new Brigade HQ and two battalions from Canada caused General Maltby to readopt the former more ambitious plan of fighting well forward on the mainland's Gin Drinkers' Line. But he could spare only three battalions, rather than the proposed division, for the eleven mile front. The remainder of his force had to defend Hong Kong Island, and in particular guard against an attack from the open sea.

Two infantry brigades were formed, each of three battalions. The Mainland Brigade consisted of the Royal Scots on the left of the Gin Drinkers' Line, covering the southern slopes of Tai Mo Shan mountain and the Shingmun Redoubt. The Punjabis covered the centre of the mainland, and the 5/7 Rajputs were on the right. (See map, page 14)

The Mainland Brigade was expected to hold the enemy for at least a week, while the dockyard and oil installations were to be destroyed if necessary. Should the enemy prove themselves to be in overwhelming strength, the Mainland battalions would withdraw towards the Devil's Peak in the south-east, from which they could be quickly evacuated across the narrow Lei Mun passage. The Devil's Peak itself would be held indefinitely by up to one battalion. The other two would take their allotted places on Hong Kong Island.

The Mainland Brigade was under the command of Brigadier C. Wallis, the previous Commanding Officer of the 5/7 Rajputs. He was a slim, tough, very determined soldier, who wore a black patch or a dark monocle over his left eye, which he had lost in World War I. He had been a trooper in the Royal Horse Guards in 1914, transferring to the Indian Army in 1917. Since his arrival in Hong Kong in 1940, he had felt there were too many cocktail parties and too little time spent on hard training. He, too, had listened to Sir Robert Brooke-Popham's optimistic views. 'I felt he must be very badly informed and making a great mistake by belittling the Japs,' he wrote afterwards. 'This sort of nonsense fitted in very nicely with what many in Hong Kong liked to hear and believe in, as they could not bear to think that their carefree, elegant life-styles could be interfered with.'[8] Shortly after taking over command of Mainland Brigade in early November, 1941, Brigadier Wallis deployed the Brigade to the battle positions for intensive training.

Major G. E. Grey was chosen to command the border force of C Company 2/14 Punjabis, with the addition of four Bren gun carriers and two armoured cars. Based on Fanling, their mission would be to ensure that all demolitions were successfully fired, and to delay the enemy's approach to the Gin Drinkers' Line for as long as possible.

Brigadier Lawson was appointed to command the Brigade on the Island, which included his two Canadian battalions and 1st Bn Middlesex Regiment, the machine-gun battalion which would occupy the concrete pill-boxes throughout almost the whole of the island.

The Artillery consisted of two Regiments of Coast Artillery, one of Anti-Aircraft Artillery, an independent Battery with a beach-defence role, and a Regiment of the Hong Kong and Singapore Royal Artillery. These regular units were reinforced on mobilization by the five batteries of the Hong Kong Volunteer Defence Force. The Hong Kong and Singapore Royal Artillery had been formed in 1841. Recruited in India, their soldiers consisted of Sikhs and Punjabi mussulmen. They were able to send their pay back to India at a rate of exchange well above the normal.

General Maltby had practically nothing for the air defence of the Colony. There were only five planes: two Walrus amphibians and three Vickers Vildebeeste torpedo bombers, all over ten years old with a maximum speed of 100 mph, and these were flown and serviced by seven officers and 108 airmen. The Chiefs of Staff had refused a request for a fighter squadron, because the aerodrome was an open target with only two World War I machine guns to protect it. Also all aircraft available were required for Singapore. The nearest British aerodrome to Hong Kong was in Malaya, nearly 1,500 miles away.

The garrison's aircraft were no match for enemy fighters, and the RAF were given orders that they were not to be flown operationally unless an opportunity occurred, either at first light or at dusk, for a torpedo attack on an enemy capital ship, or at least a large cruiser. The value of the aircraft lay in reconnaissance to give warning of a Japanese invasion.

Maltby had asked for authority to build an emergency landing ground, which might increase the chances of obtaining American air support. The political implications of 'Dominion troops unsupported from the air' was also emphasized to the War Office.

The garrison's naval power had been sadly diminished. The cruiser squadron and submarine flotilla had been withdrawn. All that were left were one destroyer, *Thracian*, four gun boats, eight Motor Torpedo Boats, seven auxiliary patrol vessels, and an auxiliary craft used for minefield duty. Naval personnel numbered about 1,300 British and 300 Chinese and Indian.

Since the Victoria dockyard was vulnerable to attack from the mainland, an alternative naval base had been prepared to the south-west of the Island, at Aberdeen. This would be sheltered from enemy artillery firing from the mainland, being protected by the massive mountain Victoria Peak.

The Navy's task was to patrol the approaches to Hong Kong, lay mines, break up enemy assaults in junks and other small craft, give fire support to the infantry, assist in the withdrawal across the channel to the Island, and generally harass the enemy wherever the opportunity arose.

As many sea approaches as possible had been mined. Hong Kong was protected from the south-west by continuous minefields, which stretched from the Island to Lamma and Lantau. The western approach between the north shore of Lantau to the mainland was similarly mined.

The only other approach to Hong Kong harbour was from the north-east through the 500 yards of the Lei Mun channel. This was covered by a boom, as was the Victoria naval base.

General Maltby, reassured by further reports on the inferior quality and material of the Japanese, and by the prospect of more reinforcements from Canada, optimistically decided to deploy almost half his force forward on the mainland. He referred, in a signal to the War Office, to holding the Gin Drinkers' Line 'permanently' in order to protect Kai Tak airfield, simplify civil defence problems and make possible eventual offensive operations. He posed the question: 'Is not the value of Hong Kong as a bridgehead increasing every day? Looking at the future, a complete mobile brigade group could undertake offensive operations to assist Chinese forces operating in Japanese-occupied territories.'[9] He saw Hong Kong as the potential spring-board for American, British, Canadian and Dutch forces to liberate South China from the Japanese.

Despite the vast distance that separated them from Hong Kong, the Chiefs of Staff in Whitehall were more acutely aware of the limitations of the Gin Drinkers' Line and the impracticalities of the General's proposal: 'The Chiefs of Staff in Whitehall are unable to agree that proposed reinforcements of Canadian troops would enable the GOC Hong Kong to hold the Gin Drinkers' Line permanently, or that use could then be made of Kai Tak aerodrome for operation of a fighter squadron.' Nevertheless they went on to say that they were prepared to recommend the increase of the Canadian force to a balanced brigade group 'subject to the assurance that no suggestion has already been made by Lawson or any other authority to the

Canadian Government that the provision of air support for the garrison is yet in view.'[10] Whitehall was determined throughout that no false promises were to be held out to the Canadians in order to obtain more troops.

By 1 December, the Canadians had carried out two intensive and successful exercises on the battle positions over which they expected to fight. They mixed well with the British and Chinese, and their general conduct received only favourable comment. It was immediately apparent, however, that although they were undoubtedly magnificent material, it would only be after prolonged training that either battalion could be regarded as being fit for modern war.

The following day Brigadier Lawson heard that *Don José*, carrying all the Canadian transport, had been rerouted by the Americans via Australia and Manila for extra security; the ship's arrival in Hong Kong would therefore be delayed until the end of December. Twenty-five Ford V8 trucks were purchased to fill the gap.

On 3 December, General Maltby and Brigadier Lawson toured the frontier and watched the Japanese through binoculars. The Japanese soldiers looked scruffy, indolent and uninterested. Nevertheless two independent reports[11] from China stated that between ten and twenty thousand Japanese troops were expected to arrive at Sham Chun, five miles north of Fanling, on 4 December for an attack on the Colony. General Maltby did not believe these reports, preferring his own intelligence sources.

Captain Iain MacGregor, Royal Scots, ADC to General Maltby, recalls that for weeks before the invasion he was constantly admitting mysterious informants through the french windows, coming to his office from the gardens of Flagstaff House: 'People of all kinds and nationalities from all over China, M16, Consular Agents, Secret Intelligence Service, cloak-and-dagger types from Shanghai, Canton and elsewhere, always came at night and they had to be shown direct to the General's study. They seemed to be fairly well-informed, and General Maltby accepted their information with cautious credulity.'[12]

The reports of the possible concentration of at least a Japanese division close to the border were contemptuously dismissed. On Sunday, 7 December, the day before Hong Kong was attacked, a remarkable intelligence summary was sent to the War Office from Hong Kong, stating that 'the reports are certainly exaggerated and have the appearance of being deliberately fostered by the Japanese who, judging by their defensive preparations around Canton, appear distinctly nervous of being attacked.'[13]

Nobody in Hong Kong knew what the Japanese were up to, what their intentions were, or of what they were capable. They were soon to find out.

4

The Enemy at the Gates

'Japan is at a loss as to which horse to back; it is impossible to back them all.'[1] This casual remark of General Tatekwa, the newly-appointed Japanese ambassador in Moscow, was quickly reported to the British Government which hoped that Japan would back no horse at all. However by early December, 1941, the German Army was occupying most of European Russia, with binoculars trained on the turrets of the Kremlin. So Japan's northern flank with Russia was secure. The prizes to be won in China no longer appeared so attractive. Japan had now become hypnotised by the prospect of unlimited rubber, tin and oil in Burma, Malaya and the Dutch East Indies. British and Dutch Colonies were waiting impatiently for their liberation. The Japanese Greater East Asia sphere promised a New Order of prosperity for all in East Asia. Every nation would be allotted its proper place amidst enduring peace and unlimited prosperity. Or so believed many in Tokyo.

The soldiers of the Japanese 38th Division were concerned with more immediate matters: to capture the Colony and smash their enemies against the rocks of Hong Kong.

Lieutenant-General Sakai, the Commander-in-Chief, had received his orders a month previously. He had gradually completed his plans with Major-General Sano, the Commander of 38th Division. The only division available to him would launch its attack the moment the operations in Malaya started.

The Division consisted of three Regiments each of three battalions. The initial move across the frontier was to be made in two thrusts (see map, page 14), each led by reconnaissance troops followed by a battalion moving across country as fast as possible, bypassing enemy positions and road blocks.

To the west the leading battalion of 230 Regiment, (Colonel Shoji), would skirt the western slopes of Tai Mo Shan thereby cutting off any British troops still on the Castle Peak Road. 230 Regiment would then break through the Royal Scots in the area of the Shingmun Redoubt and head for Kowloon.

In the centre 228 Regiment (Colonel Doi), was to move

across Laffan's Plain and then destroy the middle of the Gin Drinkers' Line, held by the Punjabis, near Tai Wai. Having done so, they would capture Kai Tak airfield.

Finally, 229 Regiment (Colonel Tanaka), on the east was to spearhead a surprise crossing of Tide Cove in sampans, force a way through the Rajputs and capture the high ground of Tates Cairn, before pushing on as fast as possible towards Kowloon Bay.

The Japanese hoped to break through the Gin Drinkers' Line quickly, with the minimum of casualties, and then hold the southern shore of the Hong Kong mainland, thereby preventing the three British battalions still on the Gin Drinkers' Line from escaping to Hong Kong Island.

General Sakai had no specific plans to capture the Island. He believed that the collapse of the only British fortified line on the mainland, and the defeat of the battalions upon it, would be sufficient to force the British to surrender the Colony, particularly when they had no water. A number of good reservoirs on the mainland and the Island gave an adequate supply of water in a year of average rainfall. General Sakai planned the early capture and destruction of the reservoirs, in particular Jubilee Reservoir by the Shingmun Redoubt which supplied water to the Island.

The Japanese were fully confident of success; eighty aircraft were promised to support them. The few contemptible Royal Air Force planes would be destroyed while still on the ground at Kai Tak in a surprise air attack before war was formally declared. Thereafter the Japanese would have complete air superiority and could switch to their secondary target, the two Canadian battalions still in their barracks at Shamshuipo, on the west of Kowloon. The Japanese were aware that they had superiority in mobile artillery which outnumbered the British by more than three to one. Even allowing for the partial destruction of roads and bridges by British demolition parties, Japanese tractors could drag their guns forward into fire positions to support their infantry.

Surprise was essential. To mislead the British, and to tie down as many of their troops as possible on needless coastal guard duties, Japanese destroyers were ordered to make threatening manoeuvres well to the south of Hong Kong Island. Meanwhile Colonel Tosaka made careful plans[2] to ensure that the Division was concentrated with the utmost secrecy in the mountainous, secluded areas well inland.

All moves were to take place at night and made to resemble a routine redeployment. Movement through the coastal areas and by sea was forbidden. Great efforts were made to ensure that everything along the border looked normal.

After the war, in 1949, Colonel Tosaka stated that his Division suffered some losses from the Chinese, due to the Japanese anxiety to break off the fighting against China without alerting the British as to their intentions. The Japanese 3rd Air Group had stopped its advance as early as the autumn of 1941, in order to co-operate with the army in its preparations for the battle against Hong Kong, which eased the pressures against the Chinese.

Colonel Tosaka later expressed dissatisfaction with the information provided by his spies in Hong Kong. Colonel Suzuki, based on the Japanese Consulate, had picked up details of where the signal cables had been laid and the location of some of the pill-boxes and guns, but his activities had been exposed. Colonel Tosaka now had to rely upon such sources as the Wanchai brothel girls, the Japanese jeweller in the Queen's Arcade, the Italian waiter at the Peninsula Hotel, and the Japanese barber at the Hong Kong Hotel who was destined to reappear after the fighting, in the uniform of a Lieutenant Commander, as the Commandant of the Stanley internment Camp. The Japanese adult population in Hong Kong, which had numbered 516 in early 1941, was rapidly decreasing.

Several hundred partially-armed Chinese fifth columnists had been infiltrated into Hong Kong. The term was coined during the Spanish Civil War, when it was said that there were four columns marching upon Madrid, while there was a 'fifth column' inside the city. In the case of Hong Kong the so-called 'fifth column' were the sympathisers of the Chinese Wong Chang Wai, who was Japan's puppet leader in conquered China. They had been recruited from Formosa (now Taiwan), and easily mingled with the mass of refugees fleeing to Hong Kong daily. They were to be responsible, once the fighting started, for sabotage, sniping at isolated posts and despatch riders, spreading false rumours and signalling to their Japanese masters the positions of guns and pill-boxes.

In June, 1941, a Japanese naval launch had carried out a reconnaissance of the small islands to the east of Hong Kong, whence British and Chinese activities were watched. In early September Japanese gunboats had destroyed Chinese junks and fishing nets in Chinese waters immediately adjacent to Hong Kong. This had resulted in a serious reduction of the fishing grounds, upon which local supplies depended. These incidents had culminated in a British ship, *Yusang*, being temporarily boarded by an officer and nine ratings from a Japanese warship.

However by November, 1941, all such incidents had ceased: nothing was to be done which might lurch the British out of their apparent complacency. When General Maltby's staff officer responsible for intelligence, Major C. R. Boxer, a Japanese linguist, proposed a baseball and football match against the Japanese border guards, they tentatively agreed.

Colonel Tosaka's curiosity about what the British were doing proved irresistible. On 5 November he authorised a Japanese naval reconnaissance aircraft to fly, at 7,000 feet, directly over the large gun emplacements and fortifications at Stanley. Similar flights had surreptitiously taken place over Malaya and Borneo.

'When war was imminent, efforts were made to learn the dispositions of installations in the fortress and the plans of the British Army, but substantial information could not be obtained,' Tosaka was to state. 'The fact that inaccurate estimates of the enemy situation were made at the time of the invasion is attributable to this lack of information concerning the fortress and the plan of the British.'[3] Even so, a Rajput patrol during the fighting killed a Japanese officer and found on him a detailed map of all Hong Kong defences, including the Colony's pill-boxes and gun positions. They had been ringed in red ink and superimposed on a map of Hong Kong which had been printed in Canton in November, 1941.

The difficulty the Japanese had in discovering the British plans is hardly surprising. The arrival of the Canadians had resulted in the Royal Scots and both Indian Army battalions now being committed forward on the mainland rather than on the Island, and many of the key British officers seemed bewildered and unfamiliar with the new plans themselves. The artillery had not yet fully registered their possible targets, and the Royal Scots were later to complain bitterly that they were fighting on unfamiliar ground.

5
'Just the Usual Crisis'

'For so many crowded years, we in Hong Kong had been living a full and cheerful life under the shadow of Japanese guns, and we accepted the menace as philosophically as one accepts an income tax demand'[1] recalls B. A. Proulx, a forty-year-old stockbroker and amateur jockey who had spent twenty-one years in Hong Kong. He had joined the Hong Kong Royal Naval Volunteer Reserve two years previously, when the Colony mobilized on the outbreak of war with Germany. 'Crises in Hong Kong had come and gone as regularly as the seasons.'

Hong Kong was a boom town. Business flourished. Even Europeans on low salaries owned a car and employed at least two servants. The business community lived on Victoria Peak or in attractive houses in the country, with at least an amah, cook, gardener, coolie and house boy. Frequent dining in hotels in white dinner jackets, and dancing, were still the order of the day. Week-ends were filled by golf, tennis and swimming in the blue, unspoilt bays. Mobilization and social life went hand in hand. The drilling of the Volunteers continued, and so did the dancing.

So far the Colony had received its greatest war scare in June, 1940. The Japanese were then fighting the Chinese just beyond the Hong Kong border, and several schools in Kowloon had been turned into hospitals for wounded Chinese, brought over in Red Cross trucks. The odour of dead bodies beyond the border was unmistakable and unbearable; they had not been buried properly, if at all. A Japanese attack was expected any day, so the Colonial Government demanded that all European women and children leave the Colony immediately. Almost overnight many enlisted as auxiliary nurses, air-raid wardens, stenographers and cypher clerks, in order to remain in Hong Kong. 'Too many wangled exemption and some deliberately flaunted the orders,' recalls one nurse who stayed. 'These were the ones who loudly bemoaned their fate later in Japanese captivity. Children were kept in the Colony and suffered the hor-

rors of war and the privations of subsequent internment, solely
through their parents' selfishness'.[2] However in June, 1940, it
appeared that almost everyone was leaving. Beyond the colour-
ful junks, the giant Canadian *Empress of Asia* stirred, her funnels
spouting black smoke, preparing to leave for Australia
crammed with evacuees. Rickshaws overloaded with suitcases
and anxious women hastened towards the Kowloon docks to
board her and *President Coolidge*.

As darkness settled over South China, husbands waved their
final farewells from the shore as the majestic ships slipped
quietly out of the beautiful harbour, led by pilot boats through
the maze of minefields. Chinese junks in the harbour glided
past, a single soft light showing in each, their patched sails
barely discernible in the darkness.

The European women who remained in Hong Kong became
increasingly involved in defence work. Signs on the Star Ferry
and elsewhere read: 'Bandage classes, European YMCA. All
helpers are welcome.'; 'First Aid Lectures. Mrs Rosenblum.'
Occasionally a notice had a particular relevance such as 'Air
Raid Precaution Lecture: Protection of your home against air-
planes.' War posters appeared in great numbers.

Later the husbands held mass meetings to demand the
return of their wives. The daily press was filled with letters criti-
cizing the Government for not allowing the evacuated women
to return, and simultaneously complaining about so-called dis-
crimination in not compelling the wives of high officials to
leave, although both Sir Mark Young and General Maltby had
set the example of not having their wives with them.

'My wife has a right to be here by my side' spoke one husband at a mass meeting. 'If I can't defend her, no one can.
Besides nothing's going to happen to so many women'.

'Darling, they've no right to break up our home this way',
wrote an evacuated wife in Australia. 'The women of London
are sticking by their husbands, so why shouldn't I? Besides it's
just the usual crisis'.

And so the alarms came and went with monotonous regular-
ity. Many felt themselves to be defenders of an 'impregnable
fortress'. Others complained bitterly that they were missing the
war against Germany. The lengthy casualty lists of those killed
in the Middle East and Europe were published frequently in
the press, copied from month-old editions of *The Times*.

Preparations for a war against Japan were well evident. A drive up to the golf course at Fanling went past barbed-wire concentration points, concrete pill-boxes and ammunition dumps nestling under camouflage nets among the hills. In Kowloon and Victoria the more important buildings, such as police stations, were darkened by walls of sandbags piled high for defence against bomb splinters. An increasing number of beaches were covered by wire fences and machine-gun posts.

The Chinese, too, knew the signs of war. Their fear of the Japanese was greater than that of the British, for they had themselves seen, or heard first-hand accounts of, the barbaric cruelty of the invaders of their country. Photographs had been published of Japanese soldiers in Manchuria gleefully bayoneting prisoners, who cowered on the ground with their hands tied behind their backs.

The Chinese shopkeepers seemed more desperate than ever to sell their goods. No longer did the merchants sit inside their shops on carved camphorwood chests and languidly wait for customers; they stood anxiously out in the street, half looking for business, half looking for Japanese planes from Fanling. 'Please buy, Missy. Please buy, the Japanese soon come. Do you think the Japanese come, Missy?' pleaded the Chinese manager of the shop selling heavily-jewelled screens to one European. The same day another Chinese girl asked her, 'Did you hear that thunder last night? I jumped out of bed thinking the Japanese had come.'

A pathetic stream of Chinese refugees still slipped across the border near Fanling, with what miserable possessions they could carry. Emergency camps of mat houses had been built for the lucky ones. Others had to join the seething masses in the towns. In the side streets of Kowloon late at night hundreds of nearly-nude bodies were to be seen on the pavements. An occasional twitch was the only sign of life until the hot morning sun would rouse them. The sleeping forms were shrouded by a blanket of mystery.

Many Chinese had enlisted in the Garrison's defence forces: in the Volunteer infantry companies and artillery batteries, and as drivers, engineers, signallers, sailors, airmen and medical orderlies. Few British officers tried to predict how the Chinese would fight. The subsequent desertion of drivers and boat hands was to be a serious blow, but most Chinese were to fight with considerable ferocity and courage.

'Happy Valley near Victoria on Saturday 6 December was
the usual scene of happy crowds of both Europeans and Chinese thronging the race course,' wrote Mrs Mabel Redwood.[3]
An Auxiliary Nurse, she was to keep a meticulous account of
the tragedy which was about to unfold. 'The band of the Royal
Scots came from Shamshuipo to play on the course. By tiffin
time there seemed to be tenseness. Military police were advis-
ing soldiers to return to barracks immediately.' The races went
on. The Jockey Club bar was crowded as gimlets and whis-
key-and-sodas were sipped, and the pretty frocks of the women
admired.

The Middlesex played rugger at the Cricket Club, and that
evening there was a large party at the Hong Kong Hotel which
went on until 4.30 am.

The same evening a Chinese charity ball was held at the Peninsula Hotel in Kowloon. The 'Tin Hat Ball' hoped to raise at
least £160,000 towards the purchase of bombers which the
people of Hong Kong were presenting to Britain. An extremely
lovely girl, Hilda Yen, with black, silky hair cascading down
her back, sang a gentle Chinese song. But the Colony had few
moments of peace left to enjoy.

'Our party last night was suddenly interrupted by telephone
calls,' wrote Phyllis Harrop the following morning.[4] She had
time off from her hospital job and was in a party with Canadian
Staff Officers. 'Major Lyndon, the Brigade Major, left immediately, Captain Bush half-an-hour later, and Colonel Hennessy
never reached the party at all. We were left with a party of
Chinese women and myself without partners.' The announcement that anybody connected with the ships in harbour
was to return immediately to duty was the last straw. Phyllis
Harrop found only the Commissioner of Police reluctant to
leave. They travelled together across the harbour on the Star
Ferry to Hong Kong Island. The Peak was usually a sparkling
Christmas tree of lights. That night it was in darkness, sullen
and unfriendly. The Royal Navy MTBs were out at sea, watching the approaches to the Colony. A sudden shiver swept the
small group in the bows of the Star Ferry. They felt that war
was imminent.

The Church Parade at St John's Cathedral in Victoria on
Sunday 7 December, 1941, started no differently from any

other. General Maltby was there with many of his officers. Hurried twitterings of conversation amongst the ladies confirmed that the Chinese Charity Ball the night before had been a great success. The latest rumours about the Japanese caused anxious, worried frowns.

The contingent of the Middlesex Regiment waited restlessly for the service to end. Their impatience was heightened when an officer suddenly entered the Church and whispered to General Maltby in the front pew. He got up and strode from the Church, followed by others. The Service had not even reached the prayers for Peace.

General Maltby was told that the Japanese were most certainly mustering near the border. The Defence Council was hurriedly summoned to a lengthy meeting at Government House.

The GOC's ADC, Captain Iain MacGregor, was left to contend for a long time with the Chairman of Hong Kong's largest and most distinguished Bank who had arrived, fuming, at Flagstaff House, demanding to see the General. 'The Chairman paced the room, all the time telling me the whole thing was bloody nonsense, and that only two days before he had received a coded cable from one of his Managers who had been dining the previous evening with the C-in-C of the Japanese Kwantung Army. The C-in-C had assured the Manager that under no circumstances would the Japanese ever attack their old ally, Great Britain. "Good God, Iain", said the Chairman, "You're a civilian really, a Far East merchant. You know how these Army fellows flap. You know our intelligence is far better than theirs. What the hell does Maltby think he's doing, calling up and deploying the Volunteers, taking more than half my staff away? Doesn't he realise it will cause a panic among the Chinese and a run on the Bank tomorrow, with only a skeleton staff to deal with it? The whole damn thing's ridiculous." I was glad indeed when the General finally returned to face the barrage. The only "run" on the Bank next morning was the mass run into the Bank to avoid the Japanese bombing.'[5]

Fortress HQ decided that war was imminent, and orders were despatched at 11.00 am to the whole garrison, including the Volunteers, to stand-to in their battle positions. The Royal Rifles of Canada and the Winnipeg Grenadiers moved from their peacetime Shamshuipo camp to their trenches along the mountainous range of Hong Kong Island. By 6.00 pm they were all in their positions. Brigadier Lawson, at his Brigade HQ at the Wong Nei Chong Gap in the centre of the Island, had his duty signaller check the line to the Battalion HQ of the Royal Rifles at Tytam Gap and the Winnipeg Grenadiers at Wanchai Gap.

On the mainland the three forward battalions, the Royal Scots, Punjabis and Rajputs, had been occupying and improving their battle positions on the Gin Drinkers' Line for almost four weeks.

The entire Hong Kong garrison was now ready. But as conclusive proof was still lacking that the Japanese onslaught was imminent, the decision to implement the numerous Civil Defence measures was deferred.

Sub-Lieutenant Lewis Bush, RNVR, had just returned from a long patrol with the 2nd MTB Flotilla. That evening he sat on the roof of his small apartment alongside the RAF base at Kai Tak. With his Japanese-born wife and their dogs they watched the harbour and quietly talked of friends and relatives. 'It was a calm and silent night,' he recorded. 'There was hardly a breath of air. The sunset was a riot of red, orange and yellow hues, and the cloud effects were weird and almost ominous as if a prelude to a disaster, much like the sort one sees before a typhoon.'[6]

6
Withdrawal to the Gin Drinkers' Line

8.00 am 8 December—9.00 pm 9 December

Major C. R. Boxer, deep in Fortress HQ, was on duty in the early hours of the morning of Monday 8 December, 1941. As an interpreter in Japanese he was able to monitor their broadcasts from Tokyo. Suddenly, at 4.45 am, he picked up unmistakable instructions to Japanese nationals abroad that war with Great Britain and America was imminent. Everyone was alerted. Major G. E. Grey, commanding the border force of C Company 2/14 Punjabis and the Engineer demolition parties at Fanling, was ordered immediately to blow all forward demolitions.

By now the Japanese had started their virtually unopposed landing on the east coast of Siam and Malaya. News of the disaster at Pearl Harbour and the invasion of Malaya was flashed to the Colony.

At 8.00 am the loud crescendo of an air raid warning ominously disturbed the bright sunny morning. Practice alerts had never taken place at that hour before. Olive Redwood was standing on the verandah overlooking the harbour. She rushed indoors to her mother and sister. 'Here they are, Japanese planes,' she screamed. They ran out in time to see the planes circling over Kai Tak airport. The loud rattle of anti-aircraft machine-gun fire mingled with the explosions of falling bombs. So sudden was the attack that some officers at first thought that 'the bloody Royal Air Force were practising for a display'.[1]

Lewis Bush, RNVR, saw the wooden buildings by the airfield crumble into sheets of flame. The Vildebeeste and Walrus RAF aircraft were blazing on the airstrip. All but one of these ancient aircraft were destroyed and General Maltby's only air reconnaissance force had disintegrated before the fighting had begun. Insufficient effort to disperse the aircraft had been

made; there were no underground shelters for them, and no attempt had been made to conceal the planes in go-downs and
fields adjacent to Kai Tak. The lesson of the German-Polish
campaign of 1939, which emphasised the necessity of dispers-
ing aircraft in protected bays, was not implemented in Hong
Kong. Wing-Commander H. G. Sullivan, the Station Commander who had arrived in the Colony on 1st December,
recalls: 'It had been suggested that dispersal bays be carved out
of the hills, but like everything else in Hong Kong these did not
materialize.'

The Japanese aircraft rapidly switched to their second objective. They had rejected the targets of the port, heavy guns or
troop emplacements on the Gin Drinkers' Line. They chose to
attack the two Canadian battalions which they thought were
still in Shamshuipo Camp, and where they believed Mainland
Brigade HQ was also located. Heavy bombs descended upon
the barracks and fighter aircraft machine-gunned the huts from
sixty feet.

Father F. J. Deloughery, the Roman Catholic Chaplain to
the Canadian Force, was saying Mass. His congregation was
very small, almost everyone having left the day before for their
positions on Hong Kong Island. There were only two Canadian
casualties – Sergeant Routledge and Signalman Fairley – the
first two Canadian soldiers to be wounded in the Second World
War. Mainland Brigade HQ was still in the building, and hurriedly moved to the still uncompleted battle HQ to the north of
Kowloon.

The Japanese had over-estimated the strength of the Royal
Air Force in Hong Kong. They later gleefully reported on
Radio Tokyo the destruction of fourteen large and twelve
medium planes.

Jan Marsman, a Dutch engineer, had arranged an early call
with the receptionists of the Hong Kong Hotel. He was schedu-
led to take the clipper to Manila from Kai Tak at 8.00 am. They
failed to call him. Still complaining, he was hustled onto the bus
for the airport. Disapproving glances from his fellow passengers
told him that he had kept them waiting. As he settled into his
seat, an excited Chinese employee of Pan-American dashed to
the bus shouting that the flight was delayed. A passenger announced that he had heard that war had been declared with
Japan; he was immediately accused of being an alarmist and

rumour-monger. The bus was diverted to the Peninsula Hotel.

The Peninsula Hotel was being stripped for action. Carpets, chairs and tables were stacked at one end of the ballroom. Red Cross nurses prepared cots for the wounded. Strips of paper criss-crossed the plate glass windows to strengthen them against concussions.

At the hotel Jan Marsman met T. B. Wilson, the President of the American Steamship Lines, whose announcement at the Chinese Ball two days before had brought such an abrupt end to the dancing. They had a cup of coffee together. Suddenly Marsman saw from the hotel window aircraft circling and diving over Kai Tak. He well remembered the scene.

'"What do you think those planes are?" I asked T. B.

'"Aw hell, just manoeuvers, Jan," T. B. said disdainfully, when I called him to the window. Columns of smoke billowed from the area.

'"Do you think they use smoke screens in manoeuvers?" T. B. demanded.'

Marsman went to the hotel lobby as the clipper crew burst into the hotel. Words tumbled over one another as they told how thirty-five Japanese dive-bombers had set their plane ablaze. The only one still on the flying-boat at the time had been a young Manila boy. He had dived overboard and swum into a drain at the waterline for safety while the clipper was engulfed in flames.

The passengers decided to return to the safety of the Hong Kong Hotel. The most popular person there was now the inefficient receptionist clerk who had failed to wake Marsman. The ensuing delay had prevented them being dive-bombed near Kai Tak, and had probably saved their lives.

The Hong Kong scene had changed dramatically. Trucks, cars, buses, wagons, carts, rickshaws still ran through the narrow streets, but air raid wardens, auxiliary nurses and uniformed Volunteers were already at their posts. 'This was war! At once everything seemed to spring into life,' recorded Mabel Redwood: 'Certainly this was the real thing, and not just another "Incident" to be treated as an exercise.

'It had been arranged in 1940 that the Jockey Club at Happy Valley racecourse on Hong Kong Island was to be used as a relief hospital. When I arrived there I found lorries were discharging equipment. Speedily we worked to get the place ready for the patients who we knew would be soon arriving. Hundreds of camp beds were brought, got into position and the surplus stored in the large betting booths. (How useful we found them later.) An operating theatre was set up on the first floor, likewise a restroom for us when off duty. Oh yes! We were going to have quite a comfortable war. How little we knew!

'Soon our patients began to arrive. Most were very old and all were very sick. We piled on blankets, but what they really needed was hot food. . . . The air raids continued spasmodically all day, but somehow being so occupied we paid little attention to them. They were not very near us anyway, and we imagined that being a hospital we were reasonably safe from attack. But unfortunately there was a military post established right next door to us in the members enclosure. We were in the public enclosure. Many planes were now coming over on reconnaissance trips. By this time our military neighbours began to get busy with their Anti-Aircraft fire. But they did little good. We expected them to turn the Japanese attention to themselves and us. . . .'

As Hong Kong prepared for its first morning of war, Churchill was dining at Chequers with Averell Harriman from Washington. News of the attacks upon Pearl Harbour, Malaya and Hong Kong had not yet reached them. Churchill was despondent. He was well aware of the vulnerability of the British colonies, and he could not yet be confident that America would enter the war. Sawyers, the butler, carried in a cheap portable radio. A programme of music was suddenly interrupted by a warning to listeners to stand by for important news. In a calm, grave voice the BBC announcer told Britain that Pearl Harbour had been attacked. The Stars and Stripes and Union Jack were now irrevocably entwined.

In Hong Kong furious work had started at 5.00 am on the demolitions at the Hong Kong railway bridges over the Sham Chun river on the border north of Fanling (see map, page 14). A platoon of the Punjabis and the Volunteer Field Engineers were responsible for the demolitions. They could see the Japanese quite clearly, scarcely three hundred yards to their front – well within shot. The Japanese made no attempt to rush the bridges or open fire, since they too were equally busy preparing their own bridge which they would push across the river when the British and Indians had blown theirs and departed.

At about 9.00 am two great explosions were heard by the forward troops. As the dust settled it was seen that both bridges had been successfully destroyed. The demolition guards pulled back towards Major Grey's covering position nearer Fanling. The Japanese eagerly rushed forward with their own replacement.

Forward observation posts reported hundreds of Japanese sweeping south in two separate thrusts, each of about a battalion's strength. To the left a force was moving initially down the Castle Peak road and over the hills. The Royal Scots Brengun carriers and patrols were well-forward. They kept them under observation and inflicted some casualties.

Major Grey's planned withdrawal route was on the right flank down the Tai Po road. His orders were to impose maximum delay and casualties on the enemy – but without getting cut off. This was becoming a serious possibility; already the Japanese appeared to be outflanking him to his right.

His next major demolition to the south, in the narrow Pineapple Pass, was equally successful. The railway line was fully blocked, as was the Tai Po road for about thirty yards. This proved no handicap to the leading Japanese, who were still bypassing the force, moving at great speed across open country to the east of Sha Lo Tung (now called Cloudy Hill). They were spotted by the Punjabis at Tai Po. The village itself was mainly deserted as the Engineers destroyed petrol pumps, demolished abandoned vehicles and removed whatever might be of value to the enemy.

The Japanese tactics were to push on at the greatest possible speed, by-passing enemy opposition which could be mopped up, half starved and cut off at their leisure in the weeks ahead. A strong Japanese company therefore swung west, after receiving some casualties, to avoid a frontal assault on Grey's Punjabis in Tai Po. This necessitated another hurried withdrawal.

At each successive retreat, the message to pull back had failed to reach Lance-Corporal A. Taylor who was serving with Signalman A. Fleet in the Hong Kong Signal Company attached to Major Grey. Within minutes of the war starting he had found that a large tub of soapy water had been deliberately poured over both his charging engine and wireless batteries –

the fifth column's first act of sabotage – right there in the middle of Border Force HQ. As they waited beneath camouflage nets for the withdrawal south of Tai Po Lance-Corporal Taylor recalls that 'Signalman Fleet got very serious and told us that he knew he would be killed in the battle for Hong Kong. He was very sincere and this depressed us. Apparently some months before, he and a couple of his friends went to the Alhambra Theatre. One of the turns was a man who could read the future merely from holding something belonging to a member of the audience. After three years in Hong Kong we were all overdue on our posting to England. Anyhow, Fleet passed up his cigarette case and asked the fortune reader how soon it would be before he left the Colony. The reply was that he would never leave Hong Kong. The entertainer was laughed off as a cheat; but the possibility of the sinister prediction being true now became immediately apparent. (Sure enough Fleet was later killed in the attack on Hong Kong.)'[2]

It suddenly occured to Lance-Corporal Taylor that all the forward troops had withdrawn, leaving nobody between him and the enemy. 'We packed up and drove like mad down the hill without lights across a bridge. Just after we crossed, it blew up with a tremendous explosion. Our own sappers had blown it not knowing that we had been left behind with a truck full of wireless gear. When we finally caught up with Major Grey, he told us that our secondary means of communication was no longer necessary and ordered us back to our unit. We drove on towards Kowloon and ran into coils of dannert wire stretched across the road. It took us thirty minutes to cut ourselves free, and we cursed the Mule Corps nearby who were responsible. Driving up the hill along the reservoir road we suddenly overlooked Kowloon and Hong Kong Island, and saw a beautiful picture of bright lights and ships in the harbour going about their various chores as they had done for the last one hundred years. Yet the enemy was just sixteen miles away, coming south fast.'

At 6.30 pm the railway tunnel south of Tai Po was destroyed, while defensive positions were taken up for the night on the higher ground to the south. A Punjabi platoon quietly lay in an ambush position to the south-west of Tai Po. They saw in the bright moonlight the leading columns of the Japanese boldly advancing towards them. The platoon's machine-guns and light automatics opened fire at a range of one hundred yards. Although some Japanese fell back in confusion with casualties, they still maintained their overall impetus and initiative. About 150 Japanese landed in sampans over four thousand yards south-east of Tai Po (close to where the Chinese University now stands), behind Grey's force. Once more he ordered a hurried withdrawal. The demolitions on the roads, railways and bridges had successfully prevented the Japanese from bringing their heavy guns and transport forward towards Tai Po; but there was no stopping their infantry, and Grey's retreat had had to be much quicker than anticipated.

The Japanese advance on the left flank towards the Royal Scots was developing equally rapidly. The speed and efficiency with which the Japanese engineers had built their own bridge at Lo Wu enabled them to get their transport and guns to Au Tau. Here they found the bridge blown, and they were fired upon by a patrol of the Royal Scots. The Battalion reported 5.9-inch guns drawn by tractors and being manhandled by the Japanese across the demolition at Au Tau.

The Japanese now abandoned the Castle Peak Road and swung south-east, across country towards Tai Mo Shan, endeavouring to cut off the Royal Scots forward patrols to the west of the mainland, just as sampans had been used to bypass defensive positions on the east. The Japanese advance indicated good knowledge of the cross-country tracks, and considerable aptitude for using them.

By dawn on 9 December, Major Grey's forward troops were between the north-east of Needle Hill, on Monastery Ridge and Sha Tin (see map, page 14). This was the last of their delaying positions. They had fulfilled their role admirably. Communications had been well maintained, over a hundred casualties inflicted on the enemy, and sixteen major demolitions carried out on the road and railway. By dusk Grey's force withdrew behind the three battalions along the Gin Drinkers' Line.

The ability of the Japanese to move rapidly and stealthily, particularly at night, disturbed General Maltby. An entry in the Fortress HQ War Diary at 2.15 am stated: 'The lesson of today is that the enemy can operate strongly on a moonlight night.' The Japanese were clearly fit, skilful and well led.

On the Island, theatres, cinemas and some restaurants still functioned normally. At the Palace Floating Restaurant, which resembled a Mississippi steamboat, however apprehensive they should have been, diners leisurely chose from lobsters, shrimps, crabs, scallops, oysters, squids, prawns and garoupa, all of which wallowed alive in large cages beneath the restaurant, a few paces from the toilets which spilt their contents into the static, stagnating water. The most fashionable of the restaurants, Gripps in the Hong Kong Hotel, was also crowded, despite the lack of its band since most of the musicians lived in Kowloon. Another band was promised for the following night.

The *South China Morning Post* on Tuesday 9 December was reassuring as always: 'Hong Kong woke yesterday to find itself at war. This was a shock for all except those who listened to the radio all night.' Skirmishes were reported at Tai Po.

'Apart from air raids, which were very frequent, we continued to live quite normally on the Island, as if we were taking part in yet another exercise,' recalls Captain A. G. Hewitt, the Adjutant of the Middlesex. 'We were not very concerned that the Japanese had advanced rapidly down the mainland and had even occupied Tai Mo Shan by 4.00 pm on the first day. On the 9th, I drove around the Island with the RSM and visited our companies and the Winnipeg Grenadiers, drinking Scotch with our people and Canadian rye with the others. Morale was high.'[3]

In the makeshift Jockey Club Hospital in Happy Valley to the east of Victoria, Mabel Redwood was as busy as ever: 'The number of patients was now increased by casualties, the results of air raids. People were arriving with messages, orders and supplies. They were eagerly besieged with questions as to the happenings in the other parts of the town. They told of fierce fighting on the border and of several of our men being brought over badly wounded. Many families' names were mentioned. I think this made us realise that we would need more than the thrill of excitement to face up to what was going to be a "not so comfortable war".'

Dr. Isaac Newton was the Government surgical specialist in Kowloon Hospital. He had been woken at 6.25 am the previous day to be told that the 'precautionary stage' had been declared. 'It was the first time I had ever heard of a precautionary stage and it meant nothing to me. I asked what it signified. I don't think it meant any more to the caller, and so I went straight to sleep again.' However three hours later he was starting the first of the twenty-seven operations to be completed that day, during which one hundred and three casualties were received.

The 9th also provided a major surprise for Phyllis Harrop, who had crossed over on the Star Ferry with the Commissioner of Police after the Charity Ball. She discovered that her post on mobilisation involved being 'attached to the Chinese secret police. They are employed by the Chinese Chungking Government, working very closely with us. I have known several of them for some time, but I did not realise that my special work was to be with them in war time.'

Although all except one RAF aircraft had been destroyed and the airstrip damaged, civilian aircraft with gallant American and Chinese pilots continued to shuttle people to safety, flying them 200 miles inland to Namyung beyond the Japanese lines. Several civilian aircraft were hidden in the Chinese quarters of Kowloon, camouflaged by day with mud and straw amongst vegetable patches.

Landings and take-offs were made in total darkness and were delicate feats of flying. The airfield was largely destroyed, but a narrow landing strip was left, so that planes could continue to operate. During the nights 8th/9th and 9th/10th, 275 Chinese and Americans, including the family of China's Finance Minister, were flown to safety.

On 7 December, Chiang Kai-Shek had sent the redoubtable Admiral Chan Chak to represent him in Hong Kong. He had earlier lost his leg in a naval action on the Yangtze River, and was to play a remarkable and unexpected role in the final hours of Hong Kong's fight for survival.

On Tuesday, 9 December, Air Chief Marshal Sir Robert Brooke-Popham, the Commander-in-Chief Far East in Singapore, issued a stirring 'Order of the Day': '. . . We are ready. We have had plenty of warning and our preparations are made and tested . . . We are confident. Our defences are strong and our weapons efficient. Whatever our race, we have one aim and one aim only. It is to defend these shores, to destroy such of our enemies as may set foot on our soil. . . .'

General Maltby's Order of the Day was: 'It is obvious to us all that the test for which we have been placed here will come in the near future. I expect each and every man of my force to stick it out unflinchingly, and that my force will become a great example of high-hearted courage to all the rest of the Empire who are fighting to preserve truth, justice and liberty for the world.'

The Canadian Minister of National Defence signalled Brigadier Lawson: 'Concurrently with Dominion's Declaration of War against Japan, I send you assurance of the complete confidence that Forces under your command will in the days that lie ahead worthily uphold the best traditions of Canadian Arms.' Brigadier Lawson replied: 'All ranks much appreciate your message. We shall do everything in our power to maintain the best tradition of the Canadian Army.'

The Canadians and the Middlesex Regiment on Hong Kong Island were issued with war scales of rations which included three days' emergency reserves. The NAAFI was absorbed by the Army, and the Royal Army Service Corps with many locally employed Chinese were responsible for distributing supplies.

Rifleman Sydney Skelton, the twenty-year-old slim, freckled Canadian from Winnipeg, high on the Tytam Gap, had a grandstand view of the dive-bombing: 'Pay Office blown up on 8 December,' he wrote in his diary. 'From where I am sitting I can see Japanese planes bombing Hong Kong. They are playing hell. Hundreds of Chinks have been killed already. Our planes have been wrecked. There must be at least fifty planes dropping bombs. Japs are raising Cain over on our barracks. On the 9th we headed up into the hills and have camouflaged ourselves with grass. . . .'

The Japanese had perfected the art of camouflage. Their uniform stitching was particularly adaptable to the insertion of twigs and grass which blended perfectly with their surroundings. They carried rolled-up camouflage nets high on their backs, which could easily be drawn down to conceal their head and shoulders.

On 9 December the Japanese closed up to the Gin Drinkers' Line. Three battalions, 2 Royal Scots, 2/14 Punjabis and 5/7 Rajputs had orders to hold the Line for at least a week. The blow was to fall on the Royal Scots' Shingmun Redoubt – the 'vital' ground to the British and Japanese alike. The first major skirmishes had finished. The battle at the Gin Drinkers' Line was about to begin.

7

The Battle for the Mainland

9.00 pm 9 December—Midday 11 December

General Maltby had visited the Royal Scots on the left of the Gin Drinkers' Line two weeks previously. At the Shingmun Redoubt he had seen round the twelve acres of defensive positions first built in 1937 and then abandoned when the defence plan changed. He walked through several of the dank, concrete, claustrophobic underground tunnels which connected the pill-boxes. The main illumination in the tunnels came from the ventilation chimneys which poked above the ground. General Maltby saw that from the embrasures in the pill-boxes most machine-guns could not be lowered sufficiently to cover the immediate, hidden approaches, for the ground fell steeply away towards the Jubilee Reservoir and a large, steep valley between Smugglers Ridge and Needle Hill (see map, page 14). The denseness of the undergrowth could permit the attacker to slip completely unobserved from one position to another.

The Shingmun Redoubt was the key to the defensive position on the mainland. It covered the southern slopes of the massive Tai Mo Shan mountain to the north-west and Needle Hill to the north-east. The redoubt was the dominating, vital ground which, if captured by the enemy, would enable them to choose the most advantageous approach into Kowloon City itself. Yet only No. 8 Platoon Royal Scots, an artillery observation post and A Company HQ could be spared to hold the redoubt, for the Royal Scots had a frontage of over three miles compared with the theoretical standard thousand yards considered a suitable length of ground for a battalion to hold. The front consisted of a confusing complex of defiles, re-entrants, bowls, sloughs and streams, varying in height between sea-level on the left and over a thousand feet on the right. There was, therefore, no prospect of many of the platoons being able to support each other.

Quite apart from the unfavourable ground and too wide a

frontage, the battalion faced another considerable disadvantage: this area was recognised to be the most malarial district in the Colony. 180 of the Royal Scots had been under treatment, and the Battalion's effective strength reduced from 735 to 600. (Due to over-crowding in the hospitals, many of the malaria victims were sent back to dig trenches and erect obstacles without the normal ten days convalescence.)

A subaltern of A Company made a 'dummy' attack on the redoubt a few days earlier to practise the defences. He had no difficulty in getting a section through the perimeter wire onto the position undetected.

Captain C. R. Jones, commanding A Company, established his HQ within the perimeter of the redoubt, in the artillery post where the observation was better to the north. The remaining two platoons of the Company were on the lower ground to the west alongside the Jubilee Reservoir. Beyond them stretched B and C Companies. D Company provided the battalion reserve in the rear to the south-west of A Company, separated from them by a thousand yards of open, precipitous country.

To the right of the Royal Scots, General Maltby had brought forward, at 6.00 am on the 9th, Captain H. R. Newton's D Company of the Rajputs from near Kai Tak. However this company's new position lay too far back between Smugglers Ridge and the Tai Po Road to be of much value to A Company of the Royal Scots although some mutual support was arranged.

The weakness of the redoubt was recognized by Brigadier Wallis who had impressed upon the Royal Scots that 'they must patrol constantly as there was much ground that could not be seen. Also that sections should be located outside the redoubt as far as possible and not caught inside.' He had also ordered that 'the redoubt was to be used largely as cover in case of heavy enemy shelling, and its defence would be achieved principally from outside positions.'[1] Nevertheless the strength of the Royal Scots in this vital area was quite inadequate for any sustained defence.

The Royal Scots clearly had more than their share of problems. But so did Colonel Doi Teihichi and his 228th Regiment, whose leading battalion was advancing towards Tai Wai at the foot of Tide Cove.

By 3.00 pm, 9th, Colonel Doi, ahead of his two other

battalions, was on Needle Hill watching the Gin Drinkers' Line. He takes up the account: 'For about two hours we carried out a reconnaissance of the main line of defence. Although no enemy was to be seen, a good view of the trenches and defensive positions was obtained, and a sighting of something like white clothes being dried gave a clue to the likely presence of enemy troops. My impression was that the enemy was still inactive perhaps because of their estimate that it would take at least several more days for the Japanese troops to approach their position.

'Heavy fog suddenly limited the visibility to about twenty metres, and as the rain began to fall and the wind was increasing it became utterly impossible to continue the recce.'[2]

To make matters worse, Colonel Doi's communications had failed and he had no information on the location of his three battalions; he was being drawn irresistibly to attack the Shingmun Redoubt which he believed to be the strongest position in the Gin Drinkers' Line, and which lay firmly in the sector of another Japanese regiment. Finally his battalions had already had an exhausting approach march, and there was no supporting artillery; it had been delayed well back due to the demolitions on the Tai Po Road.

Near Jubilee Reservoir, he ordered his 2nd Battalion on the left to recce the enemy. The 3rd Battalion were to attack at 11.00 pm with two Companies leading. Obstacle-clearing teams moved forward to clear the pathways through the wire entanglements, which would take them an hour.

'I accompanied the 3rd Battalion,' Doi wrote later. 'The troops marching in single file formation moved stealthily over rough paths towards Jubilee Reservoir. By this time the rain had almost stopped and complete darkness fell over the entire area. The men silently making their way in complete darkness in gripping tension, stumbling and falling without even raising a cry, were a grim picture indeed.'

Meanwhile the patrol of the Royal Scots No. 8 Platoon were clambering with equal difficulty over the rocks, after a weary check of the perimeter wire and a liaison visit to Captain Newton's Rajput Company.

On their return, the soldiers reported to Sergeant Robb, the Platoon Sergeant. The Platoon Commander, Second-Lieutenant J. S. R. Thomson, himself climbed up alone to his

Company Commander in the artillery observation post. While there they were told that the leader of 'Z' Force, Mr. Kendall, was coming up to them from B Company and wished to brief Captain Jones. 'Z' Force was a band of local volunteers who had been trained beforehand for work behind the Japanese lines. Dumps of arms, supplies and medical stores had been previously positioned for 'Z' Force, and Mr. Kendall would no doubt have information of value. The night was dark and misty and so a runner was sent out to guide him to the redoubt. Thomson was told by Captain Jones to remain in Company HQ to hear Mr. Kendall's report.

The Japanese attacked first.

At 11.00 pm, Corporal Laird, on sentry nearest to the Shing-mun River, saw lights and a group of shadowy figures approaching the wire. He challenged them. Receiving no reply, he opened fire with a sub-machine gun. Grenades were flung at him and his fire was returned. Laird alerted his section commander and shouted to the signaller to inform Sergeant Robb and the Company Commander, Captain Jones, of the situation. The enemy suddenly appeared everywhere at once. Sergeant Robb tried desperately to organize counter-attacks in three separate directions.

'The companies leading the attack,' wrote Colonel Doi, 'assaulted the eastern position. First a small number of troops threw hand grenades into the air ventilation chimneys of the connecting tunnels, and the infiltrating teams went into the tunnels and engaged in fierce close-quarter fighting. In the meantime each tunnel exit was blocked by several men. Although the hand-to-hand fighting was continued for more than an hour, a small number of enemy remnants continued to offer stubborn resistance. During the fighting in the eastern position, the enemy to the west mounted machine-guns in the open and suddenly opened fire and harassed the Battalion Commander and others who were not in the tunnels. Immediately our officers and men went to work to construct cover, while others were sent to assault the western position which they captured shortly afterwards.'

The artillery observation post containing the Royal Scots Company and Platoon commanders, and Lieutenant L. C. Wilcox, the artillery observation officer, was rapidly surrounded. Wilcox called artillery fire down upon the redoubt itself to drive the Japanese off the area. The enemy tossed in grenades, lights were swept off the walls and the air became dense with fumes. The Japanese blew in the main steel shutter, killing instantly two Indian signallers. By now only Thomson was unwounded. He had been out in the passage-way firing through the grating. 'He now returned and directed his fire through the wide breach in the wall,' recorded the Regimental historian of the Royal Scots.[3] 'More grenades were thrown in. One explosion sent him down on the littered floor, and then another grenade fell beside his head. He was about to sweep it aside when he realised that he would be sending it among other men who were still alive, so he tipped his steel helmet over his face and waited. On the explosion of that grenade he became unconscious. His wounds included the complete loss of one eye and the partial loss of another.' At 3.30 am Captain Newton reported that eighteen of the Royal Scots from the redoubt had reached his Rajput Company position.[4]

The last Royal Scots section post on the redoubt held out for a further eleven hours before a British shell caused the concrete of their pill-boxes to cave in. Four soldiers were dug out alive by the Japanese.

The collapse of the Shingmun Redoubt, which General Maltby had hoped would be held for a week, was one of the major disasters of the campaign, and 'really caused chaos in Fortress HQ. I have never seen General Maltby more shocked or angry' recalled one of his staff officers.

At midnight, 9th/10th, the GOC ordered the reserve company of the Winnipeg Grenadiers on Hong Kong Island to move to Brigadier Wallis' Mainland Brigade HQ on the northern outskirts of Kowloon City. However neither they, the Royal Scots reserve company, nor Captain Newton's D Company were ordered forward to counter-attack since 'the nearest troops were a mile away, the ground precipitous and broken, and the exact position around the redoubt very obscure.'[5]

Having punched a gaping hole in the Gin Drinkers' Line, Colonel Doi, to his astonishment and dismay, was ordered on the morning of 10 December by his Divisional Commander to withdraw from it immediately. Colonel Doi was told that he had flouted the orders given to him by entering 230 Regiment's sector. Doi refused to comply with two specific orders to abandon the position. His initiative was later censured. The Divisional staff officer, Oyadomani, was 'sharply rebuked' for not curbing Doi's enthusiasm. By midday, however, Doi's achievement was recognised and he was permitted to remain in the redoubt.

The Punjabis and Rajputs to the right were meanwhile receiving some shelling and mortaring. At about 4.30 pm, two sampans appeared in Tide Cove with Japanese troops disguised in Chinese dress. Both were machine-gunned from a concealed pill-box and sunk.

The Royal Scots were ordered to withdraw to a new line further to the rear between Golden Hill and Lai Chi Kok, since the Gin Drinkers' Line was irrevocably broken (see map, page 14). At dusk the Battalion slipped off quietly and apparently unobserved. Soon after midnight all troops had reached their new positions.

Second-Lieutenant J. A. Ford was ordered to establish his platoon on the highest point of Golden Hill. D Company was ordered to cover Smuggler's Ridge, to prevent the Japanese breakthrough from the Shingmun Redoubt. The appalling strain of that climb in the dark was never forgotten. The soldiers, burdened by equipment and ammunition, and weak as many of them were from malaria, were in a state of exhaustion as they crawled on hands and knees over rocks and scrub to the bare hill top. There they found a few shallow weapon pits dug over three years previously. There were no mines and the broken, rusted wire was valueless. Yet this position was to be referred to as 'the strong Golden Hill line' in the GOC's despatches.

Sentries were posted, while others tried to rest despite the bitter cold. No food could be carried up Golden Hill. Each man received a tot of rum for breakfast, while they stood-to awaiting the next Japanese attack.

The remainder of the Royal Scots, consisting of B and C Companies, two platoons of A Company and Battalion HQ, were to the left of D Company's position on Golden Hill, on lower ground.

Captain D. Pinkerton commanded D Company. 'It was his courage, his cool insistence on standing fast under merciless mortaring that gave D Company the reputation they won on Golden Hill,' recalls Second-Lieutenant Ford.[6] 'He was a tall, unbending man, sparing of words and unsparing of our

energies as well as his own. Stretching our loyalty beyond
normal human limits, he might seem at times no more than a
military martinet; but he was in truth a man of some sensitivity
and deep kindness. We were proud of him, perhaps partly because he made us proud of ourselves.'

At 7.30 am, 11th, the Japanese 230 Regiment attacked in
great strength along the whole Battalion front. 'I saw Captain
Pinkerton lead a bayonet charge to clear the top of the Golden
Hill ridge. From then on throughout the day we were heavily
mortared. That was the worst of it. There could be no fighting
back. And the mortaring was carried out with deadly accuracy.
Every time we disclosed that some of us were still alive by firing
across the Company front, we were mortared again.'[7]

Meanwhile the leading Japanese battalion fell upon B and C
Companies after a heavy mortar attack. The companies had
been unable to establish field cable communications with their
Battalion HQ. Captain W. R. T. Rose, commanding C Company, was killed and the Company withdrew towards B Company which was similarly driven back, partly because their
supporting artillery had misjudged the range and British shells
were falling in their midst. But the hard-pressed Battalion had
some successes: a mistimed Japanese thrust was caught on the
skyline and suffered heavy casualties, and a shower of hand
grenades broke up another Japanese assault on the left flank.
The platoons commanded by Second-Lieutenants F. R.
Haywood and G. C. Houston-Boswell succeeded with
machine-gun and rifle fire in pushing the Japanese back, temporarily in disorder. However, the Royal Scots were receiving
grievous casualties. Houston-Boswell was killed by the sword of
a Japanese officer in fierce hand-to-hand fighting. The Commander of B Company, Captain F. S. Richardson, was also
killed.

The Battalion Signals Officer, Captain Douglas Ford, went
forward to a southern spur on Golden Hill. He reported by field
telephone to his Commanding Officer and immediately had the
range of the supporting artillery increased. At 7.30 am, C Company had been thirty-five strong. Within three hours, they had
received twenty-five casualties. Both Companies reformed on
the two platoons of A Company, and the defence line was re-
established. At 10.00 am Brigadier Wallis told the Royal Scots
Commanding Officer and Second-in-Command that 'the good

name of the Battalion was at stake. It was emphatically stressed that further withdrawals must stop or all troops based on the Tai Po road would be liable to be cut off.'[8]

The Commanding Officer of the Royal Scots, Lieutenant Colonel S. E. H. E. White, MC, was a bluff Irishman, known to his officers as 'Scram', his favourite order of dismissal. He was a tallish man, dark-skinned from years of exposure to the sun. During the eighteen days of war in Hong Kong he was to see his battalion almost literally blown to bits. When news reached him of the virtual disintegration of B and C Companies, he went forward to meet the survivors of D Company, upon which the full Japanese attacks had now fallen; the Company was ordered to pull back to less exposed ground closer to Kowloon.

On a knoll near Golden Hill, Second-Lieutenant Ford had been left with a section of seven to cover Captain Pinkerton's withdrawal with the last of the walking wounded. An hour later he, too, was ordered to pull back. He had only one private; the rest of the section were dead. 'We tried to take one of the seriously wounded on the knoll with us, but it was rough going down to the road and he died on the way,' he recalls.

The Battalion had already received casualties amounting to about one sixth of their effective strength. The ratio of officer casualties was significantly greater. Of the four rifle Company Commanders, two had been killed and the other two wounded. Of the officers of D Company, Second-Lieutenants J. M. M. Dunlop was hit in the thigh and bled to death, J. Nicholl took a burst of machine-gun fire in the stomach and was long in dying, and T. D. Hunter had been carried back unconscious with blood oozing from arm and shoulder. Second-Lieutenant Ford's No. 17 platoon, of 26 men, that day lost 6 killed and 7 wounded. In subsequent actions, 10 more were to be wounded and 2 went down with malaria.

At 11.00 am the Royal Scots, supported by a Company of the Winnipeg Grenadiers and the carrier platoon with two armoured cars of the Volunteers, was authorized to make a partial withdrawal. Their new line extended obliquely back almost to Shamshuipo in Kowloon. On their right, the two Indian battalions were still relatively unscathed on the Gin Drinkers' Line.

A British Lieutenant commanding a reserve force of fifty Indian Army soldiers was moved to Brigade HQ, where he met

Brigadier Wallis. 'The Lieutenant looked excited and had a strange look in his eyes,' recorded Mainland Brigade War Diary. 'He spoke somewhat incoherently to Brigadier Wallis saying: "Are you sure this is necessary?" The Brigade Commander noticed the Lieutenant's hand creep to his revolver. From the look in his eyes Wallis realized this young officer was about to shoot him. He rushed the Lieutenant who was drawing his pistol, knocked it from his grip, placed him under guard and ordered him to hospital. There were other instances of loss of balance and morale as the day wore on.'[9]

Alarming reports reached Fortress HQ of a possible invasion by sea. The enemy had landed on Lantau Island, to the southwest of Hong Kong Island. They were fired on by the heavy guns at Aberdeen. An enemy party in sampans attempted a surprise landing at Aberdeen Island within three hundred yards of the Naval Base. They were driven off by machine-gun fire from a platoon of the Winnipeg Grenadiers and by 3 Battery of the Volunteers. Orders were given to the Royal Engineers to lay out personnel mines on the beaches on the southern shores.

At midday on 11 December, General Maltby made the momentous decision to withdraw all his troops from the mainland that night, except for 5/7 Rajputs which would remain on the isolated but commanding position on the Devil's Peak Peninsula indefinitely, in accordance with previous plans.

The withdrawal called for a particularly difficult move for 2/14 Punjabis, who were expected to move at night across the whole front – a distance of over twelve thousand yards of very difficult country. The speed and skill of the Japanese night fighting made such a withdrawal more hazardous.

The Kowloon denial plan was being implemented as quickly as possible. The cement works, power station and dockyards were all destroyed. Merchant ships, including a Swedish vessel, were sunk.

That afternoon the last of the Eastern Telegraph Company cables linking Hong Kong to the outside world was cut by enemy action. With the destruction of Kai Tak aerodrome's runways, Hong Kong was now totally alone.

8

Nothing but Darkness Ahead

Midday 11 December—9.30 am 13 December

The fighting crept nearer Kowloon and Hong Kong Island. The sound of gun-fire was almost constant during the daytime. At night shells whistled overhead, and red flares shot up behind where the Japanese lines were believed to be. Occasionally the distant rumble of heavy guns and intermittent bursts of machine-gun fire could be heard.

In Kowloon an unpleasant stench filled the air, since the bodies of the dead were rotting in the bright sun. Sewage seeped into the streets from broken mains. The refrigeration system had broken down in the godowns, and the goods stored there began to rot. Putrid fish and salted cabbage added their smells. Exhausted soldiers buried their faces in their arms to keep out the stench of death, excreta and putrefaction.

Doctor Isaac Newton was told on the 10th that it was the Governor's wish that the sisters, nurses and doctors should remain at their posts in Kowloon. Doctor P. S. Selwyn Clarke the Director of Medical Services in Hong Kong, also told Newton that 'it was anticipated that they might have to evacuate the mainland at 6.00 pm but if they didn't they might be able to hold it for one or two months. It was obvious that evacuation was what they really anticipated.' He wrote in his diary:

'7.30 pm. Another air raid. Tonight (10/11 December), the local news was much better, we seem to have held the Japanese at Shingmun and inflicted quite a few casualties.

'11/12 December. Unfortunately much valuable time that was spent collecting stores, food and drugs was frittered away by an order from Hong Kong to prepare a camp for 10,000 evacuees from the island. Sixty to seventy casualties admitted and two operating theatres in continuous use for 12 hours. All lights have gone except for emergency installations in the hospital.

'Terrible riots have broken out in Kowloon and it is most

dangerous to go out. As I stood in the compound this evening, I could hear the roar of the looting in the Nathan Road. It was a very nasty sound. No sooner was the camp for the evacuees stocked with food, when rioters broke in.'

The walls of many of the little shops in Kowloon had been torn wide open by the indiscriminate Japanese shelling and bombing. Chinese looters stripped the stores and hauled canned goods across the streets, in some cases before even the injured had been evacuated. Wooden shelves and even floors were ripped from the blasted buildings to be used for firewood. A few looters were shot, their crumpled bodies being left on the ground as an example to others. But law and order was disintegrating and, as the fighting got nearer, less attempt was made to control the chaos.

A refugee camp had been established in Kowloon under the control of Judge N. F. Allman, with police guards from Shamshuipo. He was an American newspaper man. To his fury the police had vanished. Judge Allman barged his way through a milling crowd into the Shamshuipo police station, but found it looted. No police were there and the telephones were smashed. A military police truck later reached the refugee camp with 300 blankets. Allman drove it round Kowloon, picking up women and children whom he found stranded in the streets. He took them to the ferry police station where hopeless confusion reigned. Many Chinese drivers and launch crews had deserted, throwing a heavy burden on the civil, naval and military administrative services.

Huge, noisy crowds swarmed along the wharves in Kowloon. Only Hong Kong Island across the harbour seemed to offer a safe refuge. The little green Star ferries shuttled back and forth like beetles. The wives and children of the Volunteers waited impatiently to cross, clutching nervously their possessions which were not permitted to exceed one suitcase. At first only people with a Governor's pass were allowed to cross, and others, including Europeans, were turned away. The Chinese, many of whom had come from where the battle was now raging, sat amid their bags and boxes. Some walked up and down the lines searching for their families or friends. One old Chinese woman, dressed in soiled black pyjamas, her feet tightly bound, sat upon a battered suitcase and wept.

When the British were seen to be finally abandoning the

mainland, and the Japanese arrival at the waterfront appeared imminent, the ferry site was a scene of panic. The last ferry stood half a mile down the concrete docks. Smoke swirled overhead as cursing, screaming Chinese swarmed towards it. Occasionally there was the crack of a pistol as shots were fired in the air to discourage rioting. There were other shots, too, as fifth columnists mixed in the crowd, shooting, stabbing, starting fires and doing everything they could to create disorder.

A Hong Kong University professor, Wenzell Brown, trapped in Kowloon without a pass, was on that last ferry, having burst through the barrier waving his American passport. Two Chinese were ahead of him in the dash for the boat. One fell with blood gushing from a bullet hole in his head. The crate which he carried teetered on the edge of the concrete siding and toppled into the water. The other Chinese leaped with the professor into the ferry as it pulled away. Brown noticed that he was still triumphantly clutching a great wooden box upon which was printed in large red letters: 'Epsom Salts', and in smaller letters of blue: 'Net weight: 50 lbs'.

Japanese shells landed close by, and the ferry came under rifle fire from the shore. Shots were fired back from the bridge. The crowd in the boat struggled to get to the bows. A European nurse was hit and lay writhing on the deck. Her husband and Wenzell Brown knelt beside her in a hopeless attempt to stop the bleeding. Slowly the ferry reached Hong Kong Island; the firing ceased, but the nurse's screams did not. The ferry tipped ominously as everyone struggled to get off at once. Japanese shells ripped into a nearby dock, and clouds of black smoke darkened the city. The ambulance took too long to reach the nurse, and she died the following day.

Only the greatest efforts prevented the situation on Hong Kong Island becoming equally chaotic. Many stores had boarded up their windows, but were still open for a few hours a day. Regulations had been introduced to prevent food being hoarded, and only emergency provisions could be purchased. A food control office ensured that supplies reached hospitals, air raid centres and army depots. Food tickets were issued to all civilian workers, which told them where and when they could obtain food. What could be served at restaurants was also carefully specified.

'While I was at home in Victoria,' recorded the Nurse Mabel

Redwood in her diary, 'some planes came circling round and suddenly there was a crash of bombs and I was sure that the flat had been hit. The sound of glass from all the windows falling into the yard below was deafening, and the amahs came rushing in saying "Missy, the kitchen has gone". The whole place was full of dust, but except for plenty of broken dishes and rubble around, the flat had escaped serious damage. Instead it was the Sikh temple which had caught the full force of the bombs. Many who were sheltering there were killed. Another raid almost immediately began in the Wanchai area, and I shuddered to think of the poor Chinese who lived in the densely populated tenement flats there, and direct hits on our Jockey Club would have annihilated all the patients.

'Next day we heard terrible tales of happenings in Kowloon. Our troops were evacuating their posts. The Japanese were at Tai Po and we were hopelessly outnumbered. Someone had started the yarn that the Japanese did not fly at night, as they could not see in the dark. This of course was a load of rubbish. They did not need to fly at night. They were doing all the damage that they wanted to by day, and without much hindrance. We had always understood that although we had nothing much in the way of air defences ourselves, planes could come to our aid, if necessary, from Singapore in a matter of hours. But unfortunately for us Singapore had plenty of her own troubles. We really knew very little of what was actually happening.'

Amongst those, who were inevitably out of touch with all but their immediate area, was Rifleman Sydney Skelton of the Royal Rifles high in the mountains above Tytam Reservoir: 'Our heavy guns can be heard now,' wrote Skelton. 'They are firing at Japanese ships. With us are the Middlesex Regiment. They are a good bunch of chaps. Two of our boys have lost their minds, gone crazy in the head. The bombing has snapped their minds. Some have been machine-gunned from the diving Japanese planes. Sixty-five per cent of us have to be awake at night and no one is allowed to undress.'

*   *   *

As darkness fell on 11 December, the Royal Scots withdrew to the ferry. 'We drove down to Kowloon Point,' wrote Ford afterwards. 'A strange journey. After all the Battalion had come through, we left the battlefield in buses, as if we were going back to barracks after an exercise on the hills. The ferry-boats were waiting for us at the pier. We looked across the water, usually ablaze with the lights of the island. That night there was nothing but darkness ahead.'[1]

By 10.30 pm the Royal Scots reached Victoria. D Company, Winnipeg Grenadiers, crossed over to the Island three hours later. All armoured cars, some trucks and nearly all the Bren carriers were successfully evacuated.

The difficult withdrawal of the Rajputs and Punjabis the same night, with all their equipment, towards the Devil's Peak Peninsula was also successful despite a strong Japanese blocking position on Tates Cairn. One group of HQ Company, 2/14 Punjabis, became lost and found themselves on the outskirts of Kowloon fighting Japanese patrols and fifth columnists. Fortunately RAF launches picked them up from the wharf just as the Japanese were closing in upon them.

By dawn, 12 December, the Rajput Battalion was holding the Ma Lau Tong defensive line, fortified earlier in the year, which was an extension of the Gin Drinkers' Line. Behind them Brigadier Wallis had his small Mainland Brigade HQ and close to the Devil's Peak jetty half the Punjabis rested while waiting to be evacuated across the Lei Mun channel to Hong Kong Island. The remainder of the Battalion had been evacuated during the night. Fresh rations, and ammunition, were ferried forward to them all.

At about 10.00 am the Japanese made a dive bombing attack on the battalion's administrative areas, but no casualties were received. At 5.45 pm, the Japanese launched a battalion attack, unsupported by their mortar and artillery, against the two forward Rajput companies. The attack was met by machine-gun and artillery fire, and it failed to penetrate the frontal belt of wire. The 6-inch battery of howitzers opened a devastating fire on the retreating Japanese until darkness obscured the targets. The Japanese casualties were heavy.

General Maltby had always planned that at least two companies of the Rajputs would continue to hold the southern tip of the Devil's Peak Peninsula, although the rest of the mainland was being evacuated. At 4.30 am, 13th, when the

Punjabis and artillery were slowly being ferried to Hong Kong Island, General Maltby changed his mind. The Rajput Commanding Officer, Lieutenant Colonel R. C. Rawlinson, received a phone call from Brigadier Wallis who asked if he was prepared to withdraw the entire Battalion that night. He replied that this was rather a tall proposition as there were only some two hours of darkness left, but that the enemy had obviously taken a nasty knock. He was told that Fortress HQ ordered a complete withdrawal because of the precarious situation due to a shortage of sea-transport. Also that the Japanese had so far failed to follow up withdrawals.

The shell fire gradually died down, but the evacuation presented problems. The reliability of the Chinese boats' crews was such that they had to be under guard to prevent them deserting. Chinese engineers had already run away, and staff officers from Fortress HQ went forward to operate the boats in their absence. The withdrawal fell behind schedule, despite the efforts of four MTBs which had been ordered forward to help in the evacuation.

At 8.30 am the last covering troops were withdrawn in broad daylight in MTBs. Brigadier Wallis was the last to leave the peninsula. The 120 mules which were with the Mainland Brigade to carry heavy equipment had to be left behind, due to the desertion of the crew of the mule lighter. There had been no Japanese air activity or any attempt to follow up the withdrawal, and the evacuation had been completed without casualties, as it had taken the enemy by surprise.

*   *   *

'Everyone at the Jockey Club hospital was discussing the shelling,' scribbled Mabel Redwood. 'It seemed from bits of news that were trickling in that the Japanese were now in full force in Kowloon, and had their heavy guns in positions in godowns all along the sea front. Observers from the Hong Kong side could see them quite clearly, and it has since been learnt that these gun platforms had been built in the godowns while they had been leased to Japanese merchants. Their batteries were set up at other strategic points, and Hong Kong was at point blank range. A good percentage of the shells were duds but those that were not did terrible damage. The gas supply was cut off and the Naval yard had several hits.'

Mabel Redwood found herself sharing a room with a foreign
and very handsome woman whom she considered reserved and
sullen. 'Before the situation had become so tense, she had spent
all her off duty times trekking up to the Gloucester Hotel, to
have hot baths and manicures, good big meals and then telling
us about it on her return. Although we only had a tiny bulb
which gave no light at all, she still went through the most elab-
orate beauty treatment before retiring. Attired in a most gor-
geous brocade housecoat, she stood and creamed and patted
and massaged, till I felt I wanted to laugh out loud. The noise
and flashes of the guns were terrifying and the shells were
screaming right over the billet.

'Suddenly she said: "Good job my husband shot himself."
This had occurred just before hostilities. I hardly knew how to
answer this peculiar observation, and before I could think of
anything to say she went on: "He would have done it tonight
anyway; he could not have stood this." Eventually we both
slept from sheer exhaustion.'

One man who received no sleep that night was Doctor Isaac
Newton in Kowloon Hospital. At 5.00 pm on the 12th, surly
Japanese with fixed bayonets entered his hospital; however a
very courteous Japanese doctor quickly introduced himself.
That night Doctor Newton recorded in his diary: 'Throughout,
in my dealings with the Japanese officers and NCOs, I found
them polite and even respectful to our civilian doctors.'

The behaviour of the Japanese battalions which overran the
Hong Kong mainland also gave no cause for criticism, and this
reassuring fact was signalled to Whitehall. Mercifully nobody
could then have guessed at the horrifying atrocities which were
to be committed on the Island in the final days of desperate
frustration.

Phyllis Harrop, in Police HQ in Victoria, wrote in her diary:
'Yesterday, 10 December, was dreadful. It was 5.30 am this
morning before the telephones stopped ringing. The Chungking Chinese certainly knew their job. Their Chief, Mr. Chu
Shu Yan, has been ordered to contact leaders of certain secret
societies and to persuade them to come over to us, on the plea
that they are not fighting for us but for their own country. We
are all in the same fight now. The secret societies don't like us,
as we have tried hard to stop their activities. The Japanese
know this and their propaganda has been aimed at that point.

But the societies are under control. The Chungking men have done wonderful work. There are thousands of Chinese living in Kowloon, and we are afraid to shell it for fear of frightening them into saying we are killing their relatives and friends in that area.

'We were all in the shower bath shelters, as low to the ground as possible, when bullets began to spatter about the floor. The Commissioner said we were being shot at through the windows and ordered us not to come out. However a few moments later he discovered that, while trying to put on his tunic in the dark, he had turned it upside down, and the bullets were really his own falling out of his pockets!

'The Police HQ compound has been painted in large blobs of green and brown, with black shadows, to represent trees. It looks weird and wonderful. . . . Arrests of fifth columnists have been carried out all today (12 December). They are very active, many have already been executed. Sand in rice is a favourite trick. Kerosene has also been found in fire buckets. One was brought in with a small transmitter taped to his chest and Japanese passes in his possession. He was found on the roof of one of the tall buildings.'

On the night of 12/13 December, at the urgent request of the civil authorities, arrangements had been made with the Harbour Master to pass nine tons of dynamite, ammunition and stores from Green Island, north-west of Victoria, to the Star Ferry for collection and distribution. It was ordered to leave at midnight and all forts, armed posts and pill-boxes were warned of the timings and ordered not to fire.

For some unaccountable reason the ship left Green Island, two hours ahead of schedule. In the dark it approached the wrong ferry and with lights extinguished. The NCO commanding the pill-box there opened fire and there was a shattering explosion. The ship, together with its entire crew, were seen no more, and there was scarcely an unbroken window within a mile of the explosion. The incident was followed by a great deal of wild firing as it was thought that it was the prelude to an attack.

On the same evening it was announced by radio that HM ships *Prince of Wales* and *Repulse* had been sunk off Singapore. 'It was staggering, and I think we all uttered cries of dismay when we heard the news. We knew now that there would be no good news for a long, long time,' was one typical comment.

The possibility of reinforcements reaching them from Malaya had previously been a forlorn hope. Now it was out of the question.

The morale of Hong Kong could scarcely be sustained by an only partly reassuring communiqué which, for a change, was accurate. 'At dusk last night, the enemy attacked our troops who still remained on the mainland at Devil's Peak. The Japanese were decisively repulsed with heavy losses. They were unable to interrupt the withdrawal of our troops to the Island. This withdrawal was consequently carried out without loss and must be accounted a local success. . . . Await events calmly. The mainland has been successfully evacuated. The position has been stabilized. The Island of Hong Kong is now in condition of full siege.'

Amid the disasters, one constant hope encouraged the garrison and civilians to sustain their efforts: the news was released that Chinese armies were marching south to relieve Hong Kong, though General Maltby was not confident that Chiang Kai-Shek's divisions could really reach Hong Kong in time, if at all. Nevertheless, according to Japanese records examined in 1946, the Chinese did step up their guerrilla campaign and attempt to divert attention from the Hong Kong operation. They also sent reinforcements to the Canton area and moved a force, about one and a half divisions strong, towards Hong Kong.[2]

General Sakai, commanding the forces attacking Hong Kong, took the Chinese threat in his rear very seriously. A Japanese regimental group, the Akari Detachment, was stationed some forty miles north-east of Hong Kong to prevent Chinese interference. They reported later that the Chinese effort to reach Hong Kong was minimal.

'There is talk that Chinese guerrillas are coming up behind the Japanese and are now at Tai Po,' wrote Mabel Redwood's pretty twenty-three year old daughter, Barbara, who also kept a diary. 'But I'm afraid to believe anything so heartening. I can see absolutely no escape, but we didn't have to stay in Hong Kong, and at least this *is* something, and we are in the war with the folks at home. . . . It's hardly worth writing a diary because I can't visualise us ever getting out of this, but I want to *try* to believe in a future.'

As the exhausted Rajputs, and the last of the guns, were

being evacuated from the Devil's Peak Peninsula, Lieutenant-General Sakai despatched a launch with a flag of truce across the harbour with a letter demanding unconditional surrender. He was confident that neither the harassed British Forces nor the civilian population could take any more of his heavy artillery and aerial bombardment.

A young American reporter of the *Detroit News*, Gwen Dew, was about to obtain one of the more remarkable scoops of her career. She had been strolling through the debris taking photographs when she saw a launch leave a wharf at Kowloon and start hurrying towards Hong Kong. Through a telephoto lens on her camera, she saw on the bow a large white banner: "Peace Mission", and ran down to the pier in time to meet a strange, mixed party disembarking. It consisted of a very pregnant lady, Mrs. Macdonald; Mrs. C. R. Lee, the wife of the Secretary to the Governor with her two dachshunds, Otto and Mitzi; and finally three Japanese. The leader politely introduced himself to Gwen Dew as Colonel Tada, of Military Information. The bespectacled, younger, stocky figure clutching a large white flag was Lieutenant Mizuno; and a dark thickset Japanese carrying a portfolio was Mr. Othsu Dak.

Mrs. Lee, while resting at the base of a pillar, told Gwen Dew that she had been sitting in her hotel by candlelight the previous evening when the Japanese told her that she would be the hostage on the peace mission. They agreed to her requests: Mrs. Macdonald could have her baby on the Island, and the dogs could also accompany them. She was promised special consideration after the surrender. The peace mission had been delayed by frequent rehearsals of their departure for the benefit of Japanese cameramen. Gwen Dew asked Mr. Othsu what the conditions were for the surrender offer. 'Equable terms for both sides and safe conduct for all' was his reply. A British officer on the pier quickly intervened: 'Let's leave the terms to the Governor,' he said. Mrs. Lee volunteered the information that the Japanese had behaved very well in Kowloon. The Japanese added smugly that the American fleet had been sunk at Pearl Harbour.

As British soldiers cordoned off the area, Major Boxer collected the peace terms and drove to the Governor. Sir Mark Young read the Japanese demands. They amounted to surrender of the Colony and severe artillery bombardment if refused. He categorically rejected them. Major Boxer returned by car with the written refusal. They shook hands. The Japanese stepped back a pace, saluted and then departed with Mrs. Lee, Otto and Mitzi.

The official Hong Kong communiqué stated bluntly: 'It can now be revealed that the Japanese who came from Kowloon under cover of a white flag brought a letter enquiring if His Excellency the Governor was willing to negotiate for surrender. His Excellency summarily rejected the proposal. . . .'

General Sakai read Sir Mark Young's reply with growing irritation: 'Not only is this Colony strong enough to resist all attempts at invasion, but it has the backing of the people of the British Empire, of the United States of America, and of the Republic of China. British subjects and all who have sought the protection of the British Empire can rest assured that there will never be any surrender to the Japanese.' Sakai reluctantly contemplated the many problems of invading the Island, believed by some to be an impregnable fortress. He wondered how many thousands of Japanese lives would be lost in the weeks ahead before Sir Mark Young could be persuaded to change his mind.

9

'Clay Pigeons in a Shooting Range'

9.30 am 13 December—7.00 pm 18 December

'We are watching day by day and hour by hour your stubborn defence of the port and fortress of Hong Kong,' signalled Churchill to the Governor. 'You guard a vital link long famous in world civilization between the Far East and Europe. All our hearts are with you in your ordeal. Every day of your resistance brings nearer our certain victory.'

The speed of the Japanese thrusts in Hong Kong and Malaya, and the success of their operations against Pearl Harbour, were also being studied by more sinister eyes. Hitler at Berchtesgarten was following with jubilation every development in the war in Asia.[1] It had already succeeded in drawing substantial British forces to Singapore. Hitler eagerly awaited his share of the plunder of tin, rubber and oil to be captured in Malaya, Burma and the Dutch East Indies. Possibly the key positions of Ceylon and Port Darwin would eventually fall too. The glittering prizes were endless.

General Maltby appeared confident that Hong Kong could be held. The battle for the mainland had not amounted to a major defeat; but the many casualties of the Royal Scots, and the speed of the Japanese advance, boded ill for the future. There was no disguising the complete Japanese air superiority, for the lack of anti-aircraft guns was such that no adequate protection could be offered at any point. The Japanese mobile artillery on the mainland was starting to destroy one pill-box after another with remarkable accuracy.

Nevertheless the Japanese had found few stores, supplies or port installations which were not destroyed, and they had received more casualties than they had inflicted. But their infantry had proved themselves to be well-disciplined and highly-trained, particularly at night. They had not yet taken advantage of their marked naval superiority. No destroyers or cruisers had approached the Island and no attempt had been made to breach the minefields at sea.

The Garrison's morale was good, although the two Indian battalions, and the Royal Scots in particular, needed rest and reorganisation.

General Maltby assessed his options. His dilemma was similar to that of all commanders who are called upon to defend a coast line or island against superior numbers with control of the air: were troops best positioned well forward to overlook the beaches, or kept back until the true strength and direction of the enemy had been determined? Lieutenant-General Percival in Singapore favoured the former course. Field Marshal Rommel's plans in the spring of 1944 to hold his Panzer Corps close to the costal defences were vetoed by Hitler, who ordered him to keep them back.

General Maltby was deterred from keeping several battalions uncommitted in the centre of Hong Kong, ready for eventualities. He had insufficient transport; the 212 Canadian vehicles were still in Manila. The roads were inadequate to move any battalion quickly in any direction. The skill of the Japanese infantry suggested that any initial foothold on the Island for the wounded. He received a curt reply that the Japanmediate area. The GOC believed that his best plan involved the Middlesex machine-gunners, supported by scattered companies, holding and if possible destroying the enemy, while 'flying columns' consisting of Winnipeg Grenadier reserve companies hurried forward.

The Japanese were expected first to attack the north-west from across the harbour, landing in Victoria. This was because the distance was short, Victoria being within easy reach of their mortars and artillery on the mainland, and the pro-Japanese Chinese and fifth columnists would assist the enemy, particularly in the congested streets. The north-east coast opposite the Devil's Peak Peninsula was considered less likely, due to the ships sunk under the demolition plan, which would hinder any approach.

General Maltby therefore decided to disperse his companies around the Island, while keeping his greatest strength in Victoria.

Hong Kong Island is divided by a narrow, winding road which leads from Happy Valley and Leighton Hill and runs between Mount Nicholson and Jardine's Lookout. From there it

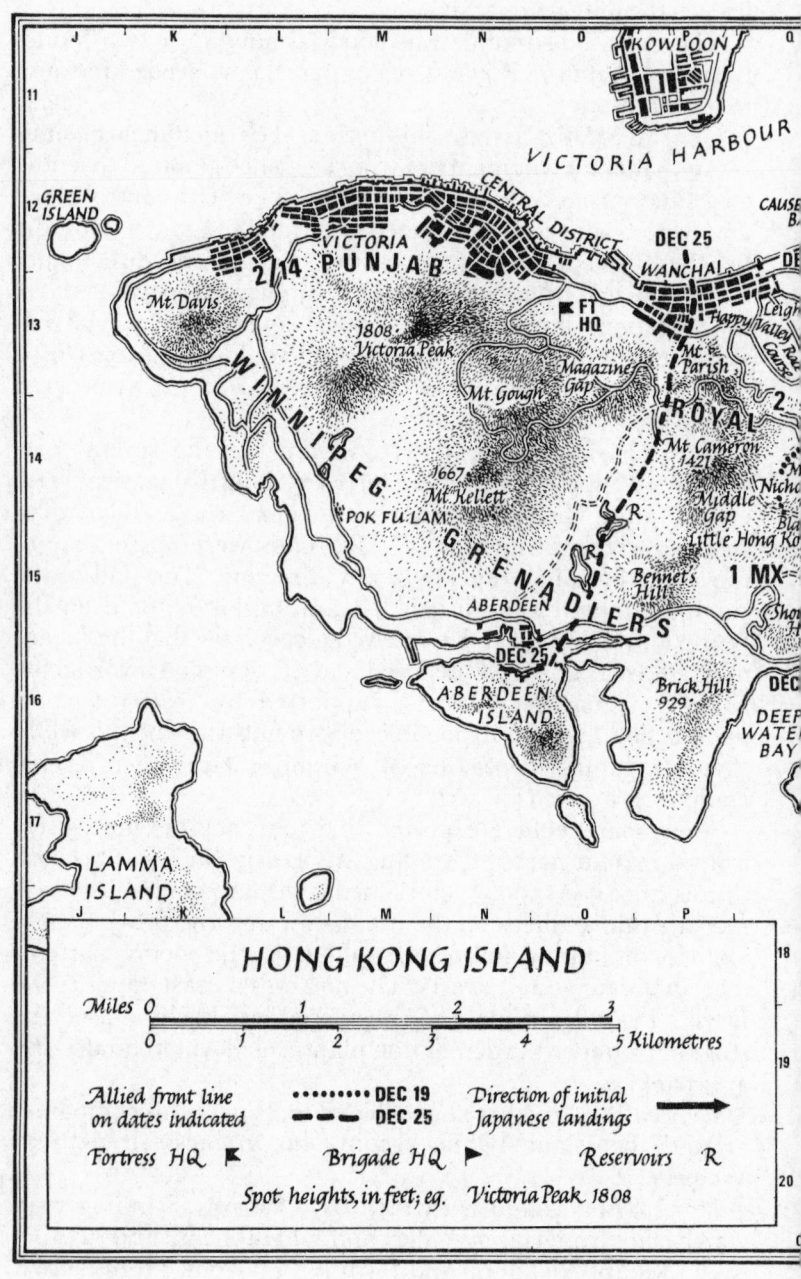

KOWLOON

VICTORIA HARBOUR

GREEN ISLAND

CAUSE. B.

CENTRAL DISTRICT

DEC 25

WANCHAI

DE

VICTORIA

2/14 PUNJAB

Mt.Davis

1808 Victoria Peak

FT HQ

Leigh

Happy Valley Rea.

Cause

Mt. Parish

ROYAL

2

Mt.Gough

Magazine Gap

WINNIPEG

1667 Mt.Kellett

Mt Cameron 1421

POK FU LAM

Middle Gap

Little Hong Ko

Nich

Bla

R.

GRENADIERS

R.

Bennet's Hill

1 MX

ABERDEEN

Sho H

DEC 25

ABERDEEN ISLAND

Brick Hill 929

DEC

DEEP WATER BAY

LAMMA ISLAND

HONG KONG ISLAND

Miles 0   1   2   3

0   1   2   3   4   5 Kilometres

Allied front line   •••••••• DEC 19   Direction of initial
on dates indicated   ⎯ ⎯ ⎯ DEC 25   Japanese landings   ➤

Fortress HQ ◤   Brigade HQ ▶   Reservoirs R.

Spot heights, in feet; eg. Victoria Peak 1808

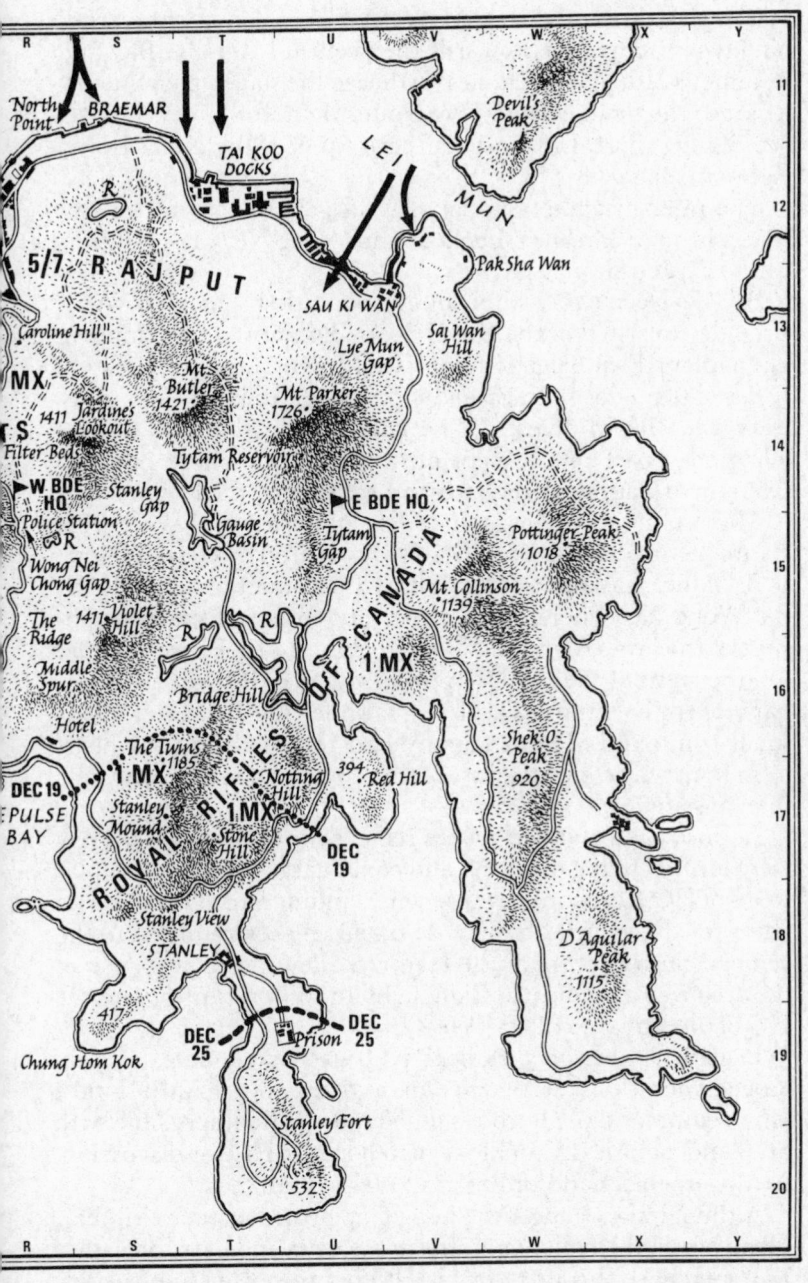

meets with three others at Wong Nei Chong Gap before dropping two hundred feet towards the beautiful Repulse Bay and
its famous Hotel. Three miles further to the south, past Stanley
Mound, the Chung Hom Kok peninsula and Stanley Village,
lies Stanley Fort, the most southern tip of Hong Kong Island
(see map, pages 68–69).

The inter-brigade boundary lay largely to the east of this
road, through Jardine's Lookout and Wong Nei Chong Reservoir to Chung Hom Kok.

By 17 December, after many confusing changes, West
Brigade consisted of the Royal Scots, Punjabis and Winnipeg
Grenadiers. East Brigade comprised the Rajputs and the Royal
Rifles of Canada. Both Brigades contained units of the Volun-
teers and the Middlesex. The latter manned the pill-boxes
along the coast line, except on the northern shore between
Lyemun to Causeway Bay, which were held by the Rajputs.

The Volunteers consisted of five batteries and seven rifle
companies in defensive positions spread throughout the Island.

Brigadier Lawson had established his small tactical HQ at
the Wong Nei Chong Gap, about one hundred yards north-
west of the large road junction and close to the Police Station.
On the right of the road, opposite Brigade HQ, was D Company of the Winnipeg Grenadiers, under the Brigadier's personal command. The Company had returned in good heart
from their successful support of the Royal Scots, with only one
man missing.

At dusk each night six trucks reported to Brigade HQ. They
were for the 'flying column', and could carry three reserve platoons of HQ Company to any enemy landing site. There was no
cover for the vehicles by day, so by dawn they returned to the
vehicle control centre at the Happy Valley race track. Also in
the area was a medical section, light anti-aircraft post, and the
HQ of the Royal Artillery (West).

Brigadier Lawson's tactical HQ was inadequate for prolonged operations, as he noted in his diary on the 12th: 'Find I
am in command of all troops on Island. Quite impossible with
Staff and facilities available. I go to Fortress HQ for discussion.
Arrangements made for East and West commands.'[2]

Although the Wong Nei Chong Gap provided poor visibility,
being overlooked by mountains to the west and east, Brigadier
Lawson chose this area for his HQ because it was on the key

road which split the Island; the harbour to the north and Repulse Bay to the south were both within fifteen minutes drive. Indeed whoever controlled the Wong Nei Chong Gap and the surrounding mountains controlled the heart of Hong Kong Island. Brigadier Lawson had placed himself on the vital ground, and within hours of the Japanese landings he was to find himself fighting for survival.

The Royal Scots were positioned in the Wanchai, the densely built-up Chinese quarters overlooking the harbour. Captain Pinkerton, insisting that he was sufficiently recovered from his wound, took his D Company to a position on the sea front. The other rifle companies, now all commanded by very young officers replacing those lost, took up positions behind D Company. Second-Lieutenant Ford had also rejoined his platoon from hospital. His pill-boxes started to receive accurate shelling, as did all those on the north shore. A near miss was usually enough to send up the inferior concrete in clouds of grey dust. There was grim hilarity among the Jocks when they saw an unexploded shell pass through both the forward and rear walls of a pill-box 'as if the prong of a fork had been jabbed through a piece of cheese'.

The Royal Scots, on the waterfront, became difficult to supply, due to the shell fire. Some loaves and stew occasionally reached them. To their surprise Chinese prostitutes came out from their quarters, oblivious to the danger, and offered thermos flasks of green tea. They had no food to give, but they supplemented the tea with little gifts of aspirin tablets and safety-razor blades. Some of the streets of the Wanchai were piled up with dead bodies, and attempts were made to cart them off for burial in communal graves. 'Refuse was gathering in heaps everywhere,' wrote Ford. 'Men tried to burn it and it smouldered slowly away, but other piles soon grew. On one of these rubbish heaps I saw a dead monkey and a dead baby, side by side. . . .'

The Middlesex pill-boxes each contained two to four machine-guns, and most were manned by a crew of nine. They were all self-contained with ammunition, grenades, food and water, and each was connected by telephone to their HQ.

A fifth makeshift Middlesex Company was formed. Commanded by Captain C. M. M. Man, it was responsible for the defence of Leighton Hill to the east of Victoria, the position being gradually strengthened with weapon pits, machine-gun emplacements and wire. No preparations previous to the war had been permitted on a ridge nearby, because the Government officials who lived there had refused to be 'inconvenienced'.[3] This hill was to become the scene of much heavy fighting. 'B' Company 5/7 Rajputs was placed well forward on its right flank, as an additional defence.

Captain Man was ordered to report on the Taikoo Docks, which were considered to be a possible enemy landing point. 'This I did, and I shall never forget the eerie sensation of walking through this large complex of sheds and workshops, all apparently empty with no sign of life. All the time I was conscious of the feeling that I was being observed. Try as I would I could not see anyone.'[4]

The Japanese had sent a patrol of four men, commanded by Lieutenant Zempei Masushima, to choose landing sites on the Island's north shore on 17 December. Dressed in Chinese clothes, they had approached the Taikoo Docks when a British searchlight spotted them. A Rajput pill-box opened fire, so the patrol jumped into the water and swam on, pulling the boat behind them. They landed by the docks, which had a six hundred yard frontage with one Rajput pill-box at each end. Lieutenant Zempei carried out a full reconnaissance of alternative landing sites that night. He noted the two Rajput pill-boxes, the location of obstacles and wire, and found several pill-boxes empty. The patrol then returned to their boat, and were fired upon once more as they recrossed the harbour towards Kowloon. Lieutenant Zempei was decorated for his bravery. 'Owing to the success of this officer's patrol it was decided to make the landings at these points', concluded the citation.[5]

Brigadier Wallis, after his withdrawal from the mainland, had established his Brigade HQ alongside the Royal Rifles' Battalion HQ at Tytam Gap, to cover the eastern half of the island.

Sir Mark Young later visited Brigadier Wallis there and asked him for his frank opinion on what the chances were. 'I told him that once again we were spread too thin with little depth,' recalls Wallis. 'That lacking air cover and with widely dispersed machine-gun posts, and as the Japanese had ample artillery and mortars while our own men had had little rest from incessant bombardment, it would only be a matter of time before we were forced back. I think Sir Mark was shocked by my reply.'[6]

The Canadian companies, like the Volunteers, were spread in defended localities throughout the Island, mainly covering the southern approaches. Parallel to them along the northern shore were the two Indian Army battalions.

In support of each Brigade were batteries of the Royal Artillery, Hong Kong and Singapore Artillery, the Volunteers, and the coastal defence guns ranging in calibre from 4 to 9.2 in. with a maximum range of 19,000 yards. Many shells had been made in the First World War. Major C. R. Templer, commanding a battery of 8 Coastal Regiment, found that several of his shells burst immediately in front of the muzzle of his guns at Stanley, with dire results. The Gunners had pre-arranged land targets, and were confident that they had inflicted many casualties on the Japanese, although it had been difficult to judge the results due to the lack of air reconnaissance and adequate communications. In many instances the civilian telephone was used to control the fire support. The only alternative was buried lines.

One Japanese cruiser incautiously came five hundred yards within the range of Major Templer's guns. His first salvo landed almost on top of the ship, which scuttled away at full speed. Each gun had been allotted twenty-five rounds for landward firing, and were to fire well over twice that number.

While the staff officers in Fortress Headquarters wearily pondered the possible Japanese assault routes, the War Office warned the Canadians in London what could be the fate of their first battalions in action in the Second World War. On 15 December, Major-General J. N. Kennedy, the Director of Military Operations, briefed the Canadian Military Headquarters in London, and emphasised the gravity of the situation. The Canadians signalled Ottawa:

'MOST SECRET
REQUEST STRICTLY LIMITED CIRCULATION
Major General Kennedy, DMO & P, has outlined Hong Kong situation as follows: Severe initial setback to both naval and air forces allows Japanese freedom of action for the moment in whole of Far East. Initial dispositions of troops were considered inadequate for war with Japan but could not be increased without serious reduction of effort in Middle East possibly leading

to cancellation of that campaign. Reinforcement of Hong Kong and despatch of *Prince of Wales* and *Repulse* to Singapore were intended to be deterrents only and were not expected to bring total forces up to size required for operations. Hong Kong has always been regarded as an outpost whose retention had both military and political significance. From strictly military point of view, the value of its retention depended on being able to relieve it within reasonable time and then use it as an advanced base for further operations. You will appreciate political significance without further comment. Decision was taken, therefore, that Hong Kong should be held and, if relief should prove impossible, the Garrison was to inflict maximum damage on Japanese. The present garrison is of strength considered proper to hold the Island only and should be capable of prolonged resistance. Reserves of food of 130 days are available and most serious weakness of situation is presence of 750,000 Chinese in City of Victoria. Possibility of early relief is considered remote since situation in Malaya is expected to deteriorate seriously rather than improve. General Kennedy emphasised Japanese freedom of action in whole area which permits them to reinforce any particular operation at will. This admitted to be purposely gloomy view of what is undoubtedly a serious situation: but Kennedy emphasised the fact that the situation could only be improved by making available the Naval and Air Forces required for advance from Singapore and it is unlikely that these can be provided.'[7]

                    *   *   *

Each day was a terrible nightmare for many Chinese. Mabel Redwood was still working day and night in the makeshift hospital at the Jockey Club race course. 'After prolonged shelling, the planes came. They seemed to be directed at the communal kitchens where Chinese were being supplied daily with cooked rice. Later I ventured home. I saw more horror in that journey than I ever want to see again. They had got the Chinese who were queueing for the Government's issue of rice well and truly; I had to step over mutilated bodies. Poor things had no chance and there were no military objectives nearby. Arriving at my house I found the amahs in a state of terror, and Ah Ting's little boy was really ill with fright. Always I told them that the Japanese would never get into Hong Kong. Now I did not feel so sure, and in answer to their tearful questioning, I could only advise them to stay in the house whatever happened. Gathering up some things I needed and tins of meat, and again explaining to them that they were safer in the house than out in the streets, I bade them goodbye. I said that I would not come home again until the war was over. This time I left by the back entrance, as I could not face the carnage that I had seen. I felt terrible leaving them but I could do no more for them, and there was much I could do at the hospital.

'I hurried along when a plane came zooming over. With a prayer that I would reach the main entrance to the Jockey Club before he dropped anything, I ran as best I could. As I got to the shelter of a wall of the paddock a small car drove up. Out jumped a nursing sister and one of the medical officers. We all sheltered while the plane circled overhead. Our conversation turned on the bad position we were in at this post, and the sister spoke of the continuous shelling to which we were being subjected. The doctor was inclined to pooh-pooh the idea that they would shell a hospital. "They are fighting a gentleman's war," he said. I have often wondered when he altered his ideas in view of what was to happen at his post. . . . By now we had had more than one hit on the hospital. The operating theatre had been wrecked. One shell which went through the top floor had taken a whole lot of rattan chairs over into the cemetery. We had a Red Cross marked on the flat roof for the benefit of aircraft, but I doubt if they ever noticed it. A large Red Cross was put on the wooden board that once showed the names of the horses and jockeys in the race, but the indiscriminate shelling continued regardless.'[8]

Many of the horses in the Jockey Club were to come to a tragic end. Fortress HQ suddenly received a panic message shortly after midnight that a large force of 'Japanese cavalry' was advancing across Happy Valley racecourse. Captain MacGregor and Captain P. Macmillan, both on duty at the HQ, were sent off to investigate with a scratch force of clerks and a Middlesex Sergeant. They climbed into a lorry with a machine-gun mounted in the front and drove to the racecourse through the dark, silent night. Captain MacGregor recalls: 'When we got to the racecourse we could dimly see the shapes of dozens of wraith-like animals, which might have been cavalry. The Sergeant was taking no chances and fired a number of bursts from the machine-guns, thus killing or maiming many of the horses which had broken out of the stables, terrified and bewildered. One of my own Australian ponies was among those killed. It seems silly and illogical now, with all the smell and sight of human death constantly around us then, to have felt so much pity, disgust and compassion for those slaughtered animals.

'We then suddenly received an urgent message from Fortress HQ: "Enemy reported landing in Wanchai area in force. Unable to make contact area pill-boxes. Investigate immediately and report". We drove as fast as possible to the sector indicated, left the lorry and crept along one of the narrow alleyways leading to the harbour. Ahead of us we could indeed see shadowy figures apparently landing from three large boats. We were just about to blaze away when we discovered that they were friendly Chinese who had managed to escape from the mainland.'[9]

There was another reported landing on 15 December. An observation post near Sai Wan in the north-east of the Island reported heavy, automatic fire and verey lights from the battery at Pak Sha Wan, and believed a landing was being attempted in rubber boats. Other batteries brought down concentrated fire on the channel. At 9.41 pm C Company Commander, Royal Rifles, near Lyemun, reported that the enemy had occupied the Pak Sha Wan battery position. 'It was later learned that this report was false,' records the Island Brigade war diary.[10] 'The report emanated from retreating gunner personnel who said "The enemy are as thick as leaves in the battery position".' The position was reoccupied without casualties four hours later. It is possible that it was fleeing Chinese rather than the Japanese who were annihilated that night.

As the Japanese indiscriminately shelled and bombed Hong Kong, their fifth columnists became increasingly active. They attacked an AA searchlight position, and incited the Chinese to riot wherever possible. They succeeded in persuading some to desert from the essential services, including transport drivers who usually sabotaged their vehicles before running away. The fifth columnists sniped at isolated detachments and despatch riders, and signalled with lamps of a primitive design operated from a dry battery, with a small but adequate mirror which directed enemy artillery fire upon suitable targets. A key observation post on Victoria Peak with direct lines to Fortress HQ was forced to move three times: each new location came under heavy and accurate artillery fire the moment the move was completed, although the positions were very well concealed. Treachery was certain.

On the north shore more than half the pill-boxes were destroyed by enemy fire. Judging by the muzzle flashes of the artillery, the Japanese guns appeared to be concealed inside the warehouses behind closed doors, which hurriedly opened for the salvo to be fired and then the doors slammed shut. Sixteen different pill-boxes were occupied, although they were not yet linked by telephone cable. More alternative pill-box emplacements had not been authorised in peace time, since requisitioning the space to build them had been thought too expensive.

The problems created for the Royal Signals by the shelling were considerable. At 4.30 pm, 14th, shells dropped in three places on the cable routes, and the cable hut was hit. All the main cables, involving 195 circuits between Magazine Gap and Fortress HQ, were cut, thereby severing all communications to the south of the Gap. The heavy-repair teams could not start until dusk, because the area was in full view of the mainland. Even then the work was slow as no lights could be used and the night was a dark one. However by dawn all joints had been made and the soldering completed.

The Japanese air force continued to be active only during daylight. Seventeen planes bombed Mount Davis on the 16th. A single bomb in one built-up area caused 150 serious civilian casualties. The following day fourteen bombers attacked the open streets of the Central District in Victoria and the Wanchai. Six different types of aircraft were identified. 'We were,' observed Gwen Dew, the American journalist, 'clay pigeons in a tiny shooting range.'

A nine-inch shell entered the Fortress HQ plotting room. It failed to explode, as did about one in three of the Japanese shells, but it did some damage to the communications. Eventually the shell was dislodged. Very plainly on the case were stamped the words: 'Woolwich Arsenal, 1908'.

As the shelling and bombing intensified, the invasion appeared imminent, and the morale of the civilian population became more unpredictable. The police maintained order in Victoria fairly successfully, except in the air raid tunnels where several armed gangs of robbers operated. Much depended upon the successful rice distribution which was a grave problem. Fresh vegetables were already too expensive for most.

The queues for the rice issue were often a block long, and disorderly. Wenzell Brown, who had volunteered to control the queues in Central Market, describes the scene: 'Women queued at one entrance and men at another. One line was able to buy ten cents of rice and another received free cooked rice mixed with beans. Into this line came all the beggars, the blind led by small boys, the diseased showing their open sores, and the insane. Many were dressed in tattered rags and nearly all went barefoot. The hot rice was carried away often in rusted tin cans, in battered hats or old pieces of crockery that had been picked up from garbage cans.'[11]

The distribution of rations to the soldiers was not proving very satisfactory, due to the desertion of Chinese drivers. Under the defence scheme it had been decided that NAAFI would open canteen services in accessible areas. This proved impractical, so it was decided that mobile canteens were to visit troops at their positions. This plan also fell through, due to the lack of vehicles. The food resupply organization included Wenzell Brown and Gwen Priestwood. The former recorded in his memoirs that he was unable to locate any of the Canadian 'food distribution centres'. Mrs. Priestwood was given a brilliant, yellow milk wagon with pictures of cows plastered on it, and was asked to move tobacco, arms and food between stores. With an armed escort she raced through air raids, past barbed wire, wrecked buildings, shell holes and road blocks. Eventually the van was painted a dull, inconspicuous grey. She missed the cows' calm, imperturbable faces.

'Reports are coming in of large bodies of looters everywhere,' wrote Phyllis Harrop from Police HQ in Victoria. It had received thirty-four hits. 'The police seem powerless to stop looting, in spite of anybody caught being shot immediately. The Gloucester Hotel is now unrecognizable. Every pane of glass in the arcades has been smashed, and window spaces have been heavily sandbagged. The Hong Kong Bank has received many direct hits. It looks as though somebody had thrown dirty balls of wet paper at the building, which had made a splash.

'Light and power failed tonight. Instructions have been

given to shoot on sight anybody who fails to answer the challenge immediately. Staircases are sandbagged and men lined up behind the bags fully armed. We have been subjected to further heavy air attacks and more machine-gunning in the streets. Food queues have been machine-gunned. Now that the power has gone there are no sirens. The only warning is when the planes appear, which is often too late. Large fires are raging at North Point.'[12]

Doctor Isaac Newton, in Japanese-occupied Kowloon, watched the tremendous bombardments of Hong Kong each successive day. 'The total absence of any news,' he wrote 'gives us a curious detached feeling regarding the war. We have absolutely no idea what is happening anywhere, except that Hong Kong still seems to be holding out. There is a cloud of smoke from the region of Kowloon. The docks this morning, and now North Point are blazing again. . . .'[13]

About two thousand yards from where Doctor Newton stood, at 9.45 am, on the 17th, two Japanese launches flying white flags emerged from Kowloon and crossed the harbour to Victoria. Major Boxer met the Japanese 'peace party' at Queen's Pier. The Japanese announced that there would be no hostilities until 4.00 pm. Sir Mark Young found that General Sakai's surrender terms were virtually identical to those already rejected on the 13th. Sir Mark dictated his reply: 'The Governor and Commander-in-Chief of Hong Kong declines absolutely to enter into negotiations for the surrender of Hong Kong, and takes this opportunity of notifying Lieutenant-General Sakai and Vice Admiral Masaichi Mimi that he is not prepared to receive any further communications from them on the subject.'

The usually inscrutable Japanese officers at the pier seemed genuinely surprised and disconcerted at this abrupt answer. They muttered to Major Boxer that future bombardments might not be so discriminate and left with glum faces. The truce was put to good use and all the communications were repaired. General Maltby attributed the offers of peace to the Japanese apprehension of attacking across the water, or perhaps the Chinese threat to their rear was taking effect.

'Jap envoys came over and said that all military installations have been destroyed, no use going on fighting,' wrote Brigadier Lawson that night. 'Governor told them to go back and destroy some more.'[14]

The Japanese had every reason to be well satisfied with their operations since their attack on Hong Kong on 8 December. They prided themselves on destroying the British aircraft at Kai Tak. However since then their plans had not gone entirely to their satisfaction: 'In spite of rendering the planes ineffective two or three British gunboats were active along the flank of our attacking unit during the offensive, menacing by bombardment and obstructing our action considerably,' Colonel Tosaka wrote later. 'Their long range fortress artillery bombardments were extremely effective. The Japanese Army was greatly hampered, especially in moving its heavy guns. Little thought had been given to an attack on Hong Kong Island if indeed the British should entrench themselves there. In actuality the British Army did not show great resistance on the expected (Gin Drinkers') line. However the Japanese Army at that time was thrown into considerable confusion in making adjustments to the situation and new attack preparations.'[15]

The plans for the invasion of the Island were decided by the Commander-in-Chief, Lieutenant-General Sakai, on the afternoon of the 17th. The orders for the attack were given out at his HQ in Kowloon direct to the regimental and battalion commanders by Major-General Sano, the Divisional Commander. Also present was Major-General Ito Takeo who commanded the infantry elements of the Division.

The landing operations were planned to commence from three points on the mainland at 10.00 pm on 18 December, all directed against the north-east of the Island. The Division consisted of three regiments, each equivalent to a brigade, and each of which was to commit two of its three battalions to the attack (see map, pages 68–69).

The Shoji Regiment (230) was to embark from a point west of Kai Tak aerodrome and land about five hundred yards east of North Point.

The Doi Regiment (228) was to embark from east of Kai Tak and land in the centre at Braemar.

Finally, the Tanaka Regiment (229) was to embark from the Devil's Peak Peninsula and land at Sau Ki Wan.

Takeo planned to accompany his HQ to North Point, shortly after midnight. Each regiment was ordered to cross the harbour in two waves: the first in collapsible rowing assault boats, each of which carried fourteen men. The second wave and follow-up troops were to cross by powered landing boats which would tow more assault craft.

One hour was allowed for the first wave to cross. 'The sunken shipping offered some concealment, but apprehension was felt that small bands of the British enemy might hide amidst the wrecks in a desperate effort to obstruct the crossing.'[16]

The battalions, once ashore, were ordered to bypass opposition, secure the high ground well inland, and take the commanding features of Mount Nicholson, Wong Nei Chong Gap, Jardine's Lookout, Mount Butler and Mount Parker. On the following night (19th/20th), they were to attack west and south-west to capture the remainder of Mount Nicholson, and Repulse Bay.

The three battalions not committed to the invasion were to remain in Kowloon to garrison the City and provide subsequent reinforcements. Minor changes were made to the Division's organization. The mountain artillery battalion attached to 228th Regiment was disbanded and replaced by independent anti-tank companies. No specific orders were issued regarding the disposal of prisoners. By standard Japanese procedure they would be sent to the points at which the regiment had originally landed, escorted by the soldiers from that unit.

The Japanese were worried that machine-gun fire and artillery concentrations might prevent them landing, particularly as the searchlights could pick out the rowing boats' slow approach, as had happened earlier.

However, according to Colonel Tosaka, the Japanese had one advantage which accounts to some extent for their early successes. He stated that a sketch of all the defensive positions and locations of the pill-boxes had been found on a dead British soldier. 'This information was disseminated to all units, especially to the heavy artillery, and the enemy installations were neutralized through fire.'[17]

The Japanese soldiers were tough, disciplined and used to hardships. Basic training was amongst the hardest in any army, and the soldiers knew that their lives were readily expendable. Most had gained valuable combat experience against the Chinese. They were indoctrinated to the belief that soldiers who permitted themselves to be captured were without honour, and that their duty was to fight to the death with a fanaticism that was scarcely human.

They had committed horrifying atrocities against the Chinese, and they were unlikely to be better behaved towards a white enemy whom, they had been conditioned to think, they had more reason to hate and humiliate than their fellow Asiatics.

To summarise: the Japanese planned to attack the northeast coastline with six battalions on the night of 18/19 December, to bypass the enemy and secure Wong Nei Chong Gap and the high ground in the east. They were to be opposed by the equivalent of eight fairly exhausted Canadian, Scots, English, Indian and Volunteer battalions which were spread throughout the island, with no air support, inferior mobile artillery and whose commander expected the blow to fall in the north-west.

*   *   *

December 18 was a cool, overcast and rather miserable day. At dawn a Japanese destroyer was seen sixteen miles south of Aberdeen; considerable small craft were reported amongst the Kowloon wharves. Three Japanese freighters were engaged by a 60-pounder gun brought up to North Point during the night. One was holed and sunk. Visibility was still obscured by heavy smoke from the large paint works at Braemar which was on fire. The Gunners nearby moved with their guns to an alternative position, lest their ammunition caught fire. Their new position was quickly located by Japanese artillery, and two 18-pounder guns were destroyed.

At 10.00 am bombers inflicted serious damage on the Central District of Victoria. Black smoke from the Anglo-Persian Company's petrol and oil storage tanks at North Point further obscured the visibility of machine gunners.

During the afternoon the Causeway Bay area was also heavily shelled. The waterfront along the north shore became a tangle of fallen tramwires and lampstands, making the road almost impassable for vehicles and despatch riders. The possibility of moving reinforcements quickly along the road to Lyemun was remote, unless the debris could be cleared.

Between 5.00 and 6.00 pm about two hundred Japanese were seen to be approaching the Devil's Peak pier from further inland. They were engaged by the Gunners. The

1a Canadian troops arrive in Hong Kong, 16 November 1941

1b Canadian signallers in an observation post before the Japanese invasion

2b Brigadier Cedric Wallis who refused to surrender the remnants of his Brigade at Stanley, maintaining 'that this action seemed to me to be locally unwarranted'

2c Major-General C. M. Maltby (*left*), the General Officer Commanding the allies in Hong Kong, meets Brigadier John Lawson who commanded the ill-fated Canadian Brigade

2a Sir Mark Young, the Governor of Hong Kong

3a Colonel Tanaka near Mount Parker looks out at Devil's Peak and Lei Mun Strait, across which his Japanese Regiment launched their attacks upon Hong Kong Island on 18 December 1941

3b Wong Nei Chong Gap, the vital ground in the heart of Hong Kong Island, where the heaviest fighting of the campaign took place

4a Stanley Peninsula (*far left*), the scene of the allies' last stand

4b Colonel Tanaka above Repulse Bay. The famous hotel which held out for almost seventy-two hours lies in the centre foreground

Japanese retaliated just before dusk with an extremely heavy bombardment on Lyemun. The soldiers in that area felt sure that the Japanese attack would come in a matter of hours straight at them, and they were right.

The two thousand Canadian troops were in little better order than those which had fought on the mainland, due to their lack of training, the long sea voyage and the ceaseless shelling and mortaring, all of which had sapped their strength.

'This day has been the worst yet. Our position has become a living hell,' wrote Sydney Skelton. 'My nerves are on edge. I could eat a horse. Shell landed thirty feet from where I was standing. One fellow got shrapnel in the side. My head swam and my nerves seem to be all gone. More lads were wounded again today. The sky is red as blood.'

Father Deloughery, the Roman Catholic Chaplain to the Canadians, who had been among the first to be bombed during his Communion service at Shamshuipo, visited the companies by day and the wounded in hospital at night. He heard confessions, administered Holy Communion, and comforted the soldiers as best he could. On the evening of the 18th, he had a long chat at Wong Nei Chong Gap with Brigadier Lawson. Both were worried about the Canadian companies, several of which had not received a hot meal for at least twenty-four hours.

At 7.00 pm three of the Brigade HQ vehicles in the open shelters close by suddenly burst into flames. Within seconds they were gutted wrecks, and two others were blown up shortly afterwards. These setbacks were attributed to the fifth columnists.

That night Brigadier Lawson decided that his Brigade HQ should move the following morning to a less exposed area on Black's Link. A new site had already been chosen and a telephone line had been laid to it.

In the gathering dusk, the Japanese soldiers silently entered their assault craft, while Rifleman Skelton scribbled in his diary: 'Huge fires are raging in Victoria. The bombardment is still on. This one day I shall never forget. Tomorrow will tell another story.' It did. He was to make but one more entry.

10
The Japanese Landings

7.00 pm 18 December—7.00 pm 19 December

At 7.00 pm on the 18th, the 2nd Battalion 228 Regiment in groups of fourteen silently embarked in the small collapsible assault craft. Colonel Doi stood at the water's edge as the first boats pushed off from Kai Tak into the darkness. He then climbed on a large barge which carried eighty officers and men of his tactical HQ.

The night was exceptionally dark. The sky was overcast with frequent showers of rain. Thick black smoke was being blown across the harbour from the burning oil tanks at North Point.

Colonel Doi gave the following account:[1] 'Halfway across the harbour, our attempt had gone undetected because the grounded ships concealed our move. But time and again the water was lit as brightly as broad daylight by the flare of burning heavy oil in the storage tanks on the opposite shore. Searchlight beams from Lyemun Point also played on the harbour. Streams of enemy machine-gun fire from the opposite shore and Lyemun Point slowed the boats, and since they failed to take a straight course, units were either mixed up or separated while they were still in the water. The resultant confusion made it almost impossible to maintain complete command of the battalion. Some boats had their oars broken and men rowed with their entrenching shovels. When exposed to enemy fire on the water, which offers no shelter, it is absolutely useless to turn the boats away from the direction of enemy fire, but perhaps it is only normal human psychology to react that way.

'It was a spectacular and grim crossing, but for the most part men went ashore on schedule. The assault boat carrying my leading battalion commander reached the spot (to the east of Braemar Point near the Taikoo Docks) where an enemy pillbox was located. He was wounded. The situation ashore was such that the squad leaders didn't know the whereabouts of platoon leaders and the latter in turn did not know the position of company commanders. It was very difficult to maintain the battalion under complete command. The only chance under the circumstances was for the men, on reaching the shore in their assault boats, to form up as a group and charge into the enemy immediately.'

As the first wave approached the Island, they signalled to the second, still at Kai Tak, to start their crossing: 'The harbour was still being illuminated by the searchlights and the flare of the burning oil. The enemy machine gun fire was all the more intense. I, the Regimental Commander, led the 1st Battalion in the crossing. When we landed I found a wire net fence, something like the one ordinarily found around a tennis court. It blocked our advance inland. Unlike ordinary wire entanglements, the net could not be cut by wire cutters, and we spent some time climbing over it with a ladder which we had brought with us.

'Enemy machine-gun fire was as intense as ever. Our second wave was forced to lie prone at the water's edge for a time after the landing. The anti-tank Company lost so many men that only one gun could be manned. It took three hours for the Commander of the 1st Battalion to regain complete control of his battalion. The main reason for the delay in restoring command was that our shouting at the time of landing invited the enemy fire. Also runners who were dispatched failed to establish contact because of rampaging enemy Bren carriers. The only alternative was to join up and regroup by a slow process of communicating from one adjoining unit to another.' Their objectives were Jardine's Lookout and beyond to Wong Nei Chong Gap.

On each side of Colonel Doi the first waves of the flanking regiments pushed inland. Colonel Shoji's 230 Regiment was soon in considerable confusion among several concrete pillboxes half a mile to the west at North Point. Shoji remained on the shore as his companies moved towards their objective Mount Nicholson to the west of the Gap. The leading platoons quickly became pinned down by artillery fire.

On the extreme east, Colonel Tanaka's 229 Regiment had a shorter crossing and landed between Sau Ki Wan and Lyemun Fort. They too headed rapidly inland with Mount Parker as one of their objectives.

As the battalions stormed ashore, stumbling over their

wounded, they were machine-gunned by the 5/7 Rajputs, although the Indians' fire was largely a matter of guesswork. 'You couldn't see a Jap at the end of your bayonet,' said one soldier. Countless bitter and bloody battles developed. While the Japanese survivors staggered to reach the high ground by dawn, those Rajputs who were·not killed by the first wave anxiously recharged their magazines and awaited the next.

On Colonel Tanaka's left flank was the Kishi Engineering Company, fighting in an infantry role, with orders to capture the AA position, held by a platoon of the Rajputs, and a searchlight at Pak Sha Wan. By midday, on the 19th, they had captured the AA position but reported that the defenders' fire was so hot that many casualties were received, including the Company Commander and his Second-in-Command. The position was finally won by a Corporal.

The Royal Engineer officer commanding the searchlight position left the searchlight on, locked up the pill-box and departed more than two hours before the Japanese arrived. The Kishi Engineering Company, however, assumed that the post was still occupied and launched a major attack upon it. Their subsequent exaggerated report of this action was to earn the Company a highly prized Citation for Bravery. It concluded: 'After much fighting for two hours they managed to break into the door, and finding the electric wires, without the least hesitation they destroyed them with explosive and extinguished the light and thus aided in the success of the landings.' One British officer, when he read the citation later in a POW camp, noted dryly that they seem to have had a hard fought two hour battle against the unoccupied searchlight.

That night Tanaka's leading battalion overran the 5th (AA) Battery of the Volunteers at Sai Wan Hill. The imminence of the Japanese approach had not been realized. Six Gunners were immediately killed, thirty escaped and twenty were taken prisoner. Tanaka's soldiers showed their ruthless contempt for an enemy which failed to fight to the finish. The prisoners were roped together and then taken out and cold-bloodedly bayoneted to death. Two survived. Bombardier Tso Hin-Chi and Private Chang Yam-Kwong had both been civilian clerks before the Volunteers' mobilisation and were now part of the Medical Section. Both received deep bayonet wounds and pretended to be dead. For three days they lay amidst the rotting corpses, but lived to give evidence before the Hong Kong War Crimes Court.

Equally appalling atrocities were to be committed by the same Regiment against the staff of the Advanced Dressing Station Medical post in the Silesian Mission at Sau Ki Wan on the 19th. Sir Mark Young had visited it the previous day, and told them that they must not leave their posts should the Japanese get close.

Major S. M. Banfill, a Canadian doctor, was in command with Captain Osler Thomas, of the Volunteers, as his Second-in-Command. Also present were members of the St. John's Ambulance Brigade, two European nurses, RAMC staff and two orderlies of the Royal Rifles. No warning of the Japanese landing had been received, although the shelling earlier had been heavier than usual. Two wounded officers of the Rajputs had been despatched by ambulance to Tytam Gap. Suddenly heavy knocks were heard on the outer door. Banfill warned his staff to offer no resistance. One of the nurses, Miss Louise Fearon, describes what happened:[2] 'A Japanese detachment of about twenty men fully camouflaged entered the building. They took us all out, and all the Army men were forced to take off their shoes, socks and tunics, and then they were searched. Some of our men put cigarettes in their mouths but these were snatched away and the men's faces slapped. . . . When the search was ended I was asked my age. I said I was thirty-nine and we gathered from the laughter that went up from the Japanese that I was too old to serve the purpose to which the Chinese girls were to be put.'

Some of the Medical Staff showed the Japanese their cards to prove that they were engaged in medical duties only; but the Japanese threw them on the floor saying: 'Soldiers first, medical second.' A Japanese interpreter named Honda warned Major Banfill that Colonel Tanaka's orders required that all prisoners should be killed. Honda, who had been educated at a Church of England school in Japan, said that he was sorry and would try to save Banfill's life. The Japanese then separated the men from the nurses. Banfill and the male staff were marched up the slopes of Mount Parker. They came across a wounded Lieutenant of the Volunteers who was crawling towards the first aid post. He was bayoneted to death by a Japanese soldier and Banfill was forced to identify his rank.

Meanwhile the nurses, V.A.D.'s and members of St. John's

Ambulance were marched up towards Lyemun Fort: 'As we walked up the winding roads towards the Fort,' continues Louise Fearon, 'we could see the men climbing up the hills on the other side of the valley. We saw them being halted and Captain Banfill alone being led up the hillside and disappearing over the brow of the hill. While the men were halted, the Japanese soldiers who were in their rear began bayoneting the men from the back. Some of our men fought back with their bare hands while others ran away only to be shot. . . . All the while we were crouched behind a low bank taking shelter against snipers who were shooting at us.' Captain Thomas takes up the horrifying account:[3] 'Suddenly the Japanese soldiers started to bayonet our unsuspecting men from the rear amidst cheers from enemy onlookers. Some had been bayoneted three times before they would fall and then their bodies were kicked into a ditch. I think at this moment panic broke out and a number of our soldiers furthest down the line ran, and these were shot. All the while, the Japanese were talking and laughing.' Those killed consisted of about eight Canadians, ten RAMC and three St. John's Ambulance men. The Japanese major led the group of nurses to Lyemun Fort 'where we were kept waiting for two hours in drenching rain,' recalls Miss Fearon. 'The major then came and told us to "go home".'

Miraculously four survived the slaughter, including Major Banfill. Captain Thomas made a run for it, was shot in the back and, drenched in blood, feigned death in a ditch. Corporal Norman Leath received a terrific blow on the neck: 'My wound was about six inches long and consistent with having been caused by a sword.'[4] He survived eight days and nights hiding in ditches by day and scavenging for food by night, before being captured. All four survived the war and in 1946 came face to face with Colonel Tanaka in Hong Kong, where they gave evidence against him at his War Crimes Trial. He was sentenced to twenty years imprisonment.

*   *   *

While Colonel Tanaka's units were bludgeoning their way towards Mount Parker and Mount Butler, Colonel Shoji's two battalions were moving to the mountainous area of Jardine's Lookout, the summit of which lay about two miles south of their landing point.

Jardine's Lookout overlooked the Wong Nei Chong Gap and lay between North Point and Repulse Bay, and also lay between the two Brigade HQ's at the Gap and Tytam respectively.

Colonel Shoji's landing proved more difficult to control than he expected. Several of his signallers were killed and his runners failed to get through, so full communications were not established for some five hours. He could hear intense rifle and artillery fire from the area of the other two regiments to the east. His leading battalion moved forward slowly in two files, along a narrow track. At 3.30 am he caught up with the commander of his 3rd Battalion on the north-east slopes of Jardine's Lookout. He was told that the pill-boxes to their front were held by Indians in unknown strength; Lieutenant Umino's raiding patrol section had captured the forward pill-box at 1.40 am, but he and five men had been killed.

Shoji gave out fresh orders to the two leading battalion commanders: 2nd Battalion was to attack east through the Lookout towards the five-road junction at the Gap, and 3rd Battalion was to attack to the right and capture the north slope of Mount Nicholson.

Jardine's Lookout had initially been held by only two platoons of the Volunteers. Captain L. B. Holmes' No. 7 Platoon was split between three positions on the northern slope, while Lieutenant Field commanded No. 9 Platoon in two pill-boxes on the south-east slope.

Brigadier Lawson had formed a 'flying column' reserve of three platoons from HQ Company of the Winnipeg Grenadiers. They were ordered forward at 2.00 am to the north, east and south slopes of Jardine's Lookout. Lieutenant G. A. Birkett found the ascent to the northern slope impossible in rain and darkness, and decided to wait until daybreak.

The leading Japanese patrol was fired upon by Lance-Corporal Hunt's section of the Volunteers and held up. Half an hour later, the main Japanese body forced Hunt to withdraw to the main platoon position which was well dug-in and protected by wire. Under a barrage of grenades the Japanese wire-cutting parties crept beneath the wire. Severe hand-to-hand fighting followed in which Captain Holmes was killed.

Brigadier Lawson decided to commit his only other reserve: A Company of the Winnipeg Grenadiers at Little Hong Kong.

He briefed the Company Commander, Major A. B. Gresham, at the Gap at 5.00 am, ordering the Company to move across Jardine's Lookout to secure Mount Butler. The Company lost their way in thick undergrowth and Major Gresham decided to wait until dawn. While there Lieutenant-Colonel Rawlinson, commanding the Rajputs, came across them. He was moving his HQ towards Tytam. He had had an agonizing night hearing one Rajput position after another being overrun. The Rajput forward platoons had fought very bravely, refusing to withdraw and inflicting considerable casualties on the enemy, but by dawn the Battalion had virtually ceased to exist.

Suddenly Rawlinson and the Canadians came under heavy fire. Major Gresham ordered his Company on to Mount Butler, where they forced scattered Japanese sections to withdraw. The CSM of A Company, J. R. Osborn, was a tower of strength amongst the Canadians. 'His manner and bearing was a great inspiration to me, which gave me confidence, myself being a young CSM,' wrote E. J. Soden of the Middlesex.[5]

At first light Lieutenant Birkett led his Winnipeg Grenadier platoon towards the summit of Jardine's Lookout. He arrived in time to find the Japanese scrambling up the other side. A desperate fight developed in which Birkett was twice hit and finally killed.

The nineteen Volunteers of Lieutenant Field's platoon on the south-east were strengthened by five Canadians, the survivors of Birkett's platoon. They listened to the battle developing around Wong Nei Chong Gap as the enemy made two attempts to advance along the catchwater which ran between Field's two pillboxes. Both attacks failed. At about midday some Japanese succeeded in crawling to the top of No. 1 pill-box and throwing grenades in through the loop-holes, but they were wiped out by the Volunteers in the other pill-box. No. 1 was now a complete wreck with all its guns knocked out, and only Lance-Corporal Hunt not a casualty. Lieutenant Field moved his remaining men into the open. By 3.00 pm, the Japanese gave up infantry attacks and relied upon an intensive mortar concentration to clear the position.

Ammunition was running low and the defenders were woefully few. Field was wounded for the fourth time. He ordered seven of his men to withdraw to safety with five wounded, and covered their withdrawal. At about 6.00 pm he collapsed from loss of blood, and at around the same time Lance-Corporal Hunt was mortally wounded.

At dusk a Japanese officer approached the position under a flag of truce and offered to spare the lives of the handful of men still there. Most had less than five rounds left, and the Japanese surrender terms were accepted. The survivors were marched off to captivity, as Colonel Shoji put it: 'after sixteen hours of hard fighting.' Jardine's Lookout had finally fallen.

Another isolated group had also been holding out with equal tenacity. Before the outbreak of war, a small but distinguished band of elderly volunteers had been formed by Colonel A. W. Hughes, the Chairman of the Union Insurance Company of Canton. The force consisted of those aged fifty-five or over and was called Hughesiliers after their founder. In his absence in England, they were commanded by Major the Hon J. J. Paterson, the Chairman of Jardine, Matheson & Co., and the senior member of the Legislative Council. He had won no less than six mentions in despatches in the First World War.

The force included Edward des Voeux, the secretary of the Hong Kong Club; the elderly 'Tam' Pearce, the Chairman of J. D. Hutchison & Co. and Secretary of the Jockey Club; Captain Jacques Egal of the 'Free French' and 'Pop' Hingston who had fought with the Canadians at Vimy Ridge and was now in his seventies.

The Company of Hughesiliers formed part of the Hong Kong Volunteer Defence Corps. They had the sedentary role of preventing sabotage of the electrical plant at the North Point power station. They were reinforced on the 16th by a platoon of forty-four Volunteers from the Electric Company and thirty from the China Light and Power Company who had escaped from Kowloon.

When Colonel Shoji's most western battalion stormed ashore, the Hughesiliers immediately found themselves cut off in the very front line. A mobile machine-gun platoon of the Middlesex and an armoured car were ordered to link up with D Company of the Rajputs who were manning the pill-boxes close by, and then to relieve the Hughesiliers. The armoured car was quickly knocked out by a Japanese mobile anti-tank gun.

The Middlesex platoon of twenty-four men, commanded by Lieutenant E. C. Graham, drove forward in three trucks; but they too came under fire and all the trucks were hit. The small force divided into three groups and ran down side streets trying to outflank the enemy. Most of the platoon reached the Hughesiliers who were preventing an enemy breakthrough. 'The delay the force caused was very valuable to me,' wrote General Maltby later.

The Japanese tossed grenades through the windows of the power station and tried with some success to burn down the main office building in which the survivors were now concentrated. The exhausted defenders tried to fight their way out. They had already been under concentrated attack for eighteen hours, but the nearest help was two thousand yards away at Leighton Hill. Some decided to make a break for it, seeking cover under a derelict bus in the King's Road outside. The elderly Private 'Tam' Pearce, aged 67, told Paterson that he would as soon be killed under a bus as roasted alive inside the burning building, and 'at the time there seemed to be quite a bit in what he said – not much choice either way.' Five men reached the bus; but all became casualties and Edward des Voeux was killed. The handful of survivors was finally overrun at 4.00 pm, when all their ammunition was exhausted and further resistance impossible. Even then a few of the Hughesiliers and two of the Middlesex managed to escape to Captain Man's Z Company at Leighton Hill.

The Hughesiliers battle was remarkable not only because of the age of the veterans who sought action rather than safety; but also because they won time for fresh defences to be established in their rear. Their courage was typical of most who fought on in isolated positions long after there was no hope of relief or reinforcements. Bullet-scarred, impersonal pill-boxes hidden by overgrown vegetation in long forgotten gulleys are today a mute reminder in Hong Kong of other less celebrated actions. The long list of 'missing in action' is indicative of their courage. All too often there were no survivors, and so there is no possibility of recording their no less gallant deeds.

11

Numb Despair

19—20 December

Nurses, air raid wardens, food and transport workers and other volunteers grimly stood to their posts as the six Japanese battalions stormed inland on 19 December. The Jockey Club, which had been the scene of so many gay, international parties, was filled with camp beds on which lay wretched Chinese patients. Efficient nurses in the grey cotton uniforms and white head-dress of the Auxiliary Nursing Service cared for the sick and wounded in the hospitals as best they could.

Their first bad blow was when the water mains were hit and the reservoirs captured. Several hospitals were fortunate to have well water, although it was brackish and unpleasant to taste and smell, but most had none. When the power station was destroyed, lamps and candles had to replace electricity.

The Gloucester Arcade in the centre of Victoria was packed day and night by Chinese, sheltering on the cold concrete for the doubtful protection from bombing that the building provided. Many seemed to remain there for the entire siege, with their only movements to change from a sitting to a squatting or a lying position. Their bodies touched their neighbours, arms and legs interlocked, until occasionally the sanitation squad ousted them for a few minutes to disinfect their squalid areas.

Trash and ruin littered the streets. More and more heaps of crumbled stone blocked the pavements, while bombs and shells damaged the buildings. Fifth columnists, gangsters and thieves were busily at work, looting, murdering and sniping, adding to the chaos as best they could.

Thousands of Chinese milled about the Central Market in Victoria, where Government stocks of rice were being sold at ten cents-worth per person. Hands snatched at the rice. Chinese university students tried to induce the crowds to form orderly lines. Women with children on their backs forced their way to the head of queues, but among the hungry there were no favours and they were pushed to the back, with sticks if necessary.

Meanwhile air raid sirens screamed in the hot sunlight. The heavy rumble of guns gradually became louder, and replaced the everyday sounds of cars, street vendors and people chattering. Japanese planes could occasionally be seen circling overhead, while shrapnel from the ineffective anti-aircraft guns pattered on the streets. When bombs fell near the rice queues, the streets quaked and the lines pushed closer to the walls, but did not break. Elsewhere air raid wardens stormed along pavements, swinging their sticks and driving people into shelters.

Numb despair crept over Europeans and Chinese alike, as the fighting grew closer. Most British families thought it too dangerous to stay in their houses, and those who could, fled to the leading hotels, although their servants were loath to see them go.

Rations of tinned fruit with dry biscuits and jam, and a hurried warm beer in the crowded hotels, became major luxuries for the civilians between their varied duty shifts. All were now committed to war work. Americans and other foreigners had joined one or other of the various Volunteer Defence Auxiliary services.

A Volunteer attempted to drive his truck from Victoria towards the Wong Nei Chong Gap, to deliver supplies to Brigadier Lawson's HQ. He was stopped by a dishevelled soldier who was running pell-mell down the mountainside: 'Good God, don't go up there,' the soldier shouted hoarsely, 'The Gap is alive with Japs.'

The retention of the strategically important Wong Nei Chong Gap was a vital factor in the defence scheme. Situated in the centre of the Island, the main lines of communication between the East and West Brigades ran through it.

When Brigadier Lawson, at his HQ at the Gap, heard of the enemy's successful landings, he ordered the destruction of all non-essential files and documents, and preparation for movement to a new HQ on Black's Link. By 2.30 am, on the 19th, he had committed the three 'flying column' platoons to Jardine's Lookout, and at 5.00 am had ordered Major Gresham's A Company, Winnipeg Grenadiers, to clear Jardine's Lookout and push on to Mount Butler, so he had no reserves left. The failure to concentrate adequate reserves in the vicinity of the Wong Nei Chong Gap resulted in the enemy being able to reach this vital point without encountering serious resistance. Instead troops had been left in their defences on the south side of the Island, despite the obvious preparations for a crossing to attack in the north.

The battalions of Colonels Shoji and Doi were moving irresistibly towards the Gap. Colonel Shoji takes up the account: 'Not only was fierce rifle fire heard from the direction of 2nd Battalion moving towards Jardine's Lookout, but suddenly from the area of Wong Nei Chong road too. At this time thick fog rolled in and even short distances could not be seen. At length reports came in from 3rd Battalion that the forward companies had encountered an advancing British force of armoured cars, and were in the midst of a fierce battle [against the Royal Scots]. The British force was steadily reinforced.' Shoji ordered his 2nd Battalion to switch their assault to the Gap in support of the 3rd. 'The general advance was made under great difficulty,' he reported to Divisional HQ near the Taikoo Docks. 'We suffered heavy losses. The sudden and fierce artillery fire from Stanley and Victoria increased in vigour.'

At 7.00 am, Lieutenant-Colonel White, commanding the Royal Scots almost two miles to the north-west at the Wanchai, received a desperate telephone call from Brigadier Lawson, who reported that the enemy had surrounded his HQ. The Brigade Commander asked for a company of the Royal Scots to be sent to break through the enemy ring and rescue them.

General Maltby himself telephoned the Royal Scots to stress the urgency of the relief operation. White replied that his men would 'go like the hammers of hell'. Thirteen minutes later Captain K. J. Campbell's A Company was speeding in trucks up the narrow, winding road towards the Gap.

On reaching the high ground level with Jardine's Lookout, they came under heavy fire. The trucks caught fire and the soldiers continued on foot; less than a dozen reached Brigadier Lawson. The enemy ring snapped shut behind them, and they were not heard of again. The rest of the Company, now reduced from seventy-six to fifteen, fell back with all the Company officers killed or wounded.

The Japanese infiltrated around the shelters of Brigade HQ, and snipers took up positions on both sides of the Gap. Two were spotted on the roof of the Medical Aid shelter, only thirty feet from Brigadier Lawson's command post. Just before 10.00 am, he realized that his position was untenable. The Brigade Major telephoned Fortress HQ to report that Brigade HQ was being evacuated to Black's Link. Brigadier Lawson told Brigadier Wallis that the HQ was almost surrounded and that he and his staff were going to get outside and fight it out rather than be killed inside like rats. The Staff Captain, H. A. Bush, was told to join D Company of the Winnipeg Grenadiers across the road to control the covering fire. The Brigade HQ telephone exchange was destroyed and the HQ abandoned. Later Captain Bush dashed back under heavy fire to the Brigade shelters to find that nobody was left.

A section of the Winnipeg Grenadiers' D Company saw Brigadier Lawson and several others run for cover shortly after evacuating the HQ. Japanese machine gunners had caught sight of him in his distinctive Brigadier's uniform, and Sergeant R. Manchester, a hundred yards away, saw him stagger and fall. Japanese machine-guns continued to fire into the small, broken group and Brigadier Lawson was never seen again. For years this very able officer had held together the frame of a largely part-time army. Had he not been chosen to command this brigade, he would certainly have reached high rank in the Canadian Army that took such an important part in the North-West Europe campaign of 1944–5.

D Company held on with great difficulty. They were reinforced by a group of seventy British and Chinese Royal Engineers sent forward earlier, and some Volunteers who had been forced to withdraw from Jardine's Lookout.

The Company Commander, Captain A. S. Bowman, organized a counter attack to clear the enemy from the area. He climbed up behind them and forced them to withdraw momentarily, but was killed on returning to his position, and stronger than ever, the enemy re-occupied the slopes on each side of the Gap.

By 10.00 am, on the 19th, the Japanese were in possession of much of the high ground in the east of the Island, including most of Jardine's Lookout, the lower slopes of Mount Butler and the northern slopes of Mount Parker. They were fanning west towards the Wanchai and Leighton Hill, and were gathering momentum for the final capture of the Gap.

The Royal Rifles' defensive positions east of Mount Parker,

although supported by 6 in. howitzers, were inadequate to act as a serious blocking force. The positions had been hastily improvised, and could easily be cut off now that the enemy was breaking through.

General Maltby discussed with Brigadier Wallis whether he should move his HQ and the Royal Rifles to the west, on the line of Tytam to Wong Nei Chong Gap. The advantage of the proposed move lay in combining the strength of both brigades; the Gap could be secured, and control of the forces simplified.

Brigadier Wallis well understood these advantages, but by 10.00 am, on 19 December, he could also see that the strength of the enemy, which had already secured most of the high ground between the two brigade HQs, and the inability of the Royal Rifles, the only unit still largely remaining to him, to move across very rugged unreconnoitered mountainous country, rendered this impossible.

'I was beginning to realize that the Battalion was incapable of real fight,'[1] recalls Brigadier Wallis. They were falling back towards Tytam from the Lyemun area unexpectedly. Their subsequent performance was to prove conclusively that the Battalion could not have succeeded in attacking west from Tytam across the high ground, however easy this move may later have appeared to those of Wallis' critics who have not walked the ground. Even a well trained, highly disciplined, regular battalion which knew the area would have found such a manoeuvre extremely difficult if not impossible in the face of such a formidable enemy.

'The great misfortune of commanding too small a force for such an extensive territory, distributed over a vast area in section posts without adequate or mobile reserves, was rapidly receiving proof,' records the Brigade War Diary.[2]

Brigadier Wallis had earlier tried to put in a counter attack, to take more pressure off Brigadier Lawson, but this had been unsuccessful. Therefore, after thorough discussion with General Maltby, it was reluctantly concluded that all Wallis' Brigade which could be evacuated should move south and concentrate in the secure Stone Hill – Stanley area.

By withdrawing to the south, the enemy was allowed to continue their penetration between the two brigades, thereby splitting the defences with all the disastrous consequences that this entailed. Despite valiant efforts, the brigades were never to reunite, and Brigadier Wallis' Brigade, cut off near Stanley, was subsequently to make no very significant contribution to the fighting, although they were to succeed in taking some pressure off other fronts and inflicted many casualties on the enemy.

A signal sent to GHQ Far East in Singapore described the situation as 'very grave' and stated that cipher books were being destroyed. Even so, General Maltby was under the impression that the Japanese had not more than two battalions on the Island, although six had landed. Accordingly he prepared his plans for a major counter attack upon the Wong Nei Chong Gap. One counter attack, meanwhile, had achieved a momentary success.

A Company of the Winnipeg Grenadiers had successfully recaptured Mount Butler shortly after dawn, on the 19th, but the Japanese moved three companies against them. 'At about 10.00 am, I noticed that our troops on Mount Butler were falling back, and almost immediately recognized Japanese troops in large numbers coming over the mountain,' relates Sergeant W. J. Pugsley. 'CSM Osborn now took charge and directed covering fire for the withdrawal. He was cool and steady and greatly helped the spirit of the men.'[3] A Company dispersed into small pockets on the open hillside, where the Japanese surrounded them.

By 3.15 pm ammunition was running out and the position became hopeless. Major Gresham, the Company Commander, decided to surrender, and stepped out of the depression holding above his head a stick with a white handkerchief tied to it. He was immediately cut down by machine-gun fire and killed.

'Grenades started to come over,' recalls Private J. D. Pollock. 'CSM Osborn kept throwing them back at the Japs every time they threw them at us.' Twice the Japanese launched major attacks, each time being driven off. The defensive position became smaller as more soldiers were wounded.

CSM Osborn's calmness and courage had a steadying effect, and the remnants of the Company stood firm. Osborn had been in tight corners before. He was a lean, granite-jawed ex-able seaman, aged forty-one. Born in Norfolk, he had joined the RNVR and fought in the Battle of Jutland. He had tried farming in Saskatchewan and working on the railroad in Manitoba, before enlisting in the Winnipeg Grenadiers in 1933. The battalion, although Militia, had a small nucleus of regular NCO's.

Sergeant Pugsley wrote afterwards: 'CSM Osborn and I were discussing what was to be done now, when a grenade dropped beside him. He yelled to me and gave me a shove and I rolled down the hill. He rolled over onto the grenade and was killed. I firmly believe he did this on purpose, and by his action saved the lives of myself and at least six other men who were in our group.'

Corporal W. A. Hall also saw the grenade fall in their midst. 'CSM Osborn on my right threw himself on it. Speaking for myself and the rest of the men who are still alive today, it is hard to say in words the admiration which we have for his gallant sacrifice.'

Shortly after CSM Osborn's death, the Japanese rushed the position, and the survivors were taken prisoner.

The citation for the Victoria Cross which was awarded to CSM Osborn is best endorsed in the language of a private soldier: 'This man sacrificed his life for the boys that might have been crippled or maimed for life. I say he was a real soldier and one of the best I've known.'

At 1.30 pm General Maltby issued orders for a general advance to commence at 3.00 pm. The 2/14 Punjabis were ordered to attack east towards North Point, to relieve the Hughesiliers at the Power Station. Lieutenant-Colonel Kidd, commanding the Punjabis, was already heavily engaged to the east of Leighton Hill with two companies, and the orders for the general advance never reached him. The Royal Scots were ordered to fight south to recapture Jardine's Lookout and the Wong Nei Chong Gap.

At 2.30 pm Lieutenant-Colonel White was told by Fortress HQ that the Gap was lightly held. He told Captain Pinkerton to take his D Company straight up the main Wong Nei Chong road, although Captain Campbell's A Company had been unable to get through that way seven hours earlier.

On Captain Pinkerton's left Lieutenant F. L. Stanier's C Company moved through the valley. Meanwhile Captain Douglas Ford's B Company moved by Black's Link track round the west side of Mount Nicholson towards the Gap. The Companies were to meet at the Gap, and then to attack Jardine's Lookout together. Eight field guns were promised for the battalion attack, but no such fire support materialized.

Captain A. M. S. Slater-Brown led the Royal Scots with their last three Bren-carriers, up the road towards the Gap. He was followed by two Vickers machine-gun sections. They reached the point about two hundred yards north of the Gap where Captain Campbell's Company had been ambushed. They found the way blocked by a tangled mass of burnt-out vehicles and corpses. 'Suddenly, without any warning whatsoever,' wrote one of his men, 'the Japs brought down on top of us everything they had.' A heavy mortar bomb hit the first Bren-carrier, killing Captain Slater-Brown and the Battalion Intelligence Officer.

D Company, on foot behind the vehicles, crouched in the ditches and scrub alongside the road. 'If one of us moved a hand, it brought down a tornado of lead on top of us from Jardine's Lookout.' The Japanese were firing from pill-boxes captured earlier from the Volunteers.

Lieutenant-Colonel White ordered his Companies to halt and wait until darkness. When night fell, the two Companies pushed on, while Captain Ford's B Company closed in from the area to the west of Mount Nicholson, where they had lain being heavily mortared intermittently throughout the day. A relief operation was launched by Brigadier Wallis from Repulse Bay. It consisted of two Volunteer armoured cars and about a hundred Indians of the Hong Kong and Singapore Artillery commanded by Major E. de V. Hunt. They reached the Police Station in the Gap and reported at 1.35 am that the enemy had been cleared from the area. However scattered Japanese section posts still remained on the higher ground on each side of the Gap. Cohesion was lost and Major Hunt's force dispersed.

Fortress HQ was still mystified as to Brigadier Lawson's whereabouts; but no new Brigade Commander was appointed to coordinate the attacks, and small, confused, ad hoc sub-units continued to be ordered to the Gap with inadequate orders, no knowledge of the situation and no artillery support. Many were fighting in an infantry role for the first time. Commander A. L. Pears led a naval party from *Thracian*. They drove up towards the Gap from Aberdeen in two trucks, and ran into an ambush. The sailors scrambled off the burning trucks under machine-gun fire. Six of them linked up with the Royal Scots eight hours later; most of the others were never seen again.

Everything now depended upon the Royal Scots. Captain Pinkerton stormed through the Gap and reached the steps of the Police Station, which had just been reoccupied by the Japanese in greater strength. Second-Lieutenant J. A. Ford found him seriously wounded on the steps, and carried him back to safety. Another attack was prepared when his brother, Captain Douglas Ford, appeared with B Company after their long approach from Black's Link.

The final battalion attack was no more successful. The leading platoon commander was blinded and the second killed. The Royal Scots stumbled back over dead Canadians and Indians. As dawn broke, they lay in the open on the lower slopes of Mount Nicholson, where they could better contest the enemy attempts to penetrate the western half of the island. Captain Douglas Ford placed his men in all round defensive positions as best he could. 'That was the worst day my men had in all the Hong Kong fighting, and as an officer in battle the worst day I experienced,' wrote a subaltern afterwards.[4] Captain Pinkerton and his command had fought courageously against overwhelming enemy strength. He was to survive the war, but was killed in action at Port Said in 1956.

Within the small perimeter of D Company of the Winnipeg Grenadiers, Padre U. Laite did his best to sustain the courage of the exhausted men. Throughout each day and night this United Church Chaplain cared for the wounded in the kitchen shelter between the trenches. Captain Bush recorded the scene during his later imprisonment: 'The position was being fired upon from all sides. It might be compared with the lower part of a bowl, the enemy looking down and occupying the rim. The main road running through the position was cluttered for hundreds of feet each way with abandoned trucks and cars. The Japanese were using mortars and hand grenades quite heavily. Casualties were steadily mounting, but at the same time reinforcements were trickling in, in the form of stragglers, so that at the end of the day, while the killed and wounded were approximately twenty-five, the effective fighting strength was about the same. . . . A platoon of Royal Scots passed through, from which later two men returned and reported that all the others had been wiped out.

'During the night 19th/20th, from midnight to 7.30 am, there was very little enemy firing, although their movement could be heard and seen. The Japanese used flash lights for signalling, and small groups called out to each other frequently, to maintain contact. We were told that B Company had been sent to relieve us. They never arrived. . . .

'A considerable amount of mortar and grenades were being used against the position. Over thirty wounded were now occupying the kitchen shelter, and water was very scarce. A lot of activity was noted on Mount Nicholson and our machine guns appeared to be inflicting losses on them. The enemy field craft was good, and camouflage excellent.'[5]

The telephone lines to the Company were cut at about 4.00 pm. Captain Billings, the Signals officer, and Captain Bush decided that they must get back to Battalion HQ to report the situation. Among the burning vehicles one stood seemingly undamaged. Just after dark they crept towards it. The driver got in while the two wounded officers pushed it round. They did not dare to start the engine or use the brakes. Fortunately the car gently coasted downhill towards the race course and safety. They eventually reached Battalion HQ, where Lieutenant-Colonel Sutcliffe, commanding the Winnipeg Grenadiers, received a full report, after which both officers were admitted to hospital.

That night Major Lyndon, the Brigade Major, made a dramatic reappearance at D Company HQ. He had last been seen with Brigadier Lawson, over thirty-six hours before. He told Lieutenant T. Blackwood, who was now commanding the Company, that he had been pinned down on the slopes of Mount Nicholson. He decided to remain with them.

The Japanese were finding the fighting more difficult than they had anticipated. The six battalions ashore by first light on the 19th had become uncoordinated, due to the initial Rajput resistance and the unfamiliarity of the ground. Nevertheless, after climbing about three hundred feet carrying full equipment, they had reached the higher ground of Jardine's Lookout, Mount Butler and Mount Parker, although behind schedule in all cases.

Colonel Shoji's 3rd Battalion had suffered the heaviest casualties, fighting through the Lookout towards the Gap which they were still unable to capture. The battalion commander had been killed.

Colonel Doi's battalions had failed to link up with Shoji for a combined attack against Mount Nicholson. Shoji sent his intelligence officer, Lieutenant Ito, to search for them. Ito later returned and reported that he had located Doi's left battalion just before midnight, 19th/20th, having their evening meal two thousand yards to the north-east; they had been delayed by heavy artillery fire. Ito received a fierce reprimand for failing to find Colonel Doi himself. Colonel Shoji was very short of ammunition, and to his intense irritation none of their wounded had yet been evacuated as the medical units had not arrived. The dying and wounded of all combatants were lying in the rain and darkness, scattered over the hillside.

At 6.00 pm, 20th, Major Oyadomari, the Divisional Staff Officer, reached Colonel Shoji and reported that 'the landing and advance had encountered unexpectedly strong resistance. There had been a hitch in the plan; contact with Colonel Tanaka had been lost, and the Divisional Commander had been greatly worried at a rumour that Shoji's Regiment had been annihilated at the Gap'.

Colonel Shoji was ordered to send a strong force to attack Leighton Hill on the following day, the 21st. Colonel Shoji apologized for having incurred so many casualties, and asked for more supplies and ammunition, and medical units to remove his dead and wounded. The sympathetic Oyadomari took Shoji's requests and apologies to the Divisional Commander at Taikoo Docks.

Colonel Tanaka's Regimental HQ had got lost and gone too far south. By midday on the 19th, he was on the east bank of the Tytam reservoir, whereas he should have been moving towards Repulse Bay, some three miles to the west. However, he quickly made up for lost time, and by 4.00 pm he had linked up with his 2nd Battalion east of Wong Nei Chong Gap. After dark they cut the only road which linked the Gap to Repulse Bay. By daybreak on the 20th, his leading company overlooked the Bay, and a platoon had captured Violet Hill. His orders were to capture Repulse Bay and then, in conjunction with Colonels Doi's and Shoji's Regiments, to sweep west and capture Fortress HQ and Government House, and so end the fighting.

*   *   *

After almost thirty-six hours a new Commander for West

Brigade was at last appointed: Colonel H. B. Rose, MC, commanding the Volunteers, succeeded Brigadier Lawson, missing presumed killed. The delay in appointing a commander for West Brigade resulted in the lack of a coordinating authority for the fighting zone during this critical period and affected the whole course of the operations over the next few days. Colonel Rose was ordered to clear the enemy from the Wong Nei Chong Gap and then to establish a strong position on the high ground to the east at Stanley Gap. His Brigade consisted of the Royal Scots, which were positioned in considerable difficulties to the north and west of the Wong Nei Chong Gap, and the Winnipeg Grenadiers. This battalion had been withdrawn from the Mount Nicholson area by their commanding officer, Lieutenant-Colonel J. L. R. Sutcliffe. He thought that his two forward companies were dispersed in too many sub-units and needed reorganizing. He had moved them to the west of Middle Gap.

Protecting the eastern approaches to Victoria was Z Company and Battalion HQ of the Middlesex on Leighton Hill. The other Middlesex machine-gun companies had barely yet been in action. There was little value in their continuing to man the coastal defences, and so two sections of A Company were sent to support the Winnipeg Grenadiers, while the remainder concentrated at Pok Fu Lam, north-west of Aberdeen. C Company was based at Little Hong Kong.

CSM E. J. Soden shared his C Company pill-box with a cook, a corporal and two privates. He was a little startled on the 20th to see some Royal Navy officers and ratings wandering over the battlefield in search of a position to defend. He took them to a house on Shouson Hill, from where they could see the Japanese on Black's Link. CSM Soden had already had a frustrating day. On being sent out to distribute dannert wire, he found it so tightly stacked from floor to ceiling in the store that he could find no way of either getting to the top of the pile, or pulling out any coils from below. The pile had to be left unused. However, the following day he successfully relieved his frustrations on a lone Japanese pilot, who dropped three small bombs while flying so low that CSM Soden could see the expression on his face. The entire Company opened fire on it. The aircraft was hit, lost height and crashed into the sea.

WO II R. R. Chaplin, the Orderly Room Quartermaster Sergeant of the Middlesex at Battalion HQ on Leighton Hill, was waging, to his disgust, a 'paper war'. He discovered that the 'B' echelon report centre was manned by Portuguese clerks, and his daily strength returns seldom got through. All communications were by telephone, so routine messages could not be accepted. Even so a sharp rebuke from the Command Paymaster reached him: the Company CQMS's had failed to close and balance their pay accounts.

Fortress HQ was inundated with civilian telephone calls at all hours from people who were cut off by the advancing Japanese. They were told to make for Repulse Bay if possible. Sometimes a duty officer, ringing round the observation posts, would be disconcerted by a Japanese answering the call.

Most of the 5/7 Rajputs, who had borne the brunt of the initial Japanese landings, had been killed or captured. B Company and some stragglers were placed under command of the Middlesex at Leighton Hill. Forty-five others were at Stanley.

The Punjabis were protecting the north-west of the Island with the forward company in the front line, between the Middlesex and the Royal Scots to their south. On the previous day, the 19th, the battalion had suffered severe losses while unsuccessfully attacking a high ridge overlooking Caroline Hill.

A series of disasters had prevented the artillery giving close support to the infantry, although the guns inflicted many casualties upon the Japanese. At Stanley Gap the Gunners had been drawn into the infantry battle, and 'four medium howitzers, two anti-aircraft guns and a warehouse in which provisions were stored, were captured in the action,' wrote Colonel Doi. 'They were of considerable aid to my regiment and the adjacent regiment in the subsequent fighting.' The Japanese quickly brought the British guns into action against the troops on Mount Cameron.

Shortly afterwards Fortress HQ received a report complaining bitterly that the Japanese artillery fire had become far more efficient; every round was going off, instead of the customary one in three being 'blinds'. Although the Japanese had sufficient artillery to support their battalions, and three times the number of British mobile howitzer batteries, the capture of these guns was a welcome bonus.

During the withdrawal of Eastern Brigade to Stanley on the 19th, several British mobile batteries had been destroyed or captured. The Battery Commander of the 4.5's in Howitzer

Battery at Red Hill had been ordered 'to get out of action'. The commander, however, read this order to be 'put the battery out of action', and he needlessly destroyed his guns. Those at Gauge Basin remained in action for too long and could not be withdrawn. 'It will be seen later,' records the Brigade Diary, 'the terrible handicap resulting from the loss of these mobile batteries. This loss went a long way towards preventing East Brigade from again joining hands with West Brigade as the infantry always found themselves confronted by enemy in commanding positions and were without the necessary covering fire to support any assault.'[6]

Despite the loss of their guns, these soldiers of the Royal Artillery, Hong Kong and Singapore Artillery and Volunteer Batteries fought as bravely as any. Colonel Doi was slow to praise courage, which was second nature to his men. However he had this to say of two Gunners: 'Two British soldiers were holding out in a small structure with its iron door closed at the (Stanley Gap) anti-aircraft gun position. Despite all our efforts to capture it and persuade them to surrender they refused, so we left them there overnight. The next morning, getting no response to our repeated call, we broke down the door and found that the two had killed themselves with their pistols. We buried those brave men with the utmost care.'

*   *   *

The Royal Navy hoped to prevent fresh Japanese troops and supplies being ferried across the Lei Mun Strait to their six battalions already on the Island. To do so, they relied largely on two Motor Torpedo Flotillas, each of which consisted of six Scott-Paine and two old Thornycroft-type boats, the latter having been acquired from the Chinese Navy. The boats were each armed with two torpedo tubes, depth charges and machine-guns. The crews were a jolly and enthusiastic crowd from all walks of life and various parts of the Far East. Prior to the Japanese attacks all of them had waited impatiently to be drafted to fight in the Atlantic or Mediterranean, instead of kicking their heels waiting for a war in Hong Kong which many felt would never come.

Since 9 December they had been in action – attacking Japanese light naval craft, shooting at Japanese positions on the mainland, helping in the evacuation from Devil's Peak, and generally being a thorn in General Sakai's open flanks, the sea.

Ten days later the Second Motor Torpedo Flotilla, commanded by Lieutenant Commander G. H. Gandy, made a determined attack upon Japanese ferry boats. The first two MTBs sped forward with machine-guns blazing. Several Japanese craft were sunk. However surprise was quickly lost, and in the brief, tragic action, of the six MTBs, two were sunk, one badly damaged and one slightly damaged. It was agreed that a similar attack by the MTBs of the other flotilla would be suicidal.

The enemy build-up in the north-east therefore continued without further interference from land, air or sea. Instead General Maltby had turned all his attention to the importance of recapturing the Wong Nei Chong Gap, and holding Repulse Bay.

At 10.00 am, 20th, A Company of the Punjabis was ordered to move through Aberdeen to check on worrying reports that the enemy had reached Repulse Bay Hotel, to where many civilians had fled.

Repulse Bay was also Colonel Tanaka's objective. Fresh from the bloody atrocities at the Silesian Mission, Tanaka's 3rd Battalion had been ordered two hours earlier to capture the Bay, and Japanese patrols were already in the outbuildings. The women and children inside were now about to experience the most fearful days of their lives.

12
'Tell my Wife I Love Her'
– the Battle for Repulse Bay

6.00 am 20 December—6.00 am 23 December

The Repulse Bay Hotel has no equal in Hong Kong for prestige and the beauty of its surroundings. Far from the din of Kowloon or the crowded watersides of Victoria, the hotel lies in isolated splendour above a beautiful, broad white beach. It is overshadowed by steep mountains.

Its wide verandah faces the attractive, unspoilt bay. On each side of the spacious main block are long east and west wings. Green lawns and gardens lie on the seaward side, and flower beds in the rear. As the shelling and mortaring in the built-up areas of Victoria became increasingly severe, the hotel was a natural refuge for all who could get there.

The troops in Repulse Bay early on 20 December consisted of a platoon of C Company of the Middlesex commanded by Second-Lieutenant P. Grounds, some naval ratings and a small party of HK RNVR; in all less than fifty.

Lieutenant Proulx, the Canadian serving in the HK RNVR, was on duty at the northern end of the hotel grounds just as dawn was breaking. He suddenly noticed in the semi-darkness, standing fifteen yards from him, a party of Japanese on the other side of the road outside the Hotel garage. He saw that they had five prisoners, including a Middlesex private who was being kicked and punched by a Japanese while others stood behind him with their bayonets ready in case the wretched soldier showed signs of resisting.

Proulx quietly called up the two soldiers on sentry nearest to him and the three of them opened fire. A Japanese officer and two others fell; the remainder ran into the garage, taking the prisoners with them.

The arrival of the Japanese had also been seen by Gloria Barretto, who was employed by NAAFI. Through a window in the half-light she saw a number of strange-looking men, fully armed and camouflaged with bits of leaf and grass. 'They looked weird,' she recalls. 'We peered down and told ourselves that they were the advance party of Chiang Kai-Shek's elusive army that we had so often been promised was coming to our rescue. But we could not repress a sickly feeling each time we gazed out.'

She watched in horror as an air-raid warden, strolling down the drive past the garage, was jumped upon by the shadowy figures and dragged inside. 'Taking a chance on appearing ridiculous, I telephoned the manageress, apologized for waking her so early, and said: "I don't know if you are aware, but there are about thirty Japanese soldiers in the Hotel garage. They have just caught an air-raid warden, and nobody seems to be doing anything about it".'

The redoubtable Miss Matheson said that she would see to it. However, shortly afterwards the alarm was raised by the noise of Proulx's shooting.

Second-Lieutenant Grounds, responsible for the defence of the Hotel, rang up Fortress HQ on the civil telephone to report that the Japanese had surrounded it. He was ordered to put the women and children on the lowest level for safety from stray bullets, and to hold the Hotel at all costs. Grounds started to organize an attack on the garage to free the prisoners, although hampered by several panicky residents who rushed outside waving white handkerchiefs. A strenuous battle developed. Although the range was short, casualties were few as there was plenty of cover among the buildings. Grounds redoubled his efforts to prevent further Japanese penetration. He was to recapture the garage, and the five prisoners were released, but he was killed leading the attack.

Meanwhile Brigadier Wallis was making a determined attempt to counter-attack out of the Stanley area towards Repulse Bay and the Wong Nei Chong Gap. At 10.00 pm, 19th, the Royal Rifles, to be supported by two platoons of the Middlesex and three Bren carriers of the Volunteers, received orders to recapture the Gap and join up with West Brigade, capturing en route Violet Hill. Brigadier Wallis pressed Lieutenant-Colonel

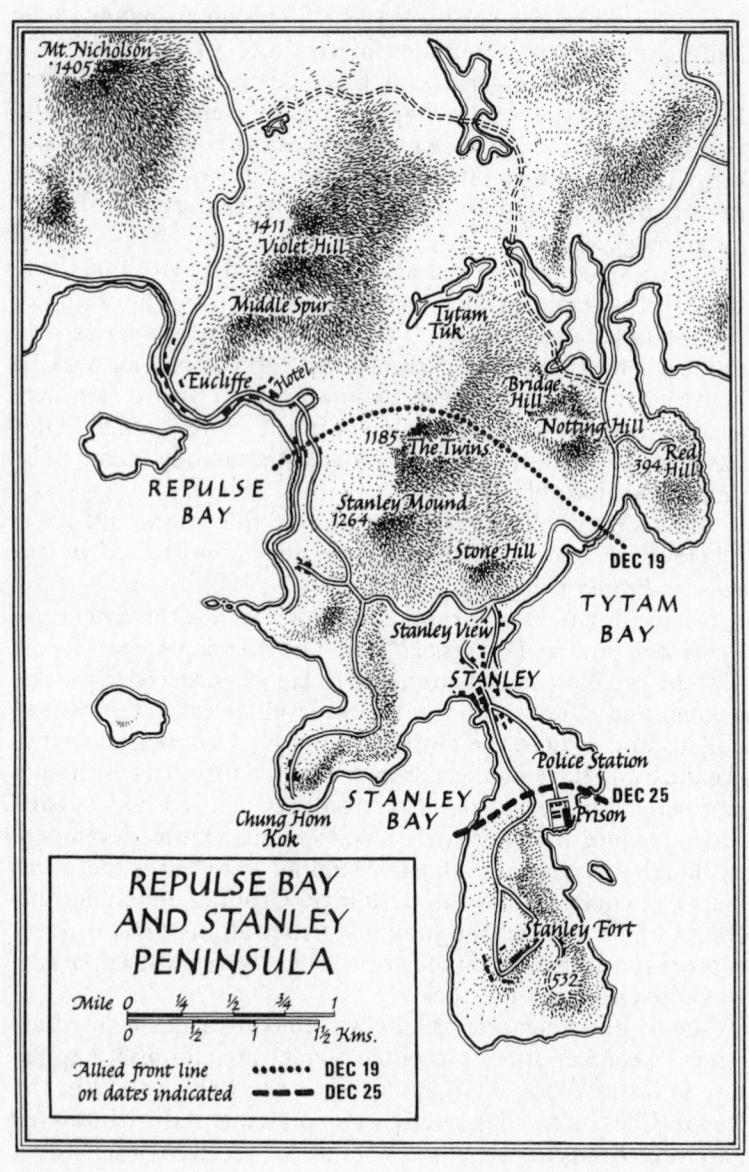

Mt. Nicholson
·1405·

Violet Hill
1411

Middle Spur

Tytam
Tuk

Eucliffe   Hotel

Bridge
Hill

Notting Hill

Red
Hill
394

REPULSE
BAY

1185·   The Twins

Stanley Mound
1264

Stone Hill

DEC 19

TYTAM
BAY

Stanley View

STANLEY

Police Station

DEC 25

Prison

Chung Hom
Kok

STANLEY
BAY

STANLEY
BAY

Stanley Fort

1532

REPULSE BAY
AND STANLEY
PENINSULA

Mile 0   ¼   ½   ¾   1
      0   ½   1   1½ Kms.

Allied front line   ••••••••   DEC 19
on dates indicated — — —   DEC 25

W. J. Home MC, commanding the Royal Rifles, to commence
his attack at 5.00 am, on the 20th. Home insisted he could not
start before 8.00 am as Companies were scattered and communications incomplete. 'The advance was slow and over-
cautious,' records the Brigade Diary.[1] 'Men were taking cover
every time a distant shot or burst from a machine gun was
heard.' By 10.00 am it was evident that a strong party of the
enemy had reached Violet Hill first. Attempts to push on to
Middle Spur failed although the Japanese were cleared from
the Repulse Bay.

Beyond the Hotel, on the north-western shore of the Bay, lies
a millionaire's castle called Eucliffe. With its grey battlements
and narrow turrets, it preserves a sinister and forbidding picture to this day, despite its swimming pool, tennis court and attractive lawn. A platoon of A Company of the Royal Rifles
occupied Eucliffe, and a patrol advanced uphill towards Wong
Nei Chong Gap, where D Company of the Winnipeg Grenadiers was still holding out against overwhelming odds. The
patrol ran into a strong Japanese force about three hundred
yards north of Eucliffe, and withdrew.

D Company, Royal Rifles, attempted to reach the Gap by
going across country on the east side of Violet Hill. An exceed-
ingly stiff climb was followed by moves of some 2,800 yards
through two water catchments. The troops came under heavy
fire from artillery, estimated to be 75 mm, from Violet Hill. The
Company gave up the attempt and returned badly disorgan-
ized, and without their 3 in. mortars, to Stanley View at
9.00 pm. Brigadier Wallis consolidated his scattered units in
the Stone Hill – Stanley area once more, leaving A Company,
Royal Rifles, in the Repulse Bay area.

By now the Repulse Bay Hotel was in an atmosphere of siege.
The prosperous Dutch engineer, Jan Marsman, who owed his
life to his having overslept on the morning that his aircraft was
bombed near Kai Tak, had the problem of finding a suitable
air-raid shelter. His firm had built many in Hong Kong, and his
professional eye quickly picked out an ideal one. A concrete
drain, eight feet in diameter, descended from a culvert in the
rear of the hotel and ran under the road to empty on the beach
near the water's edge. Marsman stuck his head out to see where
an entrance and ventilation shaft could best be chopped into it.
A bullet ricocheted off his steel helmet.

That night they completed the work, and women and children were carried down to the shelter where sandwiches and coffee were brought down the ladder inside the drain to them. 'Water was our next problem,' recalls Marsman. 'The hot water system had been turned off for lack of fuel. We found the boilers and pipes full of water which we tapped and boiled for drinking; with rationing it lasted much longer than we expected.'

In the Hotel the soldiers slept with their rifles beside them, in what previously had been the ping-pong and card room, and more were in the upstairs lounge. There had been no electricity since the 19th, so a few candles flickered in far corners. The stink of unflushable toilets pervaded the corridors.

Several dozen wounded had been brought to the Hotel and had been laid on beds in the lounge on the main floor, but there was no doctor, only Miss Mosey, an elderly nurse from Scotland who had earlier been brought out of retirement to look after the tummy aches and scratches of the hotel guests' children. Her thin reed of a body was to be seen everywhere at all hours, and her energy was truly remarkable. Frequently Fortress HQ was badgered for a doctor, but the answer was always the same: 'Sorry, but all doctors are working twenty-four hours a day on the seriously-wounded here.'

Among the ten-year-olds, there were two boys with very different backgrounds who seemed to be enjoying the siege immensely. Sing was the Hotel page-boy. He wore a round red hat, and his scarlet uniform bore a line of brass buttons. When the older Chinese boys fled, Sing regarded it as a great privilege to replace them all. Day and night, except for the moments when he napped in a chair curled up like a spaniel, Sing ran about looking after the sick and wounded and those in the drain shelter, carrying water, coffee and sandwiches.

The other ten-year-old was Jock, whose Scottish father was fighting with the Volunteers. Jock's favourite game was playing soldiers, so the siege of Repulse Bay Hotel was a dream come true. He donned stray parts of uniform and equipment and, wearing a large steel helmet, when he thought he was not being watched he hoisted a rifle to his shoulder and swaggered through the lobby and corridors as if on patrol. Such was his enthusiasm that it was difficult to prevent him sneaking out with a patrol and charging up the hillside in search of enemy snipers.

Lu was a little, old man cooked to a crisp by many years of hovering around the stoves in the Hotel's kitchens. Almost alone of the Chinese kitchen staff, he kept his kitchen open at all hours, since fixed meal times had collapsed. Helped by many of the women, he fed the soldiers, wounded and civilians at any time. Soup, coffee, sandwiches, sardines and biscuits were the staple diet. The larder was stocked with the pick of hotel delicacies – jars of caviar, tins of lobster bisque and turtle soup, smoked salmon, turkey and much more, but these stocks were being kept to celebrate happier days and were not consumed by the unfortunate residents.

By nightfall of Friday 20 December, the Canadians and Volunteers held the Bay and part of the high ground overlooking it. Beyond, Colonel Tanaka's 3rd Battalion held Middle Spur and Violet Hill, and more Japanese were moving to Stanley Mound.

Brigadier Wallis decided to make a second major attempt to recapture the Wong Nei Chong Gap, but the direct route via Repulse Bay was believed to be too strongly held by the enemy.

The night of 20/21 December was pouring with rain and visibility was very bad, the soldiers were tired and they had had little food. The break-out had therefore been postponed until 9.00 am on 21 December. Even this start time posed problems, due to a breakdown of the Royal Rifles' communications and administration. All the Brigade reserve of signals equipment had already been issued to the Battalion to replace what they had lost earlier.

Two 3.7 in. howitzers were positioned near Stanley Prison, with an observation post on a peak at Stanley Fort to the south. One 18-pounder from the beach defence role had been man-handled to fire over open sights. These three guns were the only remaining field pieces in Brigadier Wallis' Brigade. At 7.00 am, 21 December, Brigadier Wallis gave out orders to advance through Tytam Tuk, and to engage the enemy flank and rear. Major MacAuley, Royal Rifles, commanded with great energy the advance guard of one company each from the Volunteers and Royal Rifles. The remainder of the Brigade, consisting of two companies of the Royal Rifles and one of Volunteers followed. The failure to move earlier again cost the Brigade dear.

The Volunteers' carriers were slow in moving off, having failed to refuel overnight, and in the meantime the Japanese forestalled the column by occupying Red Hill – Tytam Tuk crossroads and Bridge Hill. The advanced guard came under rifle and machine-gun fire from these positions, but the attack was pressed with great gallantry. The morning was hot and steamy after the rain, and the going was hard over rocky ground and bad tracks. Notting Hill was captured at 1.00 pm and the Japanese at the crossroads were almost wiped out; they counter attacked fiercely, but were beaten off. Brigadier Wallis reported to General Maltby that 'he was very worried over the terrible slowness and lack of training of the Royal Rifles, but that they were really doing their best . . . and fighting gamely'.[2]

As dusk descended on 21 December, Brigadier Wallis' only battalion was dispersed in three different directions. Fifty survivors of Major Young's A Company were pinned down at Altamira House, close to the Ridge just south of the Gap. About sixty more Royal Rifles were in the Repulse Bay Hotel, around which Japanese sniping was continuing. The rest were scattered about one mile north-east of Stone Hill. None were making any progress against the Japanese, which was inevitable for they were opposed by two battalions which held the commanding high ground and were well-supported by their mobile howitzers and three light tanks. Major MacAuley had been wounded and all the officers of No. 1 Volunteer Company lost. It was realized that further advance was impossible. The Japanese were in strength on the Twins and Red Hill. There was a grave danger of Stanley Mound and Stone Hill being captured, in which case the enemy could cut off all troops to the east. Brigadier Wallis therefore withdrew to Stanley the force which had attempted to break out to the north-east.

This was the last serious effort made by his Brigade to recapture the Gap or break through to relieve the Repulse Bay Hotel. From then onwards both Brigades worked independently, and the forces at the Repulse Bay Hotel were on their own. There was a danger that the beleaguered garrison in the Bay might be destroyed and the women and children in the Hotel killed. Major Templer of 8th Coast Battery at Stanley was ordered at 5.00 pm on the 21st to command all troops in the area. Having secured the Bay, he was to link up with the Advanced Ordnance Depot in a group of houses on the Ridge.

Major Templer did his best to sort out the oddments of about six units which he found mingling round the Hotel, while

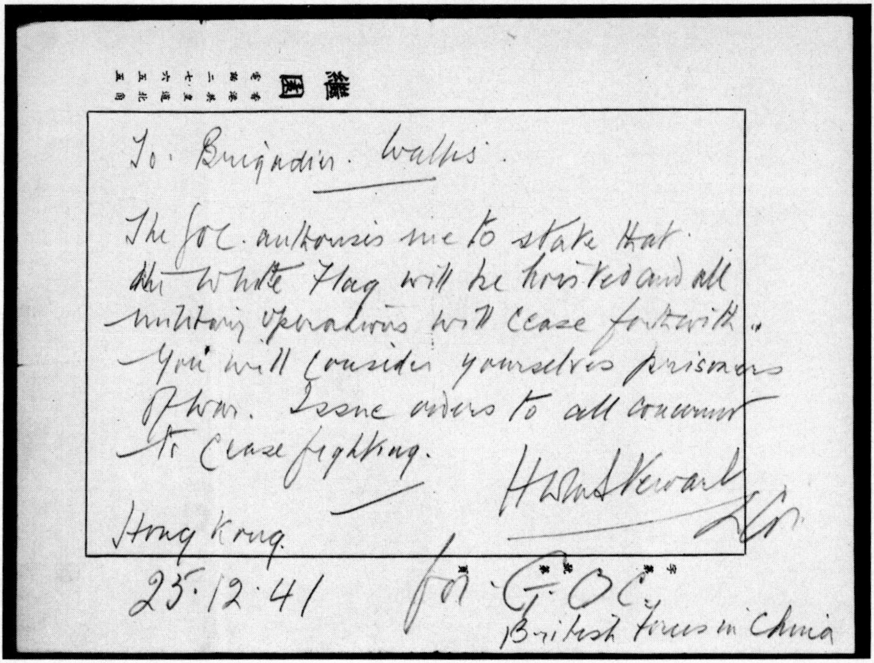

To: Brigadier Wallis.

The GOC authorises me to state that the White Flag will be hoisted and all military operations will cease forthwith. You will consider yourselves prisoners of war. Issue orders to all concerned to cease fighting.

H W M Stewart Lt Col.

Hong Kong.

25.12.41

for G.O.C. British Forces in China

5a Brigadier Wallis is ordered to surrender. (The message reads: 'The GOC authorises me to state that the white flag will be hoisted and all military operations will cease forthwith. You will consider yourselves prisoners of war. Issue orders to all concerned to cease fighting. H. W. M. Stewart, Lt. Col. for GOC British Forces in China 25.12.41')

5b Japanese troops enter Hong Kong headed by Lieutenant General Sakai and Vice Admiral Niimi

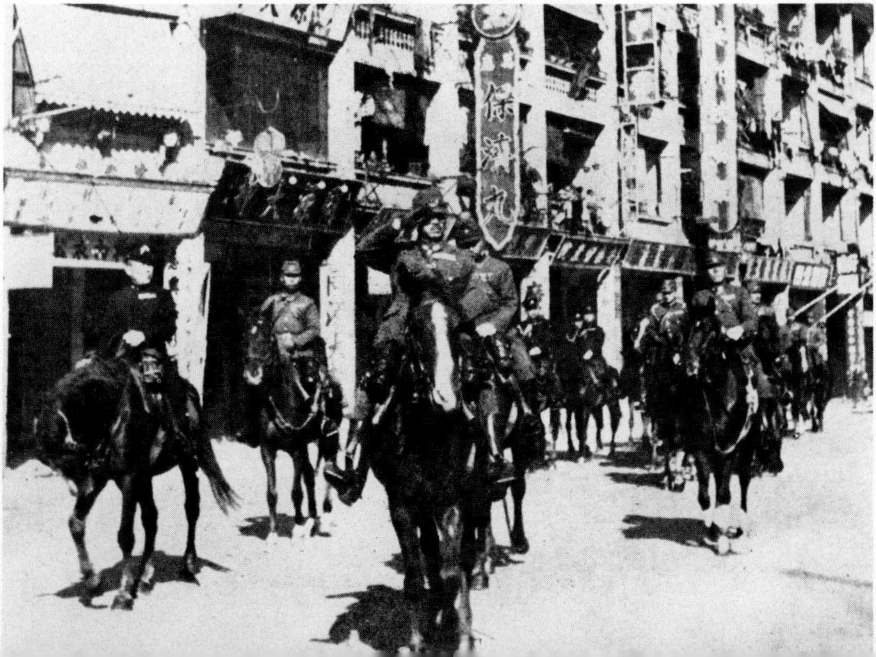

6a Silesian Mission
near Sau Ki Wan

6b The Ridge,
between Wong Nei
Chong Gap and
Repulse Bay

6c Eucliffe Castle,
Repulse Bay

6d St Stephen's College,
where allied wounded were
bayoneted in their beds

7a Colonel Toganaka,
the Japanese commander
of Shamshuipo prisoner of
war camp

7b The Japanese Commander in Chief surrenders his sword, 1945

8a Cigarettes are distributed to liberated prisoners of war,
September 1945

8b Some of the first British internees to be released from
Stanley Camp, Hong Kong

Major Young's A Company of the Royal Rifles mounted their trucks to counter-attack towards Wong Nei Chong Gap.

Major Templer recalls: 'As I drew out of the hotel a burst of enemy machine-gun fire went through my radiator and punctured two tyres of my car. A good start! However I climbed into a Royal Rifles truck, and we drove along in an eerie silence to within 300 yards of Wong Nei Chong Gap.' They passed the abandoned burnt-out trucks in which a Royal Navy party had been ambushed the previous day. About ten Royal Navy ratings lay dead in the road.

The Gap was still held by two battalions of Colonel Doi's Regiment – 'A most improbable situation for an attack mounted by one company. It was getting dark, and I planned the attack unaware of the strength with which the enemy held their position. I then received a report that the few Bren-guns which were going to cover our attack had jammed; I realized no attack could be made at that moment.' He withdrew A Company on foot to the large house, Altamira, on the other side of the Ridge, and ordered Major Young to reinforce the Advanced Ordnance Depot. 'I then pinched a bicycle and with Bombardier Guy, my orderly, cycled back to the hotel. I went round the sentries.'

The families sheltering in the drain were recovering from an unpleasant shock. They had suddenly heard Japanese voices echoing up towards them, which had caused momentary panic. It was gradually realized that the Japanese had been patrolling the beach where the big drain pipe ended – it was their noisy chatter which had been heard.

General Maltby conferred by telephone with Major Templer. They agreed to leave the families for a further night at the Hotel, in the hope that more of Brigadier Wallis' force could fight their way from the south to relieve them, and take the pressure off West Brigade by recapturing the Wong Nei Chong Gap too.

'The next day, 22 December, I got Lieutenant D. L. Prophet, who had his Volunteer platoon in great shape, to occupy the spur overlooking the hotel,' recalls Templer. 'The enemy were all around us, but did not close in. I found some 3 in. mortars, but none knew how to work them. Water was very scarce and the situation was definitely unpromising.'

Japanese aircraft occasionally flew over the bay. An abandoned MTB, disabled earlier, had been grounded on a small island within view of the hotel. The Japanese bombed it regularly several times each day.

The Hotel residents had now appointed a three-man Committee, which consisted of A. L. Shields, a member of the Hong Kong Legislative Council, Major C. M. Manners, Manager of the Kowloon Dockyard, and Jan Marsman, the Dutch engineer. They brought considerable order to the chaos.

Nobody could get any clear picture of what was happening. The Hong Kong wireless reported only that 'there was considerable activity around Repulse Bay. The battery at Stanley was holding. . . .' The news from the Philippines was encouraging. General MacArthur and General Wainwright were expected to stop the Japanese advance there.

The isolated troops in the Repulse Bay area now had only two days' food and water. The Japanese had cut off the water supplies to Stanley, by the capture of the Tytam Reservoir machinery. A suggestion was made for the civilians to be moved that night down the drain shelter to the beaches, and what boats or transport could be found would ferry them to Stanley. However the Hotel Committee quickly vetoed this proposal as too dangerous, particularly since the Japanese were patrolling the beaches at night. The inevitable noise of the embarkation might result in a massacre of all the civilians. After many confusing telephone calls, General Maltby ordered Major Templer to withdraw the troops to Stanley that night, and to leave the civilians to surrender.

It was also decided that The Ridge should be abandoned. Major Manners telephoned Lieutenant-Colonel Macpherson, who commanded the Ordnance Depot there, to tell them to withdraw that night, 22/23 December. As a security measure they spoke in French.

The Ridge had already been partly evacuated on the previous night, when a party of British, Canadians and Chinese had tried to get through to Repulse Bay, past Japanese machine-gun posts. Some only reached another house, Overbays, which lay about three hundred yards to the south. Others remained on the Ridge with Lieutenant-Colonel Macpherson.

Among those in Overbays was Private L. Canivet, Royal Canadian Ordnance Corps, who recalls: 'It was agreed that after a short rest we were to resume our move to Repulse Bay.

This was not to be, as the Japs had watched our actions and almost immediately opened fire on the house from three sides. The other side, not watched by them, overlooked the Bay and there was a steep cliff down to the road.

'An officer came upstairs to see how we were making out, and told us that it was planned to leave the house at 7.00 pm, in parties of three and four, but told us not to make any moves until he came up to see us again as he had to get the necessary authority from his HQ. About midnight QMS Singleton, RAOC, came upstairs and was very surprised to find us still there, as the others had left as arranged at 7.00 pm. He told us that he had orders to surrender the house in order to get the wounded to hospital. We decided that the best thing for us to do was to leave for Repulse Bay as soon as possible. But the house was being watched very closely, and we were told that an interpreter had told the Japanese that only wounded men were left in the house, and that we were prepared to surrender. Very few men agreed to lay down their arms and surrender, and most of us were all for picking up our rifles and taking a chance in getting through. But we were ordered by a Staff Sergeant in the Royal Army Service Corps to pile up our arms in one room and help prepare stretchers for the wounded.

'In the early morning of 23rd December, the Japs stormed the house using hand grenades and a small portable machine-gun. The wounded men downstairs were literally murdered in cold blood. Our white flag was torn down, and our interpreter was bayoneted and pinned to a door to die. The Japs came upstairs and kicked open the door of the room we were in, there being about thirty of us. First they sprayed the room with machine-gun fire and followed it up with a barrage of grenades. These were very slow in going off and we were all busy tossing them out of the windows as fast as we could. It was during the grenade barrage that I received a good sized piece of shrapnel in the jaw. Many of the men were seriously wounded and many killed.

'Two of us opened fire on the Japs with our rifles and managed to get three of them before they got away. The next thing they did was to try to pour kerosene on the ground floor and set fire to the house. We got as many of the wounded out of the windows as possible and then jumped out ourselves. Many headed down the Repulse Bay road but were immediately met with heavy machine-gun fire, so we headed for the sea. Eight of us started to swim with the Japanese firing at us. Four of us reached the other side of Repulse Bay. I was almost completely exhausted through loss of blood and excitement, to say nothing of the hard job of swimming roughly two miles.

'From here, three of us, a corporal in the RAOC, a Sapper and myself, went to a house belonging to a Mr. Ritchie who gave us clothing, bully beef and beer. We set off towards Stanley, following instructions he gave us. But we got lost. . . .'[3] Horrifying adventures were to follow.

Meanwhile Lieutenant-Colonel Macpherson's party, still on the Ridge, had attempted to surrender. He himself had gone out with a white flag, but was fired upon and ran back into the house. Captain Shellet of the Volunteers waved a white sheet, but it merely provided the Japanese with an aiming spot, and he could feel the bullets hitting the shaft. The front door to the house was next left open as a further sign of surrender. In a lull in the fighting Macpherson went out once more. He was fired upon twice and fell wounded. No more attempts were made to surrender, and as it grew dark the soldiers split up into groups, and at 9.00 pm moved off towards Repulse Bay.

The Ridge was now evacuated, apart from Major Young's A Company of the Royal Rifles, still at Altamira on the other side of the road, and the wounded with those who had remained to look after them.

As Major Templer's force prepared to evacuate Repulse Bay Hotel and abandon the women and children to the mercy of Colonel Tanaka's 3rd Battalion, the telephone wires were ripped from the walls. The liquor was destroyed, apart from two bottles of brandy hidden by the Hotel Committee. By 10.00 pm almost all were asleep upstairs, unaware that the soldiers were about to withdraw. They had not been told, to avoid panic and hysteria. Lieutenant Proulx had bid his wife and two small sons good night as if he would see them again the following day.

Down on the first floor, around a single screened candle, a few families sat in tense silence. Several women knitted to conceal their nervousness. The room was dim and foreboding. Just then lights were seen flashing in one of the rooms in the north wing; a Japanese patrol had entered the Hotel and was going from room to room.

Major Templer went to investigate with Bombardier Guy and a few others. He went to the first floor and heard Japanese conversation at the other end of the corridor. 'So I bowled several hand grenades down it, withdrawing into a doorway as they exploded,' he wrote later. 'It was a grand scene in the pitch dark! The Japs left and I resumed my post at the front door, waiting for the moon to set.'⁴

The evacuation was to be made via the drain tunnel leading beneath the Hotel to the beach, and then south along the road or across country to Stanley. Quietly the outposts around the Hotel were withdrawn, and the soldiers assembled inside it. Lieutenant Proulx was familiar with the area, and he led the first party of twenty-nine Canadians down the dark tunnel. Although everyone was in their stocking-feet, with their boots tied to their waists to make less noise, the sound of their steel helmets, bayonet scabbards and rifles knocking against the side of the tunnel made such a terrible din that, unbeknown to Proulx, Templer decided that he would risk sending the remainder of his troops out by the Hotel's side entrance.

Major Manners, his wife and Jan Marsman watched the apprehensive soldiers file out. 'Tell my wife I love her if you see her,' said one who passed Marsman an envelope into which he had slipped his wedding ring. 'Will you write to my mother and tell her we're all right?' said another. 'A picture my girl friend wanted – will you send it to where she works?' added a third.

One of the Volunteers, struggling in the rear, changed into a suit of civilian clothes and vanished upstairs. A few minutes later a neutral Swiss put on the discarded Volunteer's uniform and, seizing a rifle and bayonet, he cheerfully added himself to the last of the section.

The small group of residents awaited the arrival of the Japanese. Only the formidable snoring of Mr. Hogdon broke the sinister silence. He had been banished to sleep in a large clothes closet since he prevented anyone else sleeping. The tension grew. Marsman repeatedly called out into the eerie emptiness: 'Come in . . . Come in . . . No soldiers here! No soldiers here!' At last a door in the west wing was seen to open. Two Japanese entered menacingly; hands were raised. The Japanese were assured that all the soldiers had gone. Satisfied that this was indeed the case, the two Japanese departed to call in the others.

Just then, to the alarm and indignation of Major Manners and the others, down the staircase came a Volunteer who had fallen asleep. 'Get out! Get out!' Major Manners snapped at him, 'You've got to leave at once.' The unruffled young Volunteer replied: 'As the senior military man present, I am in charge, and I order you instantly to show me the way to the back door.'

A few seconds after he had departed, the Japanese entered the Hotel in strength, just as Lieutenant Proulx was laboriously climbing up the tunnel back into the Hotel to discover why only a few Canadians had followed him. At first he found nobody, but, hearing voices near, he went in that direction, and saw Japanese officers deep in conversation. He departed down the tunnel again with considerable speed.

Major Templer successfully led the main body straight along the beach and over the very rough hilly ground to Chung Hom Kok and Stanley Village, where they arrived at dawn. There he went to the jail and slept for the first time for forty-eight hours. Lieutenant Proulx with his Canadians also reached Stanley safely.

The successful defence of Repulse Bay for over seventy-two hours had interfered with the Japanese timetable, and delayed their drive to the south against Stanley.

When the Japanese entered the Hotel in strength, their intentions were uncertain. The families were ordered downstairs and Hogdon, the snorer, was prodded awake. The Japanese section with fixed bayonets menacingly approached a few badly wounded in their beds. The thin, elderly, white-haired figure of Miss Mosey in her white nurse's uniform barred their path. She stared straight through the Japanese, as though they did not exist. 'You will have to kill me first before you kill them,' she said. They hesitated and then abruptly turned away.

The decision to abandon the families proved fully justified. The horrifying atrocities committed previously by Tanaka's men, and about to be repeated by them close by, did not take place at Repulse Bay Hotel, due to the courage of Miss Mosey and probably because the Japanese respected the bravery and fortitude of the dejected and bedraggled families.

13

The Japanese Advance West

Dawn 20 December—Christmas Eve

By dawn on 20 December Western Brigade was holding an ill-defined and confused line. In the north was Z Company of the Middlesex at Leighton Hill with survivors of the Rajputs. The Royal Scots held the centre including Mount Nicholson. D Company of the Winnipeg Grenadiers, isolated and unsupported, hung on at the Wong Nei Chong Gap. The line then swung south through Little Hong Kong and Shouson Hill. Most of the Winnipeg Grenadiers, less D Company, had withdrawn to reorganize on the slopes of Mount Cameron.

The outlook was hardly encouraging. The majority of the troops in the Island were desperately tired, having been fighting almost without respite for eleven days.

On the morning of the 20th the Japanese began to force their way west, first against the southern end of West Brigade's Line. One of their objectives was the naval base at Aberdeen.

At midday the Japanese resumed ferrying troops in every type of craft across the straits from Kowloon. The likely points were shelled by the defenders, but direct observation of the landing points was now impossible.

Brigadier A. Peffers, Maltby's senior staff officer, tried to encourage Lieutenant-Colonel Sutcliffe, commanding the Winnipeg Grenadiers, who had been ordered to attack that night to clear Mount Nicholson and recapture the Gap. 'The Winnipeg Grenadiers', Peffers stated, 'had earlier withdrawn from its position somewhat precipitately. I spoke to Lieutenant-Colonel Sutcliffe on the trek home. He seemed tired, discouraged and distressed, saying his men were exhausted, as indeed they and everyone else were. I told him he could have six hours rest and that his Battalion must be ready after that to take its place again in the line. It did so and put up a grand show in the final days.'[1]

Captain Douglas Ford's Company of the Royal Scots was holding the exposed east slope of Mount Nicholson with the greatest difficulty. He sent two runners back to Battalion HQ, asking urgently for ammunition and food. Both men became casualties and the messages did not get through. Towards evening he considered that he would be sacrificing every man in his depleted force to no good purpose if he held on. The light was now failing; mist was blowing up and rain beginning to fall. He decided to move. He ordered his younger brother to cover their withdrawal, and then led his party back across Mount Nicholson to Battalion HQ on the road near St Albert's Hospital in Victoria.

The morning of 21st December opened badly for West Brigade. A series of disasters was reported. Doi's battalion, by capturing Mount Nicholson, had broken the defence line. Mount Cameron, to the west, was now threatened. Already the Japanese were planning its capture that night. The remnants of the Winnipeg Grenadiers on Mount Cameron were ordered to hold on at all costs, and the Punjabis, now at Wanchai Gap, were reinforced.

The next serious set-back was at sea. The MTBs had been continuing to ferry vital ammunition and supplies to Brigadier Wallis' Brigade, cut off in the south near Stanley. One boat had carried the Commanding Officer of the 5/7 Rajputs with his battle HQ from Stanley to the rest of his troops who were fighting alongside the Middlesex at Leighton Hill.

The gunboat, HMS *Cicala*, had been built in 1916, of 615 tons with a maximum speed of 14 knots. She was armed with two 6-inch guns, one 2-pounder pom-pom and eight Lewis guns, and had been firing upon the Japanese during their advance towards Brick Hill and Aberdeen. She was ordered to Deep Water Bay, where she successfully shelled enemy mortar and artillery positions. Strong air attacks soon developed against her, and stick after stick of bombs fell close by. Finally three bombs scored direct hits, and the gallant little ship was mortally hurt. With her hull shattered, steam pipes broken and her boats holed, she had to be abandoned. As *Cicala* slowly sank in Lamma Channel, MTB 10 went alongside to take off survivors. Casualties were miraculously light: one rating was killed and two wounded.

General Maltby hoped that A Company of the Punjab Regiment could break through from Aberdeen to Repulse Bay. He ordered Lieutenant-Colonel Kidd, commanding the Battalion in Victoria, to send forward a senior officer at once to lead them. Kidd decided to go himself. He collected a few naval ratings in Aberdeen en route. He found the Company only twenty-five strong with neither artillery support or machine-guns, while the enemy were in a strong position on Shouson Hill, a mile north-west of Repulse Bay. The attack started at 8.00 am on a wet, slippery slope. The Punjabis and naval ratings reached within twenty yards of the summit, but were caught there by a withering fire from the hilltop and a nearby house. There was no cover whatever, and the steep ascent made a foothold difficult to maintain. In a close and extremely fierce fight the attack failed. Courage was not enough. Of the Punjabis, only eight survived, all of them wounded. Lieutenant-Colonel Kidd was among the dead. This failure ended the attempt to break through to Repulse Bay.

The emergency hospitals were filling up rapidly. The principal military hospital on the island was at Bowen Road to the west of Leighton Hill. When the Japanese first attacked in Hong Kong on 8 December, a wholesale discharge of patients had cleared many of the wards. Among those abruptly discharged were several officers of the Royal Scots still groggy with malaria. Only those who were really ill had been allowed to remain, and these were carried to the shelters each time the air raid sirens had sounded.

A nurse with the Canadian Forces, Kathleen Christie, recalls that 'the Canadians being admitted around 20–21st were telling of being cut off from their units; and of being without food for four or five days; they had difficulty distinguishing Japanese from Chinese and frequently the sentries' challenges were answered in perfect English, only to discover too late that they were Japanese who had reached them.'[2]

Phyllis Harrop was nursing the wounded in the Hong Kong Hotel, where the lounge and grill rooms had been converted into a hospital. She recorded that 'Some Canadians reported that they have suffered heavy losses. Most of their officers have been killed. Several of the men told me tonight that they were only volunteers and have never been trained for hill fighting. Poor devils, they do not know the terrain, they have only been here three weeks. . . .'

Many of the wounded lay on the open hillside, their only chance of survival depending upon such men as Rifleman

J. D. Russel of the Royal Rifles who recalls a macabre incident: 'As I was one of the stretcher bearers, it fell to my unpleasant lot to have Capt. Gavey as my first victim, on the night of 18/19th, along with a young chap by the name of Gordon Irvine. We loaded them on the truck and took them back to the Advanced Dressing Station. On arrival there, they were pronounced dead by Dr. Lynch and taken across the road to the extermination room to await burial. Being inquisitive, I took a flash light and went into the room to see how badly they had been hit. On entering Capt. Gavey said: "Go ahead, kill me." It kind of gave me a queer feeling to hear a dead man speak. I went and informed Dr. Lynch what had happened. He told me to get him to hell out of there. We carried him out to our ambulance, loaded three more on and started for a hospital. We were told before we left they didn't think we would get through. We took the long way by Repulse Bay and, after getting around many obstacles including a land mine in a barbed wire road block, we arrived after seven hours at the Queen Mary Hospital. Capt. Gavey made his recovery after a hard fight.'[3]

Many hospitals were bombed and mortared indiscriminately. The profusion of targets around the Bowen Road military hospital perhaps made this inevitable. 'The hospital had seventeen direct hits although only one Chinese boy was injured' recalls another nurse, Anna May. 'We were surrounded by military targets: Command HQ, AA gun to the right and reservoir to the left. Our saddest day was when we were told that, with the exception of Captain Bush, our brigade staff were all killed.' Colonel Hennessey, Brigadier Lawson's senior staff officer had been about to have breakfast in a basement in Mount Austin Barracks. However he had seen smoke rising from behind the building. He and Captain Davies suspected that it might be Japanese signalling and they went upstairs to investigate. A shell burst in the room. Colonel Hennessey was carried dying to the War Memorial Hospital where both his legs were amputated in a desperate attempt to save his life. 'He was loved and respected by us all' remembers Anna May.[4]

Canada had now lost Brigadier Lawson and Colonel Hennessey, their two most senior and experienced officers.

Another nurse at La Salle had remained in Kowloon when the Japanese overran the mainland. Day Joyce remembers standing on the verandah gazing at the Island she loved, under

its heavy black smoke from the burning oil tanks. When the
Japanese arrived, the Holy Fathers and the nurses, carrying
Red Cross flags, had met them. The Japanese ordered them to
put up the Rising Sun flag replacing the Red Cross above their
building; 'but a split second after the Rising Sun flag was flying, my fury was changed to amused elation. A shell came over
from Hong Kong, then another and another. The Japanese flag
came down and the Red Cross went up again. In fact we were
ordered to make a bigger and better Red Cross.' That night she
lay on her narrow camp bed. 'I clutched a little photograph
frame in my pocket and never in my life have I felt more alone. I
had got the girls to put their camp beds together, touching, and
facing the door: I had heard about Japanese soldiers with bayonets getting between the beds. I was alongside a little Eurasian
girl, Edith. I slipped my hand out to cheer her. The current of
comfort passed in the opposite direction: I had been shaking so
much I must have rocked her bed.

'They were careless with their bayonets, and they confused
us with their barked orders. They expected us to bow to them
and all the time they smelt so. I could plot my war with an olfac-
tory graph; it is super-sensitive to me. The curve would run
along at rock bottom during this period. When interned the
next year, someone dropped and smashed a hoarded bottle of
Worth perfume, and for days my curve soared up into Heaven
each time I passed that spot.'[5]

While occasional British shells from Hong Kong Island exploded in Kowloon, Day Joyce watched the Japanese soldiers
when off duty. 'One of their favourite pastimes was to bring in a
car, all climb aboard, and try to drive it around the paths and
over the hard tennis courts. As long as it wasn't one's own car, it
was quite amusing to guess whether it would go backwards or
forwards or overturn. They always went on driving until they
crashed, when their yellow faces puckered up like children's.
My little Morris car was towed away; I minded very much and
I treasured the ignition key a long time. Later they got hold of
roller skates and were like rowdy children.'[6]

She also watched the reserve battalions train while they
waited to be called forward for the final battles on the Island.
The Japanese practised climbing obstacles, using hooks and
scaling ladders. Their superb fitness was apparent.

While standing on the tennis court at La Salle, watching the

flames in Victoria and listening to the bombing raids, Day
Joyce saw showers of leaflets descending upon the streets. One
sheet floated towards her:

'British officers and men,' she read. 'What do you expect in
your useless resistance after having been cornered in this small
Island? If you are waiting for the Chunking troops to stir up the
Japanese rear it will only end in a fool's dream. The Malaya
Peninsula and the Philippines are now under the sway of
Japanese.'

*   *   *

The British, Canadians, Indians, Volunteers and Chinese still
fighting in Hong Kong were indeed waiting for the Chunking
troops. They were encouraged to think that they were close by.
At 4.00 pm on 21 December, the Military Attaché with General
Chiang Kai-Shek had sent a message to General Maltby saying
'it is hoped that twenty bombers would operate at once against
Japanese aerodromes', but that the main Chinese attack to
relieve the Colony could not start for another ten days.

Shortly afterwards another cable was received from the War
Office emphasizing the need to destroy all installations. The
Texaco, Shell and Royal Naval oil tanks were soon ablaze.
Only the half full Secony Depot was not shelled as it was close
to a hospital wing in the women's prison.

'One day was much like another now,' wrote Mabel Redwood in the Happy Valley Racecourse hospital alongside
Leighton Hill. 'Our position was steadily worsening. We were
left with a couple of very young Chinese doctors who admitted
that they had very little experience, although casualties were
pouring in. A Methodist minister got through bringing messages and small gifts from friends. He told of heavy fighting in
Repulse Bay, but seemed to think that we were holding the
Japanese quite well.'[7] (He was later killed.)

'In fact we ourselves were in the front line, but thank goodness we did not know it. We were still quite optimistic in spite of
our difficulties. The next blow was the failure of our water
supply. This was disastrous. The sanitary situation was terrible, as not only had the flushes ceased to function but we had
no water even to clean the bedpans. There were two large
reserve tanks outside, but their keys were in the pocket of the
Doctor who was missing.

'This morning a Chinese expectant mother was led in by her mother and brother. All were in tears and the girl in labour. Quickly she was prepared for the birth and the relatives sat further up the ward. Within a couple of hours a baby – a boy – was born. The sister told me to go and inform the relatives. To my surprise, the brother, who could speak English, asked: "Does it look Scotch?" It transpired that the father was in the Royal Scots.'

* * *

The temptation for the staff officers in Fortress HQ to survive the bitter fighting by remaining in safety at their posts twenty feet underground was resisted by one and all. 'Colonel Newnham, GSO 1, was constantly everywhere seeing for himself what was happening,' recalls a warrant officer of the Middlesex. Four out of six GSO III's on General Maltby's staff had been wounded or killed. Captain Pardoe, who was a brilliant Chinese and Japanese linguist, was killed by a shell as he was visiting units. Major Boxer had been shot in the lung. Major Neve with two other staff officers had been ambushed when on a reconnaissance. As they got out of the car grenades were thrown at them. All were severely wounded, and Neve died a few days later.

These losses were irreplaceable and further increased both the strain in Fortress HQ and the difficulties of others trying to deal with the HQ. 'It was very noticeable how effectively "out of the picture" Fortress HQ appeared to be,' recorded Brigadier Wallis later. 'One had an unpleasant feeling one's reports were not trusted, that a passionate desire to minimize what was obviously a serious situation was responsible for piecemeal attacks being ordered on strongly held difficult positions with resulting failure. They did not understand that the best trained and best led infantry battalion could never have attacked dominating ground such as Violet Hill and Middle Spur with hope of success unless well supported by adequate fire. Where control of a battle takes place from an HQ in concrete shelters far from the forward positions, there may be a tendency to fail in appreciating the natural strength of ground.'[8]

* * *

'Mount Cameron was strategically located,' recorded Colonel

Doi. 'For this reason it was imperative to capture it at all costs in order to put a complete end to the enemy defence. Thus it was decided to make an attack on the night of the 22nd, although my Regiment had sustained considerable casualties and had not been sufficiently rested after taking Mt. Nicholson. In that action 'all the officers and warrant officers of the 4th Company were either killed or wounded,' Colonel Doi sombrely reported. 'The Battalion Adjutant was killed and most of the radio operators were lost.'

Doi ordered his 2nd Battalion, reinforced by a Company of the 1st, to attack Mount Cameron which was held by the Winnipeg Grenadiers, one hundred strong, and thirty Royal Engineers, all commanded by Major G. Trist.

The Canadians had been heavily dive-bombed and mortared for much of the day, receiving the normal Japanese 'softening-up' process prior to an attack. The Battalion had no tools with which to dig; in any event the rocky ground there made this impossible. They had no 3-in. mortars. 'There was no shelter and there was nothing to do except stick it out with small arms fire from behind the rocks.'[9]

At 8.30 pm, the Japanese brought down a heavy barrage of mortars and artillery on the position. Forty minutes later they attacked. Major Trist ran forward to see what was happening. The enemy had broken through on the right flank and captured a light machine gun and 2-in. mortar, which they turned to fire with deadly effect into the Engineers' flank. Lieutenant-Colonel Sutcliffe ordered a withdrawal to Wanchai Gap. Runners were sent to the other platoons telling them to withdraw with the wounded, and to destroy what they could not carry.

A counter-attack was attempted. 'One of our men, who was relieving himself to the front of our sentry line, overheard someone beyond the line speaking in a strange language' recorded Doi. The alarm was raised and the counter-attack failed. 'During the attack the enemy battery bombarded us from our rear, just as they had in our attack on Mount Nicholson, and they harassed our forward elements to a considerable extent. Our attempt to dig in was much hindered by enemy fire. Several bullet holes were made in the shelter tent of the battalion commander.'[10]

Those Japanese casualties not caused by the Canadians and Royal Engineers can be attributed to the 9.2-in. gun firing from

Stanley, and by Major H. Marsh's C Company of the Middlesex, which had fired 20,000 rounds from their machine guns
from the area of Little Hong Kong. Fortunately small ammunition convoys had successfully resupplied the Company that
day.

*   *   *

C Company Winnipeg Grenadiers were south of Mount Cameron, in the area of the Aberdeen Reservoirs and Bennets Hill.
The Company, which had one platoon detached earlier to A
Company, had not yet been in a battle. The Company Commander rang Brigade HQ when he heard that Mount Cameron
had been captured. He proposed that he should move the Company to the Battalion at Mount Gough. They suggested instead
a move to Aberdeen village. This he proceeded to do, and at
2.30 am, on the 23rd, linked up with the defenders there. They
consisted of ten sailors, one Royal Marine officer, forty-three
Dockyard Defence Corps and fourteen RAF, which illustrates
the straits into which the defences had fallen. One of the Winnipeg Grenadiers' platoons failed to find the Company after the
move to Aberdeen, which reduced his overall strength to thirty-
four. The Company Commander decided to rejoin his Battalion via Pok Fu Lam, and set off to the west away from the
enemy. At Pok Fu Lam he found No. 5 Company of the Volunteers, where he tried to telephone his Battalion and Brigade
HQ. He could get through to neither and so tried Fortress HQ
instead.

General Maltby answered the telephone. The Company
Commander reported his position and was told firmly that his
withdrawal was unauthorized. The GOC added that he was
thoroughly disappointed in his action and that he should reoc-
cupy his former position at once. The Company Commander
replied that this was impossible as his men were exhausted and
they would have to be provided with transport. Eventually C
Company reinforced by 80 more men returned to Aberdeen
Reservoir, reaching there at 8.30 pm.[11]

Another Canadian had different problems. Lance-Corporal
L. C. Speller, Royal Canadian Corps of Signals, was ordered to
deliver an important brown parcel to a British officer in a front
line position. He drove his motor cycle through the burning
streets and was shot at repeatedly. At last he delivered his

imposing package. To his utter disgust he saw the Lieutenant-
Colonel extract tins of dog food for his two animals. The Signaller roared away on his bicycle yelling abuse at the officer.[12]

*   *   *

While Doi was consolidating his position on Mount Parker,
Colonel Shoji Toshishige had ordered one of his battalions of
230 Regiment to wipe out the remnants of D Company, Winnipeg Grenadiers, at the Wong Nei Chong Gap.

It had become obvious to D Company that unless reinforcements and more ammunition reached them, their resistance could not last. On the night of 22/23rd Major Lyndon, the
Brigade Major, told Lieutenant Blackwood that he was going
to try again to get through the Japanese lines to Battalion HQ.
He went out into the darkness beyond the sentries and then un-
accountably turned back. He was accidentally shot dead by one
of the defenders.

Early next morning, the Japanese severely mortared the
Company, and Colonel Shoji's men closed in at 7.30 am.
Ammunition was completely exhausted and the remaining
men, twelve at the most, were worn out. Lieutenant Philips
passed out the order to surrender, but several decided to make a
break for it and succeeded in getting through the enemy lines.
At the time of the surrender there were over thirty-seven
wounded in the Company position. It was not known how
many seriously wounded were in Brigade HQ on the other side
of the road. There Padre Laite, being the only unwounded
officer, surrendered the position to the Japanese.

Colonel Shoji wrote afterwards: 'When the heroic defences at
Wong Nei Chong were captured . . . our medical units helped
their wounded and gave them biscuits, water and cigarettes. . . . During the departure of the prisoners, I received
reports of the discovery of the body of Brigadier Lawson. He
had died of a wound to his right leg and loss of blood.' The
Japanese medical officer, Captain Kimura, wrapped the body
of the former Commander of the Canadian Forces in the blanket of Lt. Okada, the nearest Japanese Company Commander.
'I ordered the temporary burial of the officer on the battle
ground on which he had died so heroically,' added Colonel
Shoji. 'Following this, I returned to the matter of assembling
the prisoners and in this regard gave out several cautions.'

Captain Laite of the United Church of Canada reported later: 'Shortly after the surrender I was led outside, questioned and searched. Through their interpreter, to whom I believe I owe much, they learned that I was a Chaplain. Water was asked for and was readily given, but they watched me closely as I gave each soldier his ration. When I finished my drink the interpreter said, "Oh! You give your men drink first?"

'I was then taken by an armed guard along the paths and trenches leading towards Brigade HQ, calling out to men to come out of the shelters with their hands up. During our tour I found the body of Brigadier J. K. Lawson. I later returned to the seriously wounded. Japanese private soldiers were left in charge of us. They spent most of their time trying to terrify us as well as searching kits and taking watches and rings from us.'[13] Laite was subsequently led alone through the Japanese lines by the guard who had befriended him. Small parties of Japanese which they passed wanted to kill him. Eventually his guard allowed him to go free. A Chinese gave him toast and water. Later a Eurasian woman from Macao disguised him as a Chinese. Wearing a long Chinese gown and wrapping his steel helmet in a newspaper, he was escorted by the Eurasian's maid to the safety of the Naval hospital where he met Doctor Selwyn Clarke, the Colony's Director of Medical Services.

D Company's gallantry received special praise from the Japanese: 'The enemy fire from these positions was so heavy that not only was the advance checked but our troops were thrown into confusion.'[14] The Company had held out for three and a half days with, at varying times, four Japanese battalions around them. The Canadians and stragglers with them were probably unaware of the heroic attempts of the Royal Scots and others to reinforce them. Yet they stood fast with the tenacity and gallantry of which Canada can always be proud.

Colonel Shoji apologized to his Divisional Commander for suffering eight hundred casualties, almost a third of his Regiment, between the actions at Jardine's Lookout and against D Company, Winnipeg Grenadiers.

*   *   *

The previous day the Prime Minister of Canada, Mr. Mackenzie King, had sent a message to his countrymen in the Colony: 'All Canada has been following hour by hour the progress of events at Hong Kong. Our thoughts are of each and every one of you in your brave resistance of the forces that are seeking to destroy the world's freedom. Your bravery is an inspiration to us all. Our Country's name and its honour have never been more splendidly upheld.'

Lieutenant-Colonel Sutcliffe replied very much to the point. 'Situation critical . . . casualties heavy, Lawson missing believed killed. Hennessey, Lyndon missing. But troops have done magnificent work. . . .'[15]

Winston Churchill had signalled, the first part in cypher: 'There must be no thought of surrender. Every part of the Island must be fought over and the enemy resisted with the utmost stubbornness. The enemy should be compelled to expend the utmost life and equipment. There must be vigorous fighting to the inner defences and if need be, from house to house. Ends. If cypher message cannot be sent, following shorter message should be despatched en clair: The eyes of the world are upon you. We expect you to resist to the end. The honour of the Empire is in your hands.'

The nurse, Gwen Priestwood, spoke for many when she wrote: 'Winston Churchill's order to "fight to the last man" had become known, and the implication that no help could be sent did not make us cheerful. But everybody, I think, realized that the longer we could hold out, the more we would be helping the Empire. We felt proud afterwards that Hong Kong *did* hold out longer than any other city in the Far East when subject to Japanese invasion.'[16]

London and Ottawa had been forewarned by Sir Mark Young as early as 21 December of the extreme gravity of the situation: 'Enemy hold key positions on hills, and GOC advised that we are very rapidly approaching the point at which only remaining resistance open to us will be to hold for a short time only a small pocket of City, leaving bulk of population to be overrun. I feel it will be my duty to ask for terms before this position is reached. . . .'

As the Governor's signal was being transmitted in cypher to the Colonial Office, the Director of Military Operations was briefing the CGS in London: 'Resistance could probably not be counted on for more than a few days and would be on a small scale. Therefore it would have practically no direct influence on operations in the Far East in the way of tying up Japanese forces which might be released for operations elsewhere, but if we fought to the last round and the last man at Hong Kong, we should gain an indirect military advantage in that the Japanese would judge our resistance in Malaya and elsewhere by the same standard. . . .'[17]

*　　*　　*

General Maltby later recorded in his despatches: 'Morale now had been seriously affected by the feeling that it was futile to continue the resistance with insufficient equipment, with insufficient mobile artillery support, and without both air support and air observation.' Sir Mark Young's signal to the Secretary of State for the Colonies on 23rd spoke of the courage of the defenders: 'Fighting continues all along the lines with a local success for us in the south. Small parties of our administrative military personnel, not normally equipped or trained for active combat and now fighting in advance posts, have shown great determination and courage, and in many cases they have beaten off enemy units attempting to overrun their positions, and in other cases fought to the last. The value on operations as a whole of such fine resistance by isolated parties can not be overestimated.' That afternoon the last Army wireless set was knocked out by shell fire. Communications with the United Kingdom and Singapore now depended entirely upon the Royal Navy sets.

Secret radio transmitters in China gave notice of the approach of Japanese aircraft attacking the Colony. A few minutes warning would therefore have been possible, were it not for the fact that lack of electricity silenced the air raid sirens.

A Chinese army commanded by General Yugannow was still said to be within a short distance of Hong Kong, and it was announced in the Colony that the relief of the garrison might be expected 'in the near future'. Three Chinese bombers escorted by six fighters were thought to have been seen bombing the Japanese north of Kowloon. Intelligence from Chinese sources, never very reliable at the best of times, indicated that some Japanese transport and artillery were moving north, away from Hong Kong. This was attributed to 'possible increasingly effective pressure by bodies of Chinese troops or guerrillas'[18] in the Japanese rear.

Admiral Chan, Chiang Kai-Shek's liaison officer at Fortress

HQ, had reported three days earlier, on 20 December, that he had received a wireless message from General Yu Han Mou that 60,000 Chinese troops were on the border and about to attack. This news was also relayed to the Colony: 'There are indications that Chinese forces are advancing to our aid. All ranks must therefore hold their positions at all costs and look forward to only a few more days of strain.' Alas, the hopes raised proved false.

14
The Odds and Sods

Z Company 1 Middlesex 20—24 December

'My orders were perfectly clear: "Stay where you are and resist to the last man",' recalls Captain C. M. M. Man, who was holding Leighton Hill with Z Company which consisted of the Band and the odd men discarded by other companies. 'For anyone who knows the way an army works, it is not hard to understand that Z Company was really made up of the odds and sods of the Battalion.'[1]

The war had started for Captain Man early on 8 December. Instead of the soft tread of the houseboy, Ah Yung, with the early morning tea, both he and his wife had been awakened by the heavy tread of the Officers' Mess Corporal's boots. 'Sir, we are at war with Japan,' Corporal Hughes had gravely announced in parade ground tones.

Twelve days later Captain Man found himself holding the partly built up and isolated position of Leighton Hill, which was the key to the defence of Victoria, in as much as the hill controlled the only approach to the city from the north-east where the Japanese had landed.

'Information was so vague that I was really unaware who was on my right and left and whether or not I was in the front line. There appeared to be no firm line of defence and although I sent out patrols they were unable to make contact with our troops.

'The days seemed to consist of moving only at night, and remaining inside buildings or dug in during the day. The Company received no visitors, which was to be welcomed because any movement was followed immediately by enemy mortar and shell-fire from the mainland. Casualties continued to mount and our stocks of food, and particularly water, got lower and lower. We were joined from time to time by stragglers from other units, some Indians, one or two Canadians and some Volunteers. We were hampered by enormous numbers of

Chinese thronging the streets, blocking our lines of fire in every direction, with nowhere to go and no-one to turn to.[2]

'One of my chief problems was keeping up my men's morale. I was fortunate in their Cockney spirit. I was amazed at the way they never lost their sense of humour. It became obvious that the Japanese were planning a big offensive to get into the city. To do so, they had to overrun our positions.'

Before the war Captain Man had been shown books on Japanese organizations and badges of rank. But 'there had been so many scares before, that we had come to look on invasion threats as nonsense. We had seen the Japs on the border and were taken in by their "scruffy" appearance. We had been told that they never moved or fought at night.

'I was relieved when the Japanese started their attack. For the first time we could see them and, more important to us, see the damage we were doing to them with our machine guns. I was particularly surprised at the way they kept coming. Casualties did not seem to bother them, and there was an endless supply of soldiers to keep up the impetus of their attack. The first onslaught we were able to stop, and I think they were surprised at the reception they got. The Vickers machine gun is a terrible gun when it has the right target, and this we certainly had.'

By the morning of 23 December the Company was reduced to forty men and six machine-guns. By now the Japanese were infiltrating into the houses and streets around them. A heavy bombardment had forced the withdrawal of the 5/7 Rajput Company, short of ammunition and food, leaving Man's right flank exposed.

By now it was impossible to evacuate the wounded to Bowen Road Hospital, and they had to remain in the Company position. The following day Captain Man was told by telephone to be ready to withdraw to Victoria; he was surprised to receive such an order as he had no contact with his rear. However he welcomed the possibility of withdrawal as the Company was short of men, rations, and, more important, ammunition without which they would soon be no use whatever. He wrote afterwards: 'I made plans for what I thought would be an orderly withdrawal, but I did not pass them on to the soldiers as I did not want them to start looking over their shoulders at what was bound to be a critical time for us.'

His thoughts strayed to Topsy, his wife of thirteen months. She was in the Nursing Auxiliary Service in a make-shift hospital in the Hong Kong University Buildings of Victoria. 'In the early days I used to telephone her, using the civilian telephone to let her know that I was still in one piece. She ran even bigger risks, because the Japanese had no inhibitions about bombing hospitals and butchering nurses. On one occasion, as a shell passed overhead, I said to her "Hang on a second, that was a near miss". Her reply was "That wasn't over you, it was over me!"'

'When the next attack started, I was told to evacuate Leighton Hill immediately, salvaging what equipment I could. The withdrawal at this stage was extremely difficult and I was afraid that I would have to sacrifice one gun and crew at least, if everybody was to get away. This, I am sorry to say, proved to be the case. Everyone else got out over the wire at the back of the hill, taking with them arms and ammunition and what was left of our rations. There were only a few casualties, and as a parting shot I tried to set fire to the houses by firing my pistol into cans of petrol. This being the first time that I had attempted arson, I made a hopeless mess of it, although I did manage to get a bit of a blaze going at the third attempt. As we got out, the enemy got in.'

His next position in the Wanchai 'turned out to be a Chinese VD clinic, not the most salubrious of locations, especially as it had been hastily vacated'. There Captain Man, CSM Jock Ure, C/Sgt Little and the resolute Middlesex soldiers, still accompanied by several Canadians and Indians, bitterly contested every inch of the ground, and resisted to the end. They had added fresh laurels to the Regiment's proud history.

Immediately after the surrender, Captain Man persuaded his Medical Officer to nominate him as a fake casualty in order that he could drive by ambulance under the Red Cross to say goodbye to his wife. They were not to meet again for almost four terrible years. On 2 October, 1945, the *Empress of Australia*, in which Captain Man was travelling to England with ex-POWs, docked at Colombo. He was called to the Purser's office, where he met his younger brother whom he had not seen for eight years. Captain Man was told that his wife too, by an extraordinary coincidence, was in Colombo, although she had no idea that he was there. He reached her hotel and entered the room at the very moment that she and a fellow nurse were raising their tooth glasses in a toast – to celebrate their fifth wedding anniversary.

*   *   *

By the morning of Christmas Eve, West Brigade's line stretched from the slum area of the Wanchai, bordering the harbour, through the west lower slopes of Mount Cameron, and the Wanchai Gap held by the Royal Scots, down to Aberdeen reservoir, and Bennets Hill held by C Company, Winnipeg Grenadiers. The Middlesex Company still occupied their pillboxes at Little Hong Kong. A second line running between Mount Gough and Mount Kellett was held by two companies of the Volunteers. West Brigade HQ had moved to Magazine Gap.

All spare troops had been committed. From Fortress HQ fifty Royal Artillery and Royal Scots men were despatched to reinforce the Middlesex. The Rajputs collected their lightly wounded from the hospital to strengthen their platoons. Thirty clerks, signallers and military police, commanded by Major R. E. Moody, a staff officer, also joined the Middlesex. The RAF had been fighting as infantry since the loss of their aircraft, and the Royal Navy, like the Volunteers, were involved in scattered groups almost everywhere.

The shortage of ammunition had been temporarily overcome by a brave column which succeeded in reaching the Ordnance Depot at Little Hong Kong. Six lorries were filled with mortar and gun ammunition, but there were no grenades.

The two Colours of the Middlesex Regiment were secretly buried at night in boxes in the garden of Government House by Captain MacGregor. All attempts to find them after the war failed. The Colours of the Royal Scots had been sent to the vaults of the Hong Kong and Shanghai Bank in Singapore in 1940, whence they vanished when the Island was captured. However in 1945 an army officer saw the Regimental Colour in the market. He purchased it for one dollar. It now hangs in the Regimental Museum in Edinburgh Castle.

Lieutenant L. B. Corrigan, a platoon commander of C Company Winnipeg Grenadiers, was ordered at 9.30 am on the 24th to take a small reconnaissance patrol to discover the location and strength of the enemy around the southern slopes of Mount

Cameron. 'We had gone a few yards when I heard the swish of feet moving through the grass,' related Corrigan later. 'Crouching down, I saw silhouetted in the mist a group of enemy, bent double and proceeding towards us. I dropped to one knee and fired at the chest of the closest of the Japanese who were charging us. Grasping a grenade, I pulled the pin, held it as long as I dared, then tossed it underhand into their midst. It exploded waist high behind them, their bodies acting as a shield from the shrapnel we would otherwise have received. By this time they were too close to permit the firing of my rifle, and I had to grasp it by the barrel and wield it club fashion. I had foolishly neglected to put a bayonet on it. I was able to knock the rifle and bayonet out of the hands of one of the Japanese and with his weapon I managed to run through another of the enemy, but unfortunately I had difficulty withdrawing the blade and while trying to do so I caught the flash of a sword being raised to strike me.

'Quite subconsciously I jumped for my assailant, grasped his blade in my right hand and, circling his neck with my left arm, forced his head against my chest. Locked together in this fashion we struggled, each reluctant to let go of the sword. We both lost our footing and rolled down a slope. I tried to turn his head to deliver a knockout blow. Unfortunately I had forced his steel helmet down over his face and the net result of a terrific uppercut was a sprained thumb for me. At this stage my opponent gave two shrill cries to get help from his men. Glancing up I noticed a figure nearby. I had completely forgotten that I carried a pistol, and in something of a frenzy I tried to reach it. After inserting my forefinger in the trigger guard, I found that the cut I had received when I first grabbed the sword blade had deprived it of the strength to squeeze the trigger. I tried to withdraw my finger and found that the flesh, acting much the same as the barb on a fish-hook, prevented it. However, at last I managed to fire the pistol and finally ended the weary struggle. I was much relieved to find myself quite alone.'[3]

Major-General Ito, the Japanese Commander of the Division's infantry, ordered his three Regimental Commanders to prepare to attack the remaining British positions on the following day, the 25th. He appeared dissatisfied with the progress made so far. A battalion of Colonel Shoji's Regiment reached their start line, the crest of Mount Cameron, at about 4.00 pm on the 24th. Another battalion was ordered to fight through the lower built-up area of the Wanchai along the north shore.

Colonel Doi in the centre was to attack westwards to capture Mount Gough beyond the Royal Scots. Doi ordered his 1st and 2nd Battalions to lead with the 3rd, which had just arrived fresh from Kowloon, following the 1st on the northern flank.

The Japanese attack was to be supported by batteries firing from Kowloon, and also by guns which were being dragged up Mount Cameron. Meanwhile a heavy mortar bombardment during the night was ordered. Divisional HQ were to remain near the Taikoo Docks where they had first landed.

Colonel Tanaka's three battalions had become split up. His 1st Battalion, commanded by Captain Orita Masaru, was under direct command of Division Headquarters with orders to capture Stanley Fort (see map, page 110). The 2nd Battalion had moved west round Deep Water Bay, one of the company objectives being Brick Hill.

The 3rd Battalion, commanded by Major Kenmotsu, had finally moved into Repulse Bay. 'Major Kenmotsu later reported that he had suffered heavy casualties in the vicinity of Repulse Bay, and that his Battalion had taken no prisoners' stated Tanaka.[4] It is hardly surprising that no prisoners were found, for many of Major Young's Company of the Royal Rifles had been murdered. The Company had been stranded at Altimara, close to The Ridge, after their unsuccessful attempt to get through to Wong Nei Chong Gap from Repulse Bay. Major Young wrote afterwards: 'The enemy closed in on us but we held them off for three hours until darkness came. I had the men remove their boots, and we cut our way through twenty-eight barbed wire entanglements to reach the Repulse Bay Hotel, which we found to be held by the enemy. I told the Company that from then on it was each man for himself and to try to filter through in small parties. It was almost daylight, so we had to hide among rocks and boulders until the following night. Eventually four parties each under an officer started out. Two of these officers were later found with their hands tied behind their backs – killed by bayonet wounds. Some of our men managed to get through. Others skirted the sea shores or hid for days in the hills. . . .' Meanwhile the Japanese hunted down the Canadians and the other small groups which had escaped from The Ridge and Overbays. One British officer was captured and about to be executed when a Japanese noticed that he was wearing the World War I Victory Medal which the Japanese had also received. 'Ah! Japanese decoration! Let him go' said the Japanese.

The prisoners were taken to Eucliffe, the Chinese millionaire's castle on the north shore of Repulse Bay, where the 3rd Battalion had set up its Headquarters. Company Sergeant-Major Hamlon had been captured nearby, with three riflemen of the Royal Rifles. Having been beaten up by rifle butts, their hands were tightly bound behind their backs. They were prodded with bayonets to the edge of the cliff of Repulse Bay where they were forced to sit facing the sea with their feet dangling over the edge. 'We knew that we were going to be shot, because on top of the bank were pools of blood and at the bottom of the cliff, near the sea, were dozens of dead bodies,' stated Hamlon at the War Crimes Trial. 'It was evident that they had been shot on top of the cliff and had fallen down. Then a firing squad came forward and we were all shot. Owing to the fact that I turned my head to the left as I was being fired at, the bullet passed through my neck above the left shoulder and came out at my right cheek. I did not lose consciousness, and the force of the bullet hitting me knocked me free from the others and I rolled down the cliff.'

Later fifty-three bodies were found in the area. Many had been shot, others bayoneted to death and the rest beheaded. 'Every man,' said Lieutenant W. Markey, RAOC, at the War Trials, 'had his hands tied behind his back. Without doubt they had been taken prisoner and killed later.'

Colonel Tanaka had visited Eucliffe on the morning of the 23rd and could hardly have failed to see the carnage. From Repulse Bay Hotel he watched the humiliation of the two hundred and fifty civilians who had been forced to march up the hill close by. They saw soldiers dying from bayonet wounds. Jan Marsman recalls seeing 'the Japanese Colonel burst into an angry harangue, after which the interpreter translated: 'General say: "In Japan all men fight for his country. Why you no fight? What you mean 'civilians'? Japanese men all brave fighters. Japanese lady stay home".' The interpreter grew so frenzied that most could not understand a word he said. One Japanese officer announced that the Japanese would be fully justified in shooting them all because he regarded them as soldiers who had discarded their uniforms. Eventually they were ordered to return to the hotel.

Two hours later Colonel Tanaka followed his 2nd Battalion towards Shouson Hill, where he gave orders for an attack on Bennets Hill to start at 11.00 pm.

CSM Hamlon, meanwhile, lay bleeding all day at the foot of the cliff near Eucliffe. After dark he moved, 'a mess of blood', into a cave where he met CSM S. D. Begg who had also escaped from The Ridge, with some Canadians. CSM Begg gave orders that all who could should try to swim with him across Repulse Bay to Chung Hom Kok. Some waded into the water but the phosphorescence betrayed the swimmers, and the Japanese swept the surface of the bay with machine-gun fire. Some of the swimmers were hit; some died later of cold and exhaustion in the water. It was not until 5.00 pm on the 24th that Begg and two others reached Stanley after nearly twenty-two hours in the water. CSM Hamlon remained shivering in the dank cave as Japanese sentries patrolled above.

*   *   *

'There was not much we could do for the wounded' wrote Mabel Redwood. 'Washing them was out of the question and even cleansing their wounds was difficult, as we had come to the end of our bandages. There was no chance of sterilising anything, so they have to take their chance with germs. At dusk we tried to get the pans emptied, but it needed a brave heart to steal past the sandbagged entrance to the lavatories and face the stench. There were corpses in the garage too, and the atmosphere all around was putrid.

'Suddenly we heard machine-gun fire fairly near. And it was getting nearer. What now? Nearer and nearer it came. We knew by the noise that it was right outside. Both in the main road and on the valley side. Then in the distance we heard another sound. Again machine-gun fire, but a much different tempo. This could only mean one thing. The Japanese were driving our troops back. This we thought was the end for us. Right in the path of an advancing enemy. We did not think we would survive. . . .'[5]

15
Christmas Day 1941

The Allies' grimmest Christmas of the war found the defenders in desperate straits after eighteen days of fighting. They needed rest, reorganisation, resupplies, mobile artillery, aircraft, and much else. The Christmas greetings which reached them, urging them to greater efforts, can hardly have compensated for the deficiencies.

'Christmas greetings to you all,' signalled Churchill. 'Let this day be historical in the proud annals of our Empire. The order of the day is hold fast.'[1]

Sir Mark Young's message read: 'In pride and admiration I send my greetings this Christmas Day to all who are fighting and to all who are working so nobly and so well to sustain Hong Kong against the assault of the enemy. Fight on. Hold fast for King and Empire.'

Greetings also came from an unexpected quarter, with the Japanese still keeping up their propaganda broadcasts from Kowloon. 'A Merry Christmas to the gallant British soldiers,' heard many. 'You have fought a good fight, but you are outnumbered. Now is the time to surrender. If you don't, within twenty-four hours we will give you all that we've got. A Merry Christmas to the gallant British soldiers. . . .'

General Wavell, about to become the Commander of all land, sea and air forces in the south-west Pacific, was in no state to send greetings that Christmas morning. His return to Rangoon airport after conferring with Chiang Kai-Shek coincided with an air raid by eighty aircraft; he counted seventeen bombs within fifty yards of his slit trench. In any event he was more concerned with the way the fighting was going in Malaya. Thirteen days before he had been infuriated to receive a signal from Churchill which began: 'You must now look East.' Due to the calamities throughout the Far East, he was unlikely to be looking elsewhere.

* * *

The Japanese, with their overwhelming superiority of artillery and their indifference to loss of life, brought down heavy concentrations of mortar fire on the Wanchai and Victoria. Colonel Shoji's leading platoons tried to infiltrate forward from house to house, through the defenders holding the Wanchai. Anti-tank mines were placed on the main Japanese approaches, and good use was made of the Bofers anti-aircraft guns, using them against buildings occupied by the enemy.

Communications were becoming increasingly difficult due to the breaking of cables by shelling. Fortress HQ could no longer reach Brigadier Wallis' Brigade at Stanley, nor the Royal Scots at Wanchai. It was believed that the Middlesex Company was still holding out at Little Hong Kong, and possibly the Winnipeg Grenadiers near Aberdeen Reservoir and on Bennets Hill.

The Japanese took no steps to cut the telephone cable system, possibly because they preferred listening to the conversations. The line continued working intermittently, although junction points were in enemy hands. The same applied to the civil telephone system, which was not cut until the 26th. It is to the considerable credit of the Hong Kong Signal Company that essential communications worked reasonably successfully up to within three hours of the order for capitulation.

A temporary and unexpected lull took place in the fighting. The previous day all the civilians at the Repulse Bay Hotel were marched over the mountains and through the Wong Nei Chong Gap, to imprisonment in Kowloon. During the march Major Manners and Mr. Shields of the Hotel Committee were persuaded by the Japanese to go through the British lines to ask Sir Mark Young to surrender. Not much persuasion was necessary, as they had both seen the terrible suffering of the seriously wounded abandoned on the hillsides, and the abundance of Japanese troops, artillery, horses and ample equipment.

'Three times at his headquarters we asked the Governor to surrender, and offered terms,' Shields was told by a Japanese officer. 'This time he must come through the lines to us, and surrender must be unconditional.' An officious Japanese lieutenant started pushing Shields around. 'Stop that, get me your Commanding Officer at once,' roared Shields.

The bullying Japanese surprisingly did so, and Shields made a formal protest. The more senior officer, who was so anxious that Shields should play his part in stopping the fighting, gave him some tea, after ordering the Japanese lieutenant to take off his shoes and stand in his stocking feet as a humiliating punishment.

Shields and Manners departed at 6.00 pm. However it was too late to cross the Japanese lines safely that night. They slept as best they could, while the Japanese kept shining torches in their faces to see if they were still there. The following morning they were given a large white banner to carry, and pushed towards the British-held streets. They were escorted to Sir Mark Young and the GOC.

General Maltby recorded in his Despatches what they had to say: 'They informed me of their march with civilians of both sexes from Repulse Bay Hotel via Wong Nei Chong Gap to North Point, of the "incredible" number of guns and troops seen during the last half hour of the "trek" and (in their opinion *not* put forward by the Japanese) the uselessness of continuing the struggle.

'A special defence meeting was immediately called, where it was decided that there could be no talk of surrender. The Japanese Commander sent one message that their forces would not initiate active hostilities for three hours. I conformed . . . This "impromptu" truce was difficult to stage, for Japanese planes, operating from Canton, did not conform and bombed Stanley, Aberdeen and Mount Gough. A constant service of launches was maintained over Kowloon Bay and Japanese artillery continued bombarding the Gaps.'[2]

Shields later said to the American reporter, Gwen Dew: 'We had told Maltby what we had seen, how much territory the Japanese controlled, the state of things over half the Island, and what was probably ahead of them. Yet I was told that the war would go on.' The two men, tired and depressed after the failure of their mission, returned to the Japanese lines and were imprisoned with the others.

During the truce Lieutenant-Colonel H. W. M. Stewart, OBE, MC, commanding the Middlesex, visited Fortress HQ to discover the situation.

There Captain Freddie Guest, one of the duty officers, was trying to destroy secret papers and cyphers. Petrol was splashed on bundles of documents in a corridor, but they only smouldered round the edges as more files were frantically

thrust upon them. The destruction of the cyphers proved practically impossible. They were eventually carried to a clearing
nearby, where they were buried. While doing this two men
were hit by mortar fire.

Captain Bush who had escaped, wounded from Wong Nei
Chong Gap on the 22nd, had a different problem. The key of
the safe which contained the Canadian code books had been
kept by Colonel Hennessey, who had been killed. It could not
be found and the safe resisted all attempts to break it open. In
desperation it was carried down to the harbour and dumped in
the water.

He sent a last signal to Ottawa telling of the destruction of
the cyphers. He also summarised the fate of some of the officers
and tried to indicate to his wife that he had survived: 'Killed
Brigadier Lawson Canadian Contingent Colonel Hennessey
Canadian stop,' he signalled, 'Missing believed killed Major
Lyndon Canadian stop wounded Captain Bush Canadian. . . .'
The signal was misread in Canada, and Mrs. Bush was told
that her husband had been killed.

*   *   *

The Christmas Day issue of the *South China Morning Post* was
as optimistic and irrelevant as usual. Beneath a headline 'Day
of Good Cheer', the story read: 'Hong Kong is observing the
strangest and most sober Christmas in its century-old history.
Such modest celebrations as are arranged today will be subdued, but they will be none the less light-hearted. . . . All are
cheerful in the knowledge that, for all their hardships, they
would not go either hungry or thirsty this Christmas. . . . There
was a pleasant interlude at the Parisian Grill shortly before it
closed last night when a Volunteer pianist, in for a spot of food
before going back to his post, played some well-known favour-
ites in which all present joined with gusto. . . .'

*   *   *

At midday the three-hour truce ended, and Japanese artillery
opened up punctually on a large scale. In the Wanchai, A Company of the Royal Scots was now reduced to fourteen men, and
D Company was down to seven. Alongside them was Z Company of the Middlesex. Survivors of a platoon of 5/7 Rajputs
were captured after hard fighting at Mount Parish. Fortress

HQ, guarded by only one Punjab Regiment platoon, was in jeopardy. More road blocks were erected and the last of the anti-tank mines were put out. Small parties of Royal Marines mopped up a few enemy groups which infiltrated through the crumbling lines.

A second line of defence, in the built-up area to the east of Central District of Victoria, was held by about seventy of the Middlesex. With them were men from the Royal Navy, Royal Engineers and 5/7 Rajputs, who were strengthened by fifty Punjabis. Lieutenant-Colonel Stewart, commanding this line, warned the GOC several times that his men were being slowly but surely overwhelmed. Only six guns of the mobile artillery were left in action throughout the Island.

To the west of the Wanchai Gap, the remainder of the Royal Scots, reduced to a skeleton force, were doggedly holding their position despite heavy dive-bombing. Fortress HQ was told by runner that the Gap itself had been captured.

Incendiary bombs were effectively dropped at Magazine Gap, which set the hillside on fire and burnt the field cables. This Gap was also under mortar and small arms fire. Colonel Rose, commanding West Brigade there, reported that the area could be held for about twenty-four hours.

At Stanley the Royal Rifles had been completely withdrawn into the Fort on the southernmost point of the Island. The more senior Battalion officers were convinced that their men could do no more.[3] For six days and nights they had been ceaselessly engaged. The Battalion had lost eighteen officers killed or wounded since 8 December. Most had fallen in a gallant attempt to recapture Stone Hill and Stanley Mound on the 23rd. After three attacks with grenade and bayonet, the Canadians had regained both positions, but did not have sufficient men to hold them and the Battalion had been driven back.

One Lieutenant-Colonel at Stanley told Brigadier Wallis several times that he wished to see the Governor. He felt that further resistance could only result in useless casualties which could not stave off final defeat.[4] Brigadier Wallis was shocked at such a request, and replied that General Maltby, the GOC, could not be ignored in such a fashion.

Wallis also told this Lieutenant-Colonel that the rest of the defending troops were in good heart, that he had no intention of surrendering since it was considered they could still cause the enemy heavy losses. Brigadier Wallis gave the officer two choices: to march his unit out under a white flag or to fight on.[5] The Lieutenant-Colonel decided to adopt neither course for the time being.

Food was running short. The bombing had cut the water mains, and the water tanks had been hit by shell-fire, so all the water reserves had been lost. Brigadier Wallis was determined to fight on as long as he had food, water and ammunition.

By now the forward defences at Stanley were manned by platoons of the Middlesex, Gunners and Volunteers fighting in the infantry role. 'No praise can be too great for the fighting spirit, tactical control and fine discipline of the 1st Battalion Middlesex Regiment,' wrote Brigadier Wallis later in captivity. 'Outstanding in Peace, it reaped its reward on the field of battle . . . they held their positions in the Stanley area with great bravery. Great credit is due to Lieutenant-Colonel Stewart for their achievements. . . . The artillery batteries also fought in the defence of Stanley with great stubbornness, suffering severe casualties as infantry and never retreating without orders.'[6]

The Brigade Commander also regarded the contribution of No 2 (Scottish) Company of the Volunteers as outstanding. He recommended for the Victoria Cross its Commander, Major H. R. Forsyth, a World War I gunner and peacetime chartered accountant, 'for his fine leadership, courage and devotion to duty. This brave officer though mortally wounded refused to leave his post in Stanley where he met his death when it fell into enemy hands. He stayed with his men and fought to the last.' Another whose gallantry was outstanding was a disgraced former regular officer who had been imprisoned at Stanley just before the Japanese invasion. Sir Mark Young approved his release and Brigadier Wallis wrote later that the Captain was invariably where the fighting was thickest and that 'he did the best any man can do to make up for his former shortcomings by his conduct in the face of the enemy.'[7]

                              *   *   *

Another conference took place between Sir Mark Young and General Maltby on Christmas Day. Captain MacGregor, the ADC, had just emerged from Fortress HQ and was waiting for a temporary lull in the heavy bombardment before making a dash for Flagstaff House. He suddenly saw Sir Mark strolling towards him in a beautifully cut, light-weight grey suit, grey Homburg hat and highly polished shoes. 'He was unconcernedly swinging a Malacca walking stick, as if he was playing truant from the Colonial Office and taking a quiet walk in the sunshine of St. James's Park,' recalls Captain MacGregor. 'I called out: "It's getting a bit hot along there, Sir; better take cover." He smiled and said: "Hullo, MacGregor! Lovely day, isn't it." And he strolled on, neither slackening nor quickening his pace, completely composed and apparently without a care in the world. He walked straight through the shelling and disappeared into Fortress HQ, leaving a very red-faced ADC in his wake.'[8]

Sir Mark Young told General Maltby that in his view there should be no surrender. However the GOC believed that no further resistance was possible. He later wrote in captivity that the enemy's capture of the Wanchai Gap 'thus giving him an open line of advance to the Central District, the fall of Bennets Hill, the isolation of the forces in Stanley, the deployment by the enemy of such superior forces and armament, the exhaustion after sixteen days of continuous battle with no reliefs for any individuals, our vulnerability to unlimited air attack, the impossibility of obtaining more ammunition for the few mobile guns I had remaining, the serious water famine immediately impending – these were the factors which led to the inevitable conclusion, namely, that further fighting meant the useless slaughter of the remainder of the garrison, risked severe retaliation on the large civilian population and could not affect the final outcome. The enemy drive along the north shore was decisive.'[9]

'I asked Lieutenant-Colonel Stewart how much longer his men could hold the line now occupied. He replied one hour. Captain Man of Z Company had telephoned that "the line is breaking".'[10]

Lieutenant-Colonels White of the Royal Scots and Sutcliffe of the Winnipeg Grenadiers were called to Brigade HQ. White very reluctantly left his men: 'The enemy had been steadily hammering our positions for the last five hours,' he later said. 'There appeared to be every likelihood of an attack being launched at any time.' At Brigade HQ both Commanding Officers agreed that the remnants of their battalions would fight to a finish in their present positions.

Meanwhile, as Maltby concluded in the final paragraph of his despatch: 'At 3.15 pm I advised his Excellency the Governor and Commander-in-Chief that no further useful military resistance was possible and I then ordered all Commanding Officers to break off the fighting and to capitulate to the nearest Japanese Commander, as and when the enemy advanced and opportunity offered.'

At 3.40 pm news of the surrender reached West Brigade HQ. The two Battalion Commanders were ordered to return and fly the white flag. Lieutenant-Colonel White refused to believe these instructions, and first rang Colonel Newnham, GSO I. He was told that there could be no question about it. The order to surrender must be obeyed at once, for the GOC considered that 'further fighting was useless slaughter and the white flag must be flown.'[11]

At 4.43 pm the white flag was raised. Japanese troops thought it a ruse; the flag merely drew enemy fire, and the bombing continued.

Lieutenant-Colonel White, with his second-in-command, Captain Douglas Ford, and Private G. King, an orderly, went into the enemy lines through Wanchai Gap to the Japanese, as did Lieutenant-Colonel Stewart in the Wanchai area.

When a roll was taken of the Royal Scots still in action, the total numbered four officers and ninety-eight other ranks. The casualties of the Middlesex were typical of all battalions. Of thirty-six officers serving on 8th December, ten had been killed, four wounded and two were missing, while of the other ranks ninety-four were killed, one hundred and ten were wounded and twenty-five missing. Many more were to die in captivity.

Colonel Shoji Toshishige gleefully reported that a military representative of the Governor, a British Lieutenant-Colonel, accompanied by another man with a small dog had arrived by truck. Lieutenant Ito and seven guards escorted them to Divisional HQ.

Gradually the troops disengaged and were moved to Murray Barracks. 'I suppose we had all half-expected the surrender, but we never really thought of it,' wrote Captain Man. 'We had anticipated that we would stay where we were until we ran out of ammunition, or were overrun by the Japanese. We had heard of the fate of so many of our pill-box crews, that capture was the last thing that had entered our minds. It was the anti-climax of all anti-climaxes to be told to return to Barracks almost as if it was the end of an exercise. We were even told that our arms should not be damaged and that we should return with them. This was something we were not prepared to accept, and we returned with not one single serviceable weapon.'[12]

The urgency to destroy whatever might be useful to the Japanese was universal. The Royal Scots armoured car sergeant, who had done sterling work with the Middlesex, drove each of his vehicles in turn onto waste ground and set them afire. Meanwhile the imperturbable Major (Quarter Master) Guscott, who had unfailingly resupplied the units throughout the fighting, shaved and put on his best uniform for the occasion. Guscott was one of the most popular men of the Battalion, and not least after the Christmas Dinner which he had delivered under fire the previous evening. He had started his army career as a boy in the tailor's shop. With great sadness he hoisted the Mess table cloth on the flag pole.

The Japanese of Colonel Tanaka's battalions were still loath to take prisoners, as the platoon of the Winnipeg Grenadiers on Bennets Hill discovered. 'As the Japanese overran the position, the men threw down their weapons and raised their arms above their heads,' recalls Private James Fowler who saw 'the Japanese thrusting their bayonets through the many wounded men lying on the ground.' He heard cries and screams from the wounded. The orgy of murder lasted twenty minutes.

*   *   *

The Japanese at Stanley, after the severe and costly fighting against the Middlesex and Volunteers, had no choice but to continue fighting; Brigadier Wallis, out of touch with events elsewhere, positively refused all overtures to surrender, as did several isolated section positions.

Meanwhile Sir Mark Young despatched his last signal: 'Military and Naval Commanders have now advised me that no further effective resistance can be made. I am taking action in accordance with that advice. Ends.'

16
Surrender

'By Christmas Day,' wrote Major Hector Harland, the Brigade Major of Brigadier Wallis' Brigade, 'we were still holding on but had pulled back to the end of the Stanley Peninsula. The last message we received from Fortress HQ was that there must be no surrender. After that all communication ceased. The situation was obviously desperate, and we arranged to make a last stand.'[1]

The first defensive line by the Police Station at Stanley had broken, and the Japanese were bursting through the second (see map, page 110). Final collapse appeared inevitable. Brigadier Wallis ordered a Company of the Royal Rifles to counter attack. They did so with reluctance, believing that further resistance was futile. Owing to the lie of the land no artillery support was possible. The attack failed; the Company received heavy casualties and fell back to Stanley Fort.

The defenders at Stanley had no mortar bombs, and the machine-guns of the Middlesex and Volunteers had all been knocked out. They were short of ammunition and for several days they had been on short rations of food and water. They were exhausted after so many sleepless days and nights. Only Brigadier Wallis' courage, personal example and determination had prevented a collapse. It was evident that the intensive bombardment, to which they could make no reply, was the prelude to a full-scale attack. A final line of defence was prepared at Stanley Fort on the high ground on the extreme southern tip of Hong Kong Island.

At 10.00 pm, the 25th, Lieutenant-Colonel R. G. Lamb, one of General Maltby's staff officers, drove from Fortress HQ to order Brigadier Wallis to capitulate. 'After careful consideration I decided I could not surrender at a time when this action seemed to me to be locally unwarranted, without written confirmation,' Brigadier Wallis wrote later.[2] Major Harland was sent to the GOC to obtain reliable orders in writing. Although the water supply was damaged beyond repair, and

Brigadier Wallis had no artillery or mortars fit for action and few grenades he was determined to continue the struggle.

During the fighting at Stanley many of the wounded were carried to St. Stephen's College which, like the Convents, the University and some schools, had been turned into a hospital. It was now full to bursting with Canadians, Volunteers, Middlesex and Gunners. The hospital had been shelled despite the prominent Red Cross Flag, and the operating room was destroyed. The more serious cases were evacuated to Stanley Prison hospital.

St. Stephen's was manned by three Medical Officers, Lieutenant-Colonel George Black, in his late sixties and a long time resident of Hong Kong; Captain John Whitney, a regular officer of the Royal Army Medical Corps, and Captain Hickey. The staff consisted of a British nursing sister, six British and four Chinese VAD nurses and three medical orderlies, looking after about a hundred patients. There was also Padre J. Barnett, a Canadian, who recalls: 'On Christmas Eve I went to bed in the MI room. It was not a healthy place, with broken glass and the odd bullet flying around, so I got up and dressed and went into the main ward of the hospital. This ward was lit up with two or three hurricane lamps. There was a great deal of confusion. All the sisters were there. Everyone was restless and wondered what was going to happen. Between 5 and 6 am I was preparing to hold Christmas communion, when the Japanese entered the hospital by both the north and side entrances. As they came in I saw them bayonet wounded soldiers in bed.'[3]

The Japanese drove their bayonets repeatedly into the defenceless wounded. Black and Whitney rushed forward to stop them. Both doctors were immediately shot, and 'bayoneted dozens of times' as they lay on the ground. 'All staff and patients who could walk were taken out and put in a nearby store room. We were searched and my cash and prayer book were taken from me. As it began to get daylight, we were moved to the store of a smaller room on the first floor. During this move the nursing sisters were separated from our party. About ninety men were pushed into the small room. The wounded took turns in sitting and lying down. While there a Japanese soldier took our wrist watches and rings. Another gave us a few cigarettes and a tin of milk, while yet another threw a handful of 303 bullets into our faces. Two Japanese then came in and forced two

Riflemen out in turn. We heard screams. They tried to take a
third but he slammed the door in their faces. At the request of
the men, I told the story of Christmas and read some prayers.
We all thought it was our last Christmas Day.

'Suddenly the door was thrust open and the Japanese
entered.' Instead of facing bayonets and death, Padre Barnett
saw that the Japanese faces were wreathed in smiles: 'They said
that we were now friends and let some of us move to a larger
room. They also gave us some water. On the 26th, I found the
two Riflemen dead, very badly mutilated, three nurses were
missing and the doctors had been killed. I was ordered by the
Japanese to cremate all the dead. I built a funeral pyre of
bloody sheets and blankets, old chairs and tables, but I was not
allowed by the Japanese to make a list of the dead. The missing
nursing sisters were later shown to us under a cluster of bushes
– dead, but covered with blankets. A Japanese officer had told a
sister on Christmas Day that all inmates of the hospital were to
be killed to avenge the death of the younger brother of one of the
officers attacking the College.

'I was later sent for by a Japanese officer. He spoke very good
English. During our conversation, I spoke of the murder of the
nurses. He replied that nothing could be done about such
things in the heat of battle. One of the sisters told me that some-
time between our capture and the morning of the 26th, she had
been forced to lie on dead bodies and was used by the Japanese
soldiers as they desired.'[4] Four British nurses had survived, and
four Chinese and three British had been raped and murdered.

While Major Harland was obtaining written orders to surrender, the Japanese soldiers waited impatiently among the
rocks and scrub one hundred yards from Stanley Fort. They
faced the scattered, mixed sections of Canadian, Middlesex,
Volunteers and Gunners on the higher ground above them. Occasional bursts of machine-gun fired into the darkness caused
all the weary, exhausted soldiers to crouch low. The Japanese
resumed shelling the Fort at point blank range. At last, shortly
after midnight, the Brigade Major returned with explicit orders
to capitulate forthwith. Brigadier Wallis, by now himself
wounded, composed his last message to his men: 'By order of
His Excellency the Governor and the General Officer Commanding, His Majesty's forces in Hong Kong have surrendered. On no account will firing or destruction of equipment

take place, as otherwise all lives of British hostages will be endangered. Units will organise themselves centrally forthwith. C. Wallis. Brigadier. 0045 hrs 26.12.41.' By 2.30 am all firing had stopped, and the Brigade Commander went to the HQ in Stanley of the Japanese Commander, Major M. Egashira, who treated him with courtesy and consideration.

Three days later the prisoners of war gathered in small groups at the Fort, Prison or St. Stephen's tennis court. Lance-Corporal Alf Taylor was close to St. Stephen's College when the Japanese around him suddenly sprang to attention and presented arms. A General appeared with his staff officers. Taylor was told that it was no other than General Sakai. Taylor relates that 'the General was very polite and through an interpreter asked if we wanted anything. Sergeant White, RASC, asked if it would be possible to get washing and shaving equipment as we had lost all our kit. At this the Japanese interpreter exploded with wrath saying that "the very handsome General had neither slept nor changed his clothes for several days. If he could go without, so could we". He was right. General Sakai was in a creased and crumpled uniform, his beard was sprouting from his face and he looked a very tired man.'[5]

Gradually the survivors of the fighting found their way to POW camps, or died of exposure alone and abandoned on the hillsides. Some were fortunate. Major Young led thirty-four survivors of his Royal Rifles Company down to Deep Water Bay, where they found an old, leaking motor boat, and also CSM Hamlon who had escaped from the Eucliffe murders. They set off in the boat to Stanley, but altered course to Lamma Island when they saw that the Fort had surrendered. On 28th they crossed to the Mainland. Wild plans to escape across China urged them on, but they were quickly spotted by the Japanese and taken prisoner.

Private Canivet of the Royal Canadian Ordnance Corps was among those who had been accidentally left behind near The Ridge. After swimming with two others across Repulse Bay to Chung Hom Kok, they had become lost. He resumes his account: 'My wound on my jaw dazed me pretty badly. Some Chinese boys brought us some bully beef and beer and said it was Christmas Day. They told us to get to Stanley as soon as possible, but the climb was hard and a party of six Japanese captured us. They tied us together, and when eventually we were made to crawl into a ditch, we knew that the end had arrived for us. Then the shooting started. I was hit four times and I lay very quiet, waiting and hoping that the next shot would be a clean one and have it finished. I heard my comrades die miserable deaths. Then the Chinese came along to loot our bodies. I scared them very badly by suddenly sitting up and talking. After they had completely looted all our rings, watches and money, they untied me and told me to go before the Japs came back. I started up over the hills towards Stanley. Many Chinese were coming along the road, with all their personal belongings, heading for Victoria.

'After one look at me, they all started to scream and run away. The maggots were falling quite freely from the hole in my jaw by this time and the sight was not pretty. I started to walk back to Repulse Bay where I approached a Jap officer and asked for food and medical aid, but he sent me on my way. At Wong Nei Chong Gap, the road block sentry stopped me and wanted to shoot me but I stalled him off, and he made me sit on the roadside until the sentry changed. Then an RAMC truck came along and took me to Bowen Road military hospital. I was so happy that I cried myself back into unconsciousness. Since then my wounds healed fine. I owe a great debt to Major J. Anderson, my surgeon, and also to the nursing sisters and VAD's. Their vigilance and constant hard work saved my life.'[6]

The Japanese who overran St. Albert's Auxiliary Hospital committed no atrocities, probably because of a lucky incident. 'Although all the staff were put in one room with a machine gun pointed at them, no one was ill-treated,' recalled Anna May. 'They believe that this was due to the way bearers had brought a Japanese officer in, thinking he was one of their own. During the night he died and they had him laid out and covered him with a Japanese flag. This greatly pleased the Japanese.'[7]

The nursing staff at the Jockey Club Hospital were less fortunate. On Christmas night the Japanese entered and flashed their lights on the faces of the terrified nurses. Having made their choice, the nurses were dragged from the room. One slender Irish girl mercifully fainted and was left in a pathetic heap on the stairs. About four hours later the others returned with their clothes torn, sobbing hysterically. They were comforted by Mrs. Mabel Redwood, who herself was spared. (She and her daughters were to survive the four terrible years of imprisonment. After the war and several years in England, the family returned to Hong Kong, where two daughters later married.)

'On Christmas Day we all attended Communion in the Bowen Road Hospital, where we all stood with our helmets on, as usual, while shells and bombs fell around us,' recorded the Canadian nurse, Kathleen Christie, from Toronto. 'After the surrender every patient who wished it was given beer. What remained was poured down the drains. Large quantities of tinned goods were hidden in the wards under blankets. However no Japanese appeared until the following afternoon, when an officer arrived to officially take over the Hospital which they had declared to be a POW Camp.'[8]

Many of the wounded had also been gathered at the Argyle Street Camp in Kowloon, where Doctor Isaac Newton operated day and night, making brief entries in his diary:

'24 December. 950 Canadian, British and Indian troops. 150 of them wounded. It was a hopeless task trying to do anything for them as we had no operating theatre, no instruments and only a few dressing materials, practically no drugs and no nurses. We spent yesterday dressing cases as best we could until nightfall, and carried on by candle afterwards. It was a nightmare of a game. Shells from Hong Kong were dropping round us most of last night and there are some big Japanese guns near us too, which make a huge noise and break the windows.

'Christmas Day. What a dawn! Spent from 1.00 pm yesterday until 7.00 pm dressing cases. It seemed an endless task. Most of them had been wounded about five days previously, and had only the original dressing. It is amazing how well most of them are doing. Fortunately most of the injuries are rifle bullets and hand grenades, very few bomb and shell splinters. It is certainly the strangest Christmas I have ever spent. We had 17 cases of dysentery.

'26 Dec. The surrender is probably for the best as it saves more slaughter, but goodness knows it means a pretty grim prospect for us until this war is over. You can't walk through the ward without men calling out to you for one thing or another, but they never complain and they must be suffering terrible pain. Tomorrow we are going to start operating on them, but it will be pretty primitive surgery I'm afraid. It is

awful not knowing who is left alive, and I'm afraid that when
we do know we shall find a great many have been killed, judging by the small proportion of officers to men in this camp.' One
thousand soldiers had now been crammed into a space built for
three hundred Chinese.

'28 Dec. I am beginning to find the stench of pus pretty
trying. The mortality is going to prove terrific. . . .'[9]

*   *   *

On Christmas morning MTB 08, in which Sub-Lieutenant
Lewis Bush, RNVR, was serving, was blown up when a bomb
fragment entered the fuel tanks. Miraculously there were no
casualties. At 4.00 pm the signal reached them that the
Governor had surrendered. 'It was a grim and tragic moment,'
recalls Bush. 'Further resistance was quite hopeless and ridiculous. The Royal Navy knew not surrender. The word is not in
the Navy vocabulary. Most of us sighed with relief, and surely
there must be something sacred about human life and values.
For us amateurs who came from all walks of life it was not so
bad. We could face the facts, and consoled ourselves that we
had done our best and need have no shame. But for the older
professional sailors, the whole bottom had fallen out of their
world.'[10]

Lewis Bush planned to escape in the remaining MTBs, but
he was ordered to report instead to Government House to be a
liaison officer. He spoke Japanese well, having married a
Japanese and taught for many years in schools in Japan
before the war.

He listened to the firing from the direction of Stanley, as
he walked towards the Naval Base outside which bands of
Chinese looters had gathered. He waited at the main gate
for the Japanese while looters threw rocks at him, and
within the base hundreds of bottles of liquor were destroyed. It was almost dark when a Japanese corporal and
private arrived. They both seemed relieved when Bush
spoke to them in Japanese. The corporal smiled 'and
pointed to his bandaged neck and said that he had been
wounded by one of our bullets. He asked if there was anything they could do for us. I pointed to the crowd of ruf-
fianly looters. The Corporal caught the ringleader and tied
him to a tree.'

Bush went to Government House, which he found surrounded by Japanese sentries: 'There was no electricity and General Maltby, with about twenty officers, was in the lounge which was bathed in a soft light of candles. It was a heartrending meeting, for me one of the most tragic and impressive moments of my life. . . .' There he also found his wife, Kaneko, who had been forced to accompany the Japanese to interpret. Earlier in the day she had been taken to Wong Nei Chong Gap, where she had been sickened and horrified by the sight and smell of the dead.

Once already that day Sir Mark Young and the GOC had met the Japanese Commander after the surrender, at Queen's Pier. The Japanese launch had, as previously, carried European women in the bows. General Sakai was smartly dressed with a large display of medals. His ceremonial sword was studded with jewels and his staff officers were similarly dressed. Sakai had a stubborn face and appeared very sure of himself.

Sir Mark Young had stepped forward with some papers. General Sakai quickly passed them to one of his staff. Soon the quick ceremony was over and the launch departed. The second meeting in the evening at Government House was only a little longer. Sub-Lieutenant Bush witnessed the scene:

'General Maltby asked if it was the practice of the Imperial Japanese army to rape nurses, and to shoot and bayonet the wounded in their beds. The Japanese replied that, if it was true, the culprits would be found and shot. But the Japanese claimed that the shooting of the wounded at Stanley was justified because the firing had come from St. Stephen's College Hospital and armed men were found inside, and that they could not know who were wounded or who were shamming and waiting to shoot any Japanese who approached.'

Lieutenant-Colonel Lindsay Ride, Commanding the Volunteers' Field Ambulance, requested permission to scour the Island for the wounded. He received a curt reply that the Japanese could be trusted to look after all the wounded. Nevertheless, grudgingly, the necessary authority was given. Ride and the senior Canadian doctor, Major J. N. Crawford, started to organize search parties as best they could with the little resources at their disposal.

Gradually, the groups in Government House dispersed into the night. Sir Mark Young and General Maltby were taken by the Japanese to captivity in Kowloon. Kaneko Bush was given numerous messages for wives, and promised to try to find the Scotch terrier of the General's ADC.

That night the soldiers, concentrated in Murray Barracks, received their first full night's sleep since 8 December. Wives and sweethearts elsewhere waited in fear through the night to discover which of their loved ones were still alive.

*   *   *

Two of the GOC's staff officers were amongst those determined to evade capture. Captain Peter MacMillan was an officer of the Royal Artillery in his late twenties. He was a robust, red-faced, clean-shaven Old Etonian. Both he and Captain Freddie Guest had earlier made good friends with Admiral Chan Chak.

As the surrender was ordered, the Battle Box of Fortress HQ gradually emptied, and the group of officers finalized their escape plans. They asked Captain Iain MacGregor to persuade General Maltby to accompany them. The ADC went to his very weary and dispirited General. 'Sorry, Iain' General Maltby said, 'a Commander should not desert his men. I must stay with the Garrison, come what may. The others have my permission and approval to get away as planned.'[11] They all shook hands. MacMillan and Guest then left the HQ to seek out Admiral Chak. They found him in the Gloucester Building nearby, disguised in ordinary Chinese clothes and carrying a small hold-all. Henry Chan, the Admiral's henchman, had gone in search of some form of transport. He returned a few minutes later with an old four-seater Austin with a canvas top. The four of them jumped in and sped off towards Aberdeen which had not yet been taken over by the Japanese.

After a frantic search, a twenty-five foot boat was found. They clambered aboard. By now their party had gathered ten more. The little engine started up. They slowly chugged at about five knots into the Lamma Channel. 'It was all very quiet except for the throb of the engines,' recorded Freddie Guest 'and I was beginning to think that we were safe, at least from the land, when suddenly through the stillness of that lovely evening there came the crack of a single shot, quickly followed by others. We stared at each other with startled looks and I yelled: "My God! Sighting shots!" The next second came the frightening rattle of a machine-gun. The first burst hit the boat

and in a second the Norwegian engineer fell on top of me riddled with bullets. I received a splinter in my face which bled
profusely. By this time the boat had stopped and water was
pouring in from all sides.'

They started to swim. The Admiral unstrapped his wooden
leg and jumped into the sea. The Japanese were still firing from
the beaches about a thousand yards away. The bullets fell like
hail stones around them. The Admiral was hit, but continued
to swim, leaving a small trail of blood in the water. Fortunately
the water was not too cold and this area of Hong Kong was not
shark-infested. Instead giant sixty pound jellyfish abounded
with fierce stings. They swam through a shoal of them. An hour
later eight of them reached the rocky shore of Lamma Island,
after a swim of about two miles. But the Japanese had been
watching their progress through binoculars and shelled the
beach as they staggered ashore. Guest helped the Admiral
climb over the rocks. Chak was still bleeding profusely from his
left arm, and with only one leg he was completely unbalanced.

For two hours they slept. When Guest awoke he saw an MTB
motionless in a bay not far off. He swam out to it, brought it in,
and within a short time the Admiral was carried aboard. Filled
with hot rum and cocoa and dressed in the complete uniform of
a Lieutenant Commander of the Royal Navy, Admiral Chak
looked very bright and cheerful, despite the bullet still in his
arm.

The MTB was part of the flotilla still at sea. They had orders
to rescue the Admiral, but had no idea of his whereabouts.
They had also been told to scuttle each of their ships, should
there be no alternative.

They decided to make for the Chinese mainland at Mirs Bay
to the north-east of Hong Kong that night. There they sank
their boats and struck inland towards Chungking, led through
Japanese occupied territory by a Chinese guerrilla leader. The
Admiral was carried by Chinese coolies, while the British
officers and Royal Navy MTB crews encouraged each other to
keep moving towards safety and freedom. Eventually the whole
party split into smaller groups and made their way to Chungking. Captain Guest was less fortunate in obtaining lifts and
arrived last, to be warmly welcomed by the British Ambassador, Sir Archibald Clark Kerr, and later entertained by
Madame Chiang Kai-Shek. The Russian military mission

showed the greatest interest in him; after a prolonged feast as their sole guest, they questioned him throughout the night. Guest was later flown to Delhi where he met MacMillan once more and lectured on the fighting. The Royal Navy crews had already been flown to Rangoon.

*   *   *

26 December was a beautiful day. Some Chinese and Europeans alike were almost blinded by the sun after hiding for so long in air raid shelters. They noticed steel helmets, gas masks, arm bands and badges of rank lying discarded in the gutters, where they had been thrown when the capitulation had been announced.

Hong Kong looked a sorry spectacle. Damaged cars and trucks were sprawled around the streets. Large white sheets hung limply from the Hong Kong Bank, Lane Crawford's and the Exchange Building. Many others flew the Rising Sun. The streets were filthy; the sewer mains were broken and gave off a dreadful stench. There was hardly a building which was not pock-marked by shell splinters.

Chinese squatters were beginning to set up hundreds of stalls of looted merchandise of every description: tins of Australian mutton, Singapore pineapples, soap, toothbrushes, pipes and sweaters. Wayside bars dispensed looted whisky and champagne in Chinese tea cups, but occasionally the bottles of whisky were found to contain cold tea. The shops did not dare to open for fear of looting mobs which roamed the streets and ransacked houses, whether occupied or not. Scavenging mobs of men, women and children were later to tear out the plaster from walls and ceilings to remove the wooden laths, take locks off doors, extract nails and tear up floors and window frames. Such houses looked as if millions of giant ants had been at work.

One Japanese sentry close to the Peak was to be seen wearing a very handsome lady's mink coat. Captain Man's flat nearby was amongst those ransacked. Neither he nor his wife was ever to see the flat again, nor his proudest possession, his Edward VIII engraved sword which he had left in his golf bag.

Phyllis Harrop, who spoke Cantonese, had been summoned on 28 December to Lieutenant-Colonel Iguchi, the Japanese Director of Medical Services. He wanted to discuss proposals for brothels. He produced the finest maps she had ever seen.

Everything of military significance was carefully marked, and various objectives had been indicated in different colours according to their importance. She also noticed by his elbow the British blue Staff books.

Many others recall their activities in those bitter days of defeat. Lewis Bush, RNVR, had been sent with the Japanese to persuade a remarkable Australian serving in the Royal Engineers to surrender. The Australian refused to do so, although it was over forty-eight hours after the capitulation. He and a small party were hiding in the ammunition magazines near Little Hong Kong, and were to blow up all the munitions and explosives. They were almost out of water, but were surviving on an abundance of chocolate. Eventually Bush persuaded them to surrender. The thirty Japanese around the building regarded the Australian and his party as heroes. They were taken to Aberdeen, where a Japanese officer filled them with beer and whisky.

On 29 December the two senior officers of the Volunteers' Field Ambulance, Lindsay Ride and John Crawford, came across The Ridge in their search for the wounded. Lieutenant-Colonel Macpherson with his British, Volunteer and Canadian soldiers had held out there, before being ordered to surrender with their wounded. The doctors found a dozen bodies slumped close together at the base of the cliff below the house. They were already badly decomposed. 'I decided that these men had been lined up against the base of the cliff and shot,'[12] stated Ride. He found twenty more bodies a hundred yards away, and a further fifty near Wong Nei Chong Gap. Many of their hands and feet had been tied. This also applied to corpses found in the machine-gun pill-boxes manned by the Middlesex on the south coast of the island. Many of them had died of bayonet wounds.

However some Japanese soldiers behaved very well. Wenzell Brown, the University lecturer who had been responsible for distribution of food, was stopped with his companion, Larry Clyron, by a Japanese soldier who asked them the time. Brown indicated that their watches had been stolen. The Japanese led them at gun point up the street: 'We followed behind in considerable trepidation,' relates Brown. 'He led us to a jewellery store and knocked heavily on the door. A fearful coolie opened it. The Jap forced his way in and told Clyron to take his pick from a display of watches behind a glass case. Clyron chose one.

The Japanese soldier slapped down some money on the counter, picked up the watch, presented it to Clyron, led us out of the shop, bowed, hissed and departed.'[13]

At the Argyle Street Hospital on the same day, 29 December, Doctor Newton saw the Japanese guard turn out and salute when a dead British soldier was carried out of the camp. They saluted again when the body was buried. The Doctor was unimpressed; he wished they had taken more trouble with the living.

17
Imprisonment

On 31 December, 1941, the survivors from Stanley were marched sixteen miles across the island to imprisonment at North Point Camp, which consisted of damaged wooden huts originally built as a temporary shelter for 300 refugees. The Japanese had used the camp to stable their horses and mules. It was to become the home for 1,800 prisoners-of-war.

Brigadier Wallis addressed his men before they left Stanley. He reminded them of their traditions and that the soldier was at his best when faced with the most adverse conditions. They found North Point Camp to be a dirty hole with thousands of flies, no lights, water or latrines. More prisoners were brought in as isolated groups were rounded up. Soon dysentery made its appearance and spread rapidly. However, gradually sanitary conditions improved, water being laid on, a stove built and two-tier bunks constructed. On 15 January many from North Point joined the other prisoners at Shamshuipo in Kowloon, where conditions were equally bad. Most officers were separated from their men in April, and were sent to Argyle Street Camp.

Three weeks after the surrender, search parties were still finding bodies on the hills, although they were too decomposed to be identified. 'A parcel of identification discs was brought in this morning, but the smell was so bad that they had to be sent back to the Medical Department for disinfectant,' wrote Phyllis Harrop on 18 January, 1942. 'If only we had been allowed to collect our wounded, we should not have had such a high death roll. Wounded men lay on the hills for days and we could not get them in; the Japanese would not allow us to take ambulances and collect them. I suppose they wanted to clear their own before anyone had a chance to see them.'

The Japanese decreed that all businesses and shops should re-open, the double-decker trams should run, and public buildings should be restored. However thousands of Chinese were starving, and the Japanese rice distrbution was deliberately inadequate, for they had no wish to feed Chinese. Queues began forming at the distribution centres usually at 4.00 am and extended seven or eight abreast for miles. The centres quickly ran out of food almost as soon as the distribution began.

In the crowded Chinese quarters, some sort of life started up under Japanese masters. Only dirty little children playing in the gutters seemed not to notice the strange smell of decaying, rotten food, human excrement, and unburied dead which hung over the area like a poisonous fog.

Many shops were turned into Japanese beer halls. Japanese soldiers drank with Chinese, Russian and Eurasian prostitutes while Philippino musicians played popular music. For anybody with money to spare, there were some extraordinary bargains such as antiques, rare perfumes and valuable books. The libraries had all been looted and many leather-bound gold-embossed first editions were being sold by their weight to use for lighting fires.

The Japanese ordered all English signs to be removed from streets, shops and hotels. At first some of the shop owners, feeling that maybe it was a little premature to destroy English signs, pasted paper strips over them with Chinese lettering. However these had to be ripped off, the English painted out and the Chinese signs went up. The streets received long, unpronounceable Japanese names. The British Military Hospital at Bowen Road became Dai Ichi Bun In, Kirishima Doi.

The Japanese rounded up not only the military but also arrested prominent Chinese who were thought to be sympathetic to the British. They also decided to intern all British, Dutch, American and other Allied nationals, regardless of sex or age. Many were already imprisoned in sparse Chinese hotels in Kowloon and Hong Kong where there was totally inadequate food, and the sanitary arrangements indescribably foul. After three weeks of humiliating treatment, the internees were moved to Stanley, most marching part of the way.

Phyllis Harrop remembers seeing on the march a small boy of five or six, with blue eyes and fair hair. 'He wore a blue overcoat and from its belt hung everything his mother thought he would need: an enamel jug, a spoon, knife and fork, a small chamber pot, scissors, an enamel saucepan and other things.' Most Chinese who watched them stood silent and apathetic. Others showed their sympathy in small gestures. Phyllis

Harrop was not interned because she had formerly been married to a German. She fled to Macao, disguised as a Portuguese, and afterwards travelled 1,200 miles to Chungking. Before she left Hong Kong she noticed that the big, bronze lion statues outside the Hong Kong Bank had wooden tags around their necks inscribed: 'This is the property of the Japanese Imperial Government.' The squat statue of Queen Victoria rested in a great pile of scrap metals such as torn up tram tracks, iron window frames and smashed cars, all awaiting a boat for Japan.

Phyllis Harrop was fortunate to miss the horrors of Stanley Internment Camp where 1,100 men, 1,000 women, 340 children and 80 infants were dumped unceremoniously and left to shift for themselves.

Evidence of violent fighting was still around them. Roofs of houses, corners of buildings, windows and roads had all been scarred by shell or shrapnel. The dead had been left to decay in gullies and under bushes – wherever they had fallen. The Japanese ignored the rotting bodies. For months there was one dead soldier on the beach just beyond the barbed-wire barricade, whom nobody could reach. Each day a young English girl went as close as possible – for it was her brother. Soon his face, constantly covered by a solid mass of flies, was unrecognisable. The khaki cloth turned to mouldy green and the putrefying flesh rotted from the bones.

The internees roamed the hills, paths and roads inside the camp, which was on the rocky peninsula. Fortunately it included apartment houses built for prison warders, a few bungalows, a college and school into which the internees moved. As many as twenty men lived in each of the class rooms, sleeping on the floor, or on improvised beds made out of doors or boxes. Some of the primitive toilets were shared by up to eighty people.

The 350 American internees were fortunate to be in the only area with a complete kitchen in running order. The British had to build their emergency kitchens from rubble.

The food was completely inadequate. Meals usually consisted of a small bowl of broken, weavily rice with three-quarters of a cup of thin gravy at ten in the morning. At five a similar issue of rice, with all manner of peculiar greenstuffs, was cooked. Very occasionally the diet included buffalo meat and fish heads, but such delicacies were apt to be diseased. One volunteer in the kitchens vividly remembers pouring bad rice over a table and seeing it actually undulating with the movement of the worms and weevils in it. Most ate out of tin cans found in garbage bins. It was a sad, dreary sight to see the ragged internees line up each day with their tin pails or cans for food which was dissatisfying and disagreeable, to eat just to stay alive.

According to the Geneva Convention it was specified that civilian prisoners were to receive 2,400 calories a day. For a three-month period the diet averaged 850 calories a day. The Japanese had signed but not ratified the Convention.

As weeks went by, the lack of clothing, and shoes in particular, became a serious problem. Gwen Priestwood made cardboard soles when the rubber ones wore out. The cardboard collapsed a few hours later and cloth ones disintegrated. Finally she cut soles out of old biscuit tins – and that was perfect. They outlasted the uppers. She occasionally thought of her evening gowns, pretty afternoon frocks and dozen pairs of high-heeled shoes which she had last seen amidst the bombed rubble of her flat in Victoria.

There were a number of pretty young girls in camp, many of them wearing the briefest of shorts and bras, due to lack of material. The cemetery was popular with lovers, for there was shelter from prying eyes among the trees, rocks and headstones. The Japanese were said to have issued an order: 'Sexual intercourse is prohibited, except between husband and wife or close friends.'

A new aristocracy sprang up which was different from the old class system of Hong Kong. The privileged groups were now the physically strong, the politically dexterous and those who had smuggled in large sums of usable money. Some former directors of influential firms, university professors and wealthy widows were on the edge of starvation. What mattered most was whether they had bedding, tobacco, black tea or whatever small comfort made life worth living for them.

The internees came from every walk of life. When the Japanese had bombed Chungking, Sir Arthur Blackburn, Counsellor at the British Embassy, had been wounded in the face. He had been flown for treatment to Hong Kong before the invasion, where he was injured again. He and Lady Blackburn now lived in a small room with eight others, including a number of children, most of whom slept on the floor.

There were people of every variety. All the Government officials were there, with the exception of Sir Mark Young who was imprisoned in Kowloon and later moved, in November, 1942, to Formosa. Mr. F. C. Grimson, the former Colonial Secretary, was elected representative of the internees for dealing with the Japanese. And so it was that humble salesmen and clerks lived and starved alongside the former leaders of society who had once been conscious of their high social positions. Most of the internees were kind and decent people, who bore their lot with great good humour and fortitude.

The camp contained a small building used as a hospital, although there were few medicines. At times a large number were extremely ill with dysentery, and the volunteer staff worked day and night to save them. There were some deaths, and also a number of births. One nurse had delivered a child a few weeks earlier, close to the window so that she could see now and then by the gun flashes.

The camp elected representatives to be in charge of the garden, small library, drains, food, and for other chores. A Town Crier announced events in the camp, and what war news had been smuggled in. The Japanese provided a daily two-page propaganda sheet which told of fantastic Japanese and Axis victories. Occasionally hints of the truth emerged, for example adamant statements were made such as that 'Tokyo had not been bombed, the damage was very slight and only a few fires had been started. Three American planes brought down over Tokyo were on exhibition. No raid had taken place.'

Rumours abounded: the Pope had flown to see Hitler to plead for peace; the British had landed in Holland and the Americans in Formosa. But when the Japanese propaganda sheet announced gleefully that Singapore had surrendered, most realized it was true. On the other hand nobody believed that a tiger had been seen digging in the dustbins, until one was shot close to the camp. It had escaped from a circus during the invasion.

One night the internees were herded into the school to watch films of the Japanese victories. There was no applause, although another film showing Japanese brewing Asiahi beer drew some ironic cheers. After the film the Maryknoll fathers, a group of American Catholic priests who were also interned, organized a sing song. There was little enthusiasm: hunger was gnawing at everyone, and the thought of all that beer . . .

The thirty-two priests seemed to miss cigarettes as much as everyone else. They collected many of the butts and mixed them with pine needles and tea leaves. The cigarettes became known as 'Padres Specials.' Many other tobacco substitutes were tried, including dried grass, ground bark and dried hibiscus blossoms. All kinds of paper were used as coverings in which the tobacco substitutes could be rolled.

Part of the camp was awakened one morning by an irate wife giving an unforgettable tongue-lashing to her husband, who had used their much-needed supply of toilet tissue for the luxury of smoking.

The Japanese largely ignored the internees. Mr Yamashita, who had been the second barber in the Hong Kong Hotel for twelve years, and Mr. Nakazawa, a former tailor's assistant, shared command of the camp. Most of the guards were Sikhs of the former Hong Kong Police. One old Sergeant, who wore medal ribbons of the First World War, whispered to one internee that he was ashamed at serving the Japanese, but he had a wife and children in the Colony and feared for their safety. At night a few Sikhs surreptitiously crawled to the camp wire and sold food to the internees at exorbitant prices. Others smuggled gifts of shoes, shirts and food to their friends in captivity.

One afternoon a group of internees were playing softball, although weak from malnutrition. Four Japanese officers watched the game. One grabbed a bat. He hit the ball high and a girl caught it. 'Out!' she sang triumphantly. The officer stayed in, grinning. Other players ran over to him yelling: 'You're out – out – out!' The officer shouted back in broken English: 'Not out! No! Singapore broken – not out!'

Morale gradually declined as everyone became weaker from hunger, and the hope of early release evaporated.

Quite suddenly the Japanese announced that the Americans were to be repatriated. The British, and the Dutch who numbered fifty, were to remain at Stanley. Confusion and anxiety mounted as the departure date was continually postponed. However on Sunday, 29 June, 1942, the *Asama Maru*, with white crosses on her side, anchored off-shore. Sunset flushed the sky with scarlet and gold as the ship sailed with the Americans that night. They stood by the railings, waving good-bye to those they could hardly see through their tears. The British and Dutch were left behind, standing on the rocky peninsula, bravely watching, waiting, weeping. The Canadian internees were repatriated in September, 1943.

Singapore, Corregidor and Burma had fallen. General MacArthur had left the Philippines for Australia, the Japanese had lunged into the Indian Ocean, and Colombo had been bombed. But the Battle of Britain had been won, and very soon the Allies could expect the benefit of the full weight of American war production.

'The young children in the camp,' recalls Barbara Redwood, 'led a carefree and happy life, digging in the sandy soil, and wearing the minimum of clothing. Brown as berries, many of them remembered no other life. "When I grow up," one small girl said, "I'm going to have four children – one to grind the rice, one to do the washing, one to go to the canteen, and one to collect the water." Obviously she expected to live in the camp forever. There were plenty of school teachers in camp and some children passed exams set to matriculation standards.'[1]

The internees were perpetually worried about their husbands, fathers, brothers, sweethearts and friends who were imprisoned in the POW camps on the mainland, and no contact with them was permitted.

Conditions for the POWs were very much worse.

New arrivals to the North Point Camp early in 1942 had been horrified by the broken, spiritless, dirty, slovenly, unshaven gaunt-looking spectres who stared at them with unfriendly, unwelcoming eyes. In the first few months of captivity, when bodies were becoming adjusted to a totally altered and hopelessly inadequate diet, morale in the prison camps was at its lowest.

Many had had their hopes sustained during the fighting by false claims of help coming from China. So they started their captivity with a cynical attitude of disillusionment, critical of the leadership and of the many deficiencies in their equipment.

The hardships everyone had to endure were greatly overcrowded quarters, a basic diet of rice of the poorest quality and increasingly diminished quantity, a plague of flies, bed bugs and lice, inadequate sanitation, the arrogance of the Japanese, and no mail or communication from home.

In August, 1942, the first letters from about five hundred Canadian POWs reached the censors in Ottawa. Each was closely examined for any clue as to the fighting, their capture or the conditions under which they were imprisoned. However the POWs had to follow a standard format in their letters, which permitted no divergence. A scant half-dozen made any reference to their capture and then it was only in the most guarded terms: 'We've had a little trouble, but it's all over now.' Almost all letters said that they were being well treated. The Canadian authorities concluded correctly that they were merely writing what they were told to. More ominously, at that stage less than a third were writing at all.

There was a great deal of sickness, especially beri-beri, one form of which was known as 'electric feet'. The sufferers from this unpleasant disease were to be seen with their feet in buckets of water, for this was the only way they could obtain relief and, for most of them, sleep was impossible. The lack of it was to be seen in their sunken eyes and ghastly pallor. Dysentery was the other terrible scourge. There were usually about fifty inmates in a special ward, most of whom were in a serious condition. The stench was horrible, but the spirit of the sufferers was wonderful; they joked about their condition, and even had bets on who would die first. None complained unreasonably, and all were conscious that everything humanly possible was being done by their medical staff to get them well.

Throughout the Japanese occupation of Hong Kong, one British military hospital, at Bowen Road, near Victoria, remained a going concern. The Japanese supplied it with some medical supplies and rations, and regarded it as a show piece for the Red Cross representatives, both international and Japanese. The staff and patients fared much better than many other prisoners in Japanese hands, the credit for which was largely due to Major D. C. Bowie who was made senior medical officer by the Japanese at less than twenty-four hours notice, on 7 August, 1942. The previous commander was bundled off with the more senior officers to a POW camp.

The years of captivity fell loosely into four parts. First, the period of the infections including wound sepsis, dysentery and a very serious outbreak of diphtheria. Then came the period of deficiency diseases. This was followed by the long, long period of slow decline which lasted until about March, 1945. Finally came five months of relative stability until the Japanese surrender. All were characterized by sub-standard nutrition, including serious vitamin deficiencies.

During 1942, 1,225 patients were admitted, the rations were poor and deaths frequent. By the end of the year the natural resilience, as the acute epidemics subsided, the arrival of a Red Cross parcel per head, and food gifts to the hospital from friends in Hong Kong, brought about some lightening of the clouds. Dr. P. S. Selwyn Clarke was deeply committed to the welfare of Hong Kong's Chinese citizens of all classes, and also to the allied prisoners. He was not interned because the Japanese feared a major epidemic as much as the allies. He arranged for the delivery of gifts of food to the hospital twice a week, until his arrest on a charge of spying in May 1943. Dr. Selwyn Clarke was confined to the cells of the Supreme Court in the utmost squalor for twenty months of intensive interrogation. However he survived. After the Japanese surrender he returned to his office in Hong Kong to reestablish medical and health control in the Colony.

Mr. R. Zindell, a neutral Swiss citizen, was in charge of the Red Cross organization in Hong Kong. The Japanese allowed him no scope to help the prisoners. However his tenacity and skill enabled the hospital to hold emergency stores of food, as the arrival of rations proved equally erratic for the allies and Japanese guards alike. He was not allowed to investigate atrocities, the news of which was now filtering through to the outside world. The Viceroy of India strongly deprecated references to assaults on women in Hong Kong, stating that they would have an unsettling effect in India. He was overruled by the War Cabinet who favoured publicity because world opinion might put a stop to the atrocities and 'the fighting men will know how they will be treated.'[2]

Early in 1942 the Japanese began to pay commissioned allied officers, many of whom subscribed on a voluntary basis to provide extra diets and other necessities for hospital patients.

Colonel Tokunaga, the commander of all the POW camps in Hong Kong, was thick-set, fat and a little over average height. He never spoke to a patient, and due to his gross negligence he was largely responsible for many deaths. He was sentenced to be hanged by the War Crimes Court in Hong Kong in 1946, a sentence later commuted to life imprisonment, and later still to twenty years. Tokunaga lived in a splendid house near the Argyle Street POW camp in Kowloon, with a Chinese mistress. Every Saturday she contrived to send parcels from his store to her old friends in the POW camps.

A Japanese army doctor, Lieutenant Saito, was in immediate charge of the Bowen Road Hospital and medically of all the POW camps. He acquired an evil reputation, partly due to his haphazard selection of patients for hospital. He seldom saw them, and many who might have survived if sent to hospital were not chosen. Saito, too, was condemned to death, but this sentence was later commuted to fifteen years.

Japanese officers and NCOs usually wore swords and field boots. The guards later were Formosan (Taiwanese) and were pettily officious and quick to take offence. They sometimes slapped patients for no apparent reason. The guards did not appear well fed, and their clothing was poor quality. A brisk business sprang up between them and the patients, in negotiations for which neither side had any confidence in the other. On one occasion a sentry wanted to take a patient's article away for valuing before making his offer, but the patient would not agree to this. Eventually a compromise was reached; the sentry left his loaded rifle with the patient as a surety, while the article was valued. The patient kept the rifle in his bed and in due course the sentry returned and a bargain was struck.

The acute shortage of medicines accounted for many deaths. However by an extraordinary stroke of good fortune, the lack of medicines was marginally solved due to a diseased prostitute. The curse of the Shamshuipo Camp was Kinawa Inouye, a Canadian born in British Columbia of Japanese parents who was known to the prisoners as Slap Happy or the Kamloops Kid. He was a sadistic pigmy responsible for a number of murders, for which he was executed after the war. One night he came to Sub-Lieutenant Bush with a painful venereal disease. He asked to be cured by Major Ashton-Rose, since he was too scared to report to the Japanese medical authorities. The British doctor willingly treated him, having first secured more than enough medicines to do so. More infected Japanese followed, and a steady flow of drugs was surreptitiously received. After that night Slap Happy appeared more subdued and gave considerably less trouble.

On 28 November, 1942, the first Red Cross food parcels were delivered. They were magnificent, containing jam, sugar, meat puddings and other delicacies. A shipment of cereal from India made a fine porridge, and helped those suffering from beri-beri.

Two months earlier the greatest single tragedy of the campaign had occurred. On 25 September, 1942, 1,816 British prisoners-of-war were assembled at Shamshuipo Camp and addressed by Lieutenant Hideo Wada: 'You are going to be taken away from Hong Kong,' he said, 'to a beautiful country where you will be well looked-after and well-treated. I shall be in charge of the party. Take care of your health. Remember my face.'[3]

Two days later they sailed in the *Lisbon Maru*, crammed into three holds. The ship was armed, carried Japanese troops and bore no signs that she was a POW ship. At 7.06 am 1 October she was hit by the fourth torpedo of USS *Grouper*. The Submarine Commander saw no damage through his periscope, and fired two more at 8.45 am. Gradually it became clear to the prisoners in the holds that the ship had been disabled and was listing. At 9.00 am Wada had the hatches to the holds sealed down. The prisoners had received no food for 24 hours and their water was exhausted.

Morale was maintained by the leadership of Lieutenant-Colonel Stewart, the Commanding Officer of the Middlesex. The water was rising in one of the holds, and several patients died. The extreme heat and shortage of air caused some to lose consciousness. Stewart organized a break-out. At 9.00 am, on the following day, when the air was dangerously foul and the ship appeared to be sinking, the hatches were forced. The Japanese guards opened fire from the bridge, but were overwhelmed. The other Japanese had already been taken off by other ships. Captain N. H. Cuthbertson, Adjutant of the Royal Scots, wearing his Glengarry, was the last to leave his hold, after ensuring that everyone had escaped from it. Major L. W. D. Walker, Second-in-Command of the Royal Scots, gave his lifebelt to a non-swimmer and was not seen again. Those who could, swam five miles to the nearest of the Sing Pang Islands off the coast of Chekiang Province. Although Japanese were in the area, the Chinese villagers set off in junks and sampans to rescue all they could. The following day the Japanese landed and collected all the prisoners except three, who eventually escaped to Chungking.

843 were killed or drowned in this disaster. Of those who survived, a further 244 died working as slave labour in Japan. In February, 1949, thirteen survivors revisited the Island and witnessed the Governor of Hong Kong presenting a motor fishing launch to the islanders, who had saved so many lives. One survivor of the *Lisbon Maru* who died of exhaustion and malnutrition in captivity shortly afterwards was Lieutenant-Colonel Stewart. He was given the Distinguished Service Order, an extremely rare honour when awarded posthumously. 'Die-Hard' was a fitting Regimental motto for this very gallant soldier.

In August, 1943, a further group of about five hundred mainly Canadian POWs were despatched to Japan. They were fortunate to be accompanied by Sub-Lieutenant Lewis Bush, RNVR who, as already mentioned, knew Japan from before the war and was fluent in the language, and also by Matsuda, a Japanese guard, nicknamed Cardiff Joe because he spoke English with a Welsh accent. He had once been an officer in a British merchant ship and hated all Germans. He was one of the handful of guards for whom the POWs developed both respect and affection.

On their arrival in Osaka in September, 1943, the POWs noticed that everything was drab and the people looked shoddy, the women mostly in dirty, grey kimonos, the men in the dreary-looking national uniform. Nobody seemed cheerful despite the fact that, according to Imperial HQ, the Japanese were enjoying victories on every front. Gone was the scenic beauty, smiling geishas and women in bright kimonos wearing big obi bows like butterflies perched on their backs.

Most of the Winnipeg Grenadiers in the group ended up at Niigata. Over one hundred of these fine Canadians died there during their first winter through sickness, and a tragic avalanche which almost buried the camp. They now lie in the British Commonwealth Cemetery at Hedogaya, near Yokohama.

*   *   *

Early in 1942, the Japanese segregated Indian POWs for political reasons. The majority were separated from their officers and doctors, and sent to a special camp in Kowloon. Doctor Newton recalls: 'There was no-one who could instil any discipline into them. As a result the dysentery cases among them used the whole camp as a latrine and this made the fly menace appalling. There were armies of maggots crawling up and down the concrete gutters around the huts, presumably because they were warm in the sun. The Indians did not wash themselves and the smell of dirty humanity combined with that of a number of dysentery cases lying on the floor, added to the smell of pus, made the most revolting conditions.'

However, as with the British and Canadian POWs, self-respect and discipline soon replaced the shock and humiliation of surrender, and conditions improved. So much so that the Indians later smuggled to the British officers a parcel that contained a large sum of Japanese money. The gesture was much appreciated, but the money was returned. Many of the Indians had Chinese friends and they were able to arrange to have some food parcels sent to the British camp.

The Japanese put great pressure on the Indians to turn traitor against Britain. The vast majority remained loyal and were sent to Canton, Hainon and Swatow. There they were subjected to incessant propaganda and extremely harsh treatment. Their leaders were beaten in front of their men. They were all employed on heavy manual labour and given insufficient rations, without adequate medical care or Red Cross supplies.

The Indian soldiers had distinguished themselves in the fighting, and they did so once more in their appalling captivity.

Captain M. A. Ansari, whose company of the 5/7 Rajputs had held the rearguard at the Devil's Peak Peninsula, was starved and tortured by the Japanese in an attempt to seduce him from his loyalty to the British.

Captain Ansari was a tall, good-looking officer, nicknamed the 'Brown Bomber' by his brother officers. He was extremely popular, although before the war he was often in trouble in fights with other officers. 'I was warned by the GOC that if I wished to remain in command (then of the battalion) I must control him,' recalls Brigadier Wallis. 'I replied that once the fighting started Captain Ansari would render a good account.'[4] Had he changed his allegiance to the Japanese, others would have followed his example. However he held firm, and he was eventually beheaded. He was subsequently awarded the George Cross.

A very young soldier, Gunner Mohd Afsor, although hung upside down by his heels for many hours, refused to collaborate. Finally the Japanese took him down, saluted him and said: 'You very brave man.' He was later awarded the British Empire Medal.

*   *   *

A few prisoners in Hong Kong were in touch with the British Army Aid Group run by British officers in China, and also with the Hong Kong resistance groups which consisted of very dedicated and courageous Chinese.

Major Price, Second-in-Command of the Royal Rifles, on discharge from hospital had been sent to Argyle Street POW camp. When he was about to rejoin the Canadians at Shamshuipo, he was asked by Colonel Newnham to smuggle an innocuous packet of Japanese tooth powder to Captain Douglas Ford of the Royal Scots. He was transferred to Shamshuipo in February 1943 and handed over the precious packet, the contents of which he never discovered. He recalls meeting Captain Ford: 'A young, fair-haired Scotsman, sturdy, serious, with a strong character, full of courage, determination and resourcefulness. Douglas Ford proved to have all these qualities in abundance, and in addition a modesty unusual in one who undertook such dangerous responsibilities and grave risks – there could not be found a better comrade or finer gentleman.' It was Ford who was organising the smuggling of precious medicines and messages into the POW camps with the help of several other British and Canadian POWs who were in touch with the Chinese while working at Kai Tak airport under the Japanese.

On 1 July, 1943, during a softball game, Japanese guards arrested three key couriers, Sgt. Routledge, Royal Canadian Corps of Signals, Sergeant Hardy, RAF, and Flight Lieutenant H. E. Gray. Japanese search parties hunted unsuccessfully for incriminating evidence which Ford had concealed in an old football hanging on the wall of his room. Two Chinese contacts beyond the wire, known to Major Price only as No 58 and 71, were tortured and executed. Ten days later Captain Ford and Colonel Newnham were arrested too. All were held in solitary confinement on starvation rations at Stanley undergoing prolonged interrogation and torture. They refused to implicate anyone and accepted the whole responsibility themselves. Hardy and Routledge were sentenced to fifteen years imprisonment and despatched to a Chinese prison in Canton, where they were lucky to survive the war. On 1st December, 1943, the three officers were tried on a charge of espionage and condemned to death. For eighteen days Newnham, Ford and Gray lay in their cells with no medical attention, no hope of reprieve, and forbidden to write a note of farewell to relatives and friends. The long period between sentence and execution was designed to break their nerve. It failed utterly. On 18 December, 1943, they were taken out almost too weak to move, to face a firing squad. All three were subsequently awarded the George Cross in recognition of their gallantry and courage, both moral and physical, during their terrible ordeal. 'I had recommended Gray for the Victoria Cross,' recalls Wing Commander Sullivan. 'The Air Ministry reminded me that this was awarded for bravery in the face of the enemy, to which I replied that many VCs were won in the heat of battle surrounded by one's comrades. Gray, Newnham and Ford had deserved theirs in the cold of the torture chamber.'

General Maltby and Brigadier Wallis discussed what to do with an officer they were certain was a Japanese informer in their midst. 'We considered whether I should walk round the camp with him on the exercise circuit and accidentally see to it that he fell into the live wires,' wrote Brigadier Wallis later. A Doctor planned a more sinister death for the traitor. 'We decided against any such action, feeling that in the end God would bring him to his just deserts.'[5]

* * *

Between 27 and 29 July, 1943, the Americans bombed Japanese positions and oil depots in Hong Kong. Morale soared. Heavy bombing raids were maintained intermittently throughout the next two years.

In one unfortunate incident an American plane, attacking the Japanese batteries at Stanley, dropped a bomb which killed fourteen internees. The prisoners announced collectively that they had no bitter feelings towards the Americans; on the contrary, they had nothing but admiration for the air crews. Those captured had been drenched in petrol by the Japanese and burnt to death.

General Maltby had obtained a promise from General Sakai at the surrender that he could share imprisonment with his men. However he and thirteen other senior officers were moved to Formosa on 4 August, 1943, as a punishment for the successes of a few very determined and courageous men and women who had escaped from the horrors of imprisonment.

18
They Escaped

Those in the POW camps who favoured escape were few, due to the certainty of the reprisals against the remaining prisoners, the danger of being caught and then executed, and their deteriorating physical strength. Most escapes were in the months immediately after the surrender, when the POW camps were least organised.

Colonel Lindsay Ride was a professor at Hong Kong University who had commanded the Volunteers' Field Ambulance. He had been accompanied into Shamshuipo Prison by Francis Lee Yiu-Piu, his Chinese clerk in the university physiology department who was also a Corporal in the Volunteers. 'Francis' devotion was such that he wanted to help me,' recalls Ride. After only a few days in prison Yiu-Piu escaped on a sampan, having arranged to return twenty four hours later to collect Colonel Ride, who meanwhile sought others who wanted to escape. He eventually persuaded two studious lecturers at the Hong Kong University, both officers in the HK RNVR, to accompany him. Their escape was successful due to Yiu-Piu's loyalty and courage. The following day the Japanese interrogated Major Crawford, the former Second-in-Command of the Field Ambulance. 'Where is Ride, the senior Medical Officer?' they demanded. Crawford replied that he had never heard of such a man and that he, Crawford, was the senior Medical Officer. The Japanese left thoroughly perplexed. Colonel Ride remained in China for the duration of the war, to organise the British Army Aid Group which rendered vital assistance to other escapers and to civilians fleeing from the Colony. He was also instrumental in having supplies and information smuggled into the camps. Yiu-Piu later returned to Hong Kong carrying secret messages. He was arrested and sentenced to death, but escaped once more. After the war he was commissioned into the Volunteers.

Privates D. Hodges and J. Gallagher of the Royal Scots also escaped from Shamshuipo. Hodges, aged twenty-nine, came from Cork and had served in India, Egypt, Sudan and Palestine. Both successfully made their way together to Chungking, although they had no friends to help them and no knowledge of the country. They were each awarded the Distinguished Conduct Medal, fought in North West Europe and remained in the Regular Army after the war. Gallagher was killed in Korea in 1951.

Captain A. G. Hewitt, the Adjutant of the Middlesex battalion, Captain Douglas Scriven, the battalion's Medical Officer, and Pilot Officer D. Crossley from New Zealand, escaped from the same camp on 1 February, 1942. In the weeks of preparation beforehand they had bought a prismatic compass for twenty cigarettes, obtained a sketch map of the Japanese positions, hoarded a small stock of tinned food, and done their best to get physically fit. General Maltby gave them $800 and messages for the British Ambassador in China.

The sentries were very active that moonlit night, firing several shots at shadows and at dogs outside the camp. The three officers escaped by sampan, but the coolie paddling them demanded 'tea money' so noisily that the sentries opened fire. 'We flung ourselves on the bottom of the sampan as bullets brushed over our heads, some hitting the water just in front of us. But the moon clouded over and the coolie resumed paddling as fast as he could to a beach,' recalls Hewitt.[1] By 3.00 am they found they were lost in a maze of small hills and broken country. They felt too exhausted to go any further and slept in an old grave. Shortly after dawn, in a thick mist, they met a Chinese who warned them of Japanese patrols nearby. After hiding them in a valley, he took Captain Hewitt's watch and some of their money and promised to return a few hours later to help them. Nothing happened until shortly after midnight, when suddenly seven Chinese armed with choppers and bayonets jumped upon them.

After a desperate struggle the Chinese turned and fled, leaving Hewitt badly injured by bayonet cuts. It was now very dark and raining heavily. They hid throughout the second day. Fortunately Scriven, who spoke Cantonese fluently, succeeded in persuading friendly Chinese to provide them with bowls of rice, fish and vegetables. Scriven's appearance caused the Chinese great amusement, for he wore extraordinary khaki drill pantaloons which came down over his knees, and a monocle which earned him the nickname 'Three Eyes'.

That night the three officers set off again, avoiding Japanese patrols. But they were ambushed once more by armed Chinese ruffians who beat them, stole their kit, money, food, watches and General Maltby's messages. After an impassioned speech by Scriven, the compass was returned. They crossed into China on the fifth night, and there met a very big Chinese, Percy Davis, who was half Jamaican Negro. He had owned a radio shop near Shamshuipo Camp and recognized them all. He led them to a group of seventeen bandits, who searched the officers thoroughly. All were well-dressed, in new Homburg hats and new dark European suits. Each carried two pistols, three or four watches, Parker fountain pens, and had gold fillings in their teeth. Banditry was obviously a profitable profession.

Captain Hewitt recalls: 'They were friendly and said they would lead us through to the Chinese Army. Over to our left we could hear Japanese trucks moving up and down the road. After marching for much of the day we had a long wait, with sentries all round us and a bandit sitting in front of us twirling a Smith and Wesson six-shooter round his finger by the trigger guard. It was fully loaded and I never knew why it didn't go off.' At dusk they watched a wedding ceremony, which included a coolie beating an enormous gong while an ardent young Communist lectured them.

After resuming their march north, they met Communist guerrillas who said that the officers had no right to pass through their territory. 'We spent a week with the guerrillas, closely guarded but well fed with ducks' eggs and rice. They questioned us continually about arms dumps in Hong Kong and asked us to stay and fight with them. This we refused, but Scriven lectured on first-aid and sanitation. I gave them instruction on care and maintenance of arms and other odd subjects and Crossley sang to them at night round the camp fires. We found that many of our tunes were patriotic songs to them: the "British Grenadiers" and the "Eton Boating Song" were especially popular.' They later had a long march in pitch dark and bitter cold, with the Japanese close by. On Chinese New Year's Eve vast quantities of rice wine were washed down with goose. When the guerrillas were too drunk to carry on, the three officers 'borrowed' their blankets and slept in comfort.

They eventually reached the Chinese Army HQ in Waichow,

a large and once beautiful Chinese city of lakes and artistic bridges and pagodas. After eleven days on a boat going up the East River and four more on a bumpy truck, they reached Kukong, where the party broke up. Crossley was sent on quickly to India where he spent three months in hospital, and later fought in North Africa. After a rest of ten days, Scriven returned to the Japanese-occupied territories, to repay the Communist guerillas who had helped them and to organize an escape route for others. Although nearly recaptured by the Japanese, he succeeded in getting his beautiful Chinese girl friend out of Hong Kong to India. He now practises in Hong Kong once more. Finally, Captain Hewitt, after five weeks in a Methodist mission hospital, set out alone on a two-month trek of a thousand miles to Chungking. After reaching the city on the vast yellow waters of the Yangtse-Kiang River, he flew over the jungles and mountains of Burma and Tibet to Calcutta, accompanied by American pilots who had bombed Tokyo in April, 1942.

Lieutenant F. H. Fairclough had been serving with 17th Heavy Anti-Artillery Battery, Hong Kong and Singapore Royal Artillery, before the surrender at Brick Hill near Aberdeen. On Christmas Eve he had disbanded the fifty Chinese artillery recruits who were completely untrained and had been sent to the gun sites on the out-break of hostilities. After encouraging them to infiltrate through the Japanese lines, his thoughts turned to his Christmas lunch which was to be accompanied by half a bottle of Plymouth gin, a tin of excellent potatoes and the last of his Balkan Sobranis. However at 4.00 am on Christmas morning the Japanese attacked in strength.

The Punjabis to the front of the guns held up the enemy for twenty minutes before turning and fleeing back, leaving their arms and ammunition in the trenches. The 3.7 anti aircraft guns were used in the ground role and by keeping up rapid fire the Japanese were held off for three hours before over-running the position by a bayonet charge. Fairclough was shot in the chest and collapsed. On recovering consciousness he recalls 'looking up straight into the eyes of a Jap soldier who, realising that I was still alive, took careful aim and shot me again.' He was left for dead, and it was not until about twelve days later that he was imprisoned, eventually at Shamshuipo.

One corner of the POW camp jutted out into the harbour and, by cutting down a partition, Fairclough built a small raft with Captain J. Wedderburn. They pushed it through the wire one dark night, but discovered it would not float let alone carry anything, and so they took the floats out of toilet tanks which were fixed beneath the raft. Just as they were about to push off the following night, Wedderburn had such a severe attack of diarrhoea that the escape had to be postponed once more. However the next night they jumped into the sampan of some Chinese who were surreptitiously selling food through the wire. They were rowed to safety, and after many adventures made their way overland to India.

Those who escaped were apprehensive, with good reason, of the repercussions on those left behind. The morning after one escape the senior RAF officer was among those arrested. Wing-Commander Sullivan had seen his aircraft destroyed in the first few minutes of the Japanese invasion, after which, according to him, he 'had spent an inglorious battle doing odd jobs in Fortress HQ.'[2] After Hewitt's group had escaped he was sent with three other RAF officers, Wing-Commander H. T. Bennett, Flight Lieutenant H. E. Gray and F. Hennessey, to a Saigon jail where they were thrown into an eighteen by fifteen foot cell full of so many Japanese defaulters that they could not lie down. Sullivan soon fell seriously ill with amoebic dysentery and was removed to a Japanese military prison where he was given fruit and illustrated papers by friendly Japanese patients who had been wounded in Malaya. 'After three weeks I was returned to jail still in very poor shape,' he recalls. 'On 9 February, 1942, I was given a banana to celebrate the fall of Singapore, and on the Emperor's birthday we received seaweed as a great treat. In July we were returned to Hong Kong on a freighter with a gaping hole in her side where she had been torpedoed.' The voyage was remarkable for the kindness of the Japanese crew, soldiers and 'comfort girls' who continuously offered the RAF officers sweets, fruit, whisky and cocoanuts. 'This pleasant interlude came to an abrupt halt when we returned to a cell in Hong Kong,' recalls Sullivan. 'Why did they send us to Saigon: to obtain information from us or to punish us for assisting in the escape? The Japanese were a weird crowd!'[3]

Several groups also escaped from Stanley internment camp. The first to do so consisted of the pretty English girl, Gwen

Priestwood, accompanied by a police superintendent, Anthony Bathurst, a missionary's son born in China. He had a map, compass, Colt .45 and spoke Cantonese, and so made an ideal companion for the dangers ahead.

On 19 March, 1942, the night before the escape, Gwen Priestwood put on all her rings, pearls, rubies and diamonds for the last time. The following day she sold all but the pearls to raise money for the journey. No Cantonese would steal pearls for they are sewn into burial robes to light the dead to the next world, and a stolen pearl will give no light. That night the two escapers crawled through the barbed wire. Immediately Gwen Priestwood's thirty-pound pack caught in the fence, but they eventually wriggled it free.

Within a few hours they had become hopelessly lost. After an exhausting climb, they sheltered for much of the night in a disused pill-box. To their dismay they discovered the following morning that they were twelve hundred feet above the internment camp, but still barely two miles from it. They watched a Japanese patrol boat shelling Chinese fishing junks. As the junks' crews took to their lifeboats, the Japanese machine-gunned them, and not a boat reached shore. The blue-clad bodies floated a little while and then sank. The two pushed on again that night with this vivid reminder of the barbarity of their enemy.

The following night they met a sympathetic fisherman who arranged for his nephew to take them across to the mainland in a sampan. The Chinese refused all payment and warned them of robber bands. The two escapers were next befriended by villagers who had converted a junk into a small warship, with a machine-gun on a high poop. Every member of the crew wore tattered clothing and a dirty towel around his head. They glowered and spat thunderously at frequent intervals, and seemed to expect a Japanese attack at any moment. After a day at sea, Bathurst and Gwen Priestwood struck inland through wild, attractive country. Eventually they met a smartly dressed Chinese officer, Captain Chung Mao Hing, who provided them with bicycles, and coolies to peddle them while the escapers sat pillion-style behind. Bathurst's coolie was so small and the progress so slow that he reversed their roles. The sight of a white foreigner giving a coolie a free ride caused much amusement and questioning. Both coolies gravely announced that the policeman was completely insane – an explanation which was readily accepted.

Several days later Bathurst decided to stay to fight with the Chinese guerrillas, and Gwen Priestwood sadly went on alone. She still had over a thousand miles to go to Chungking and was suffering occasionally from malaria. Her crumpled, dirty clothes were riddled with lice. Nevertheless she completed the journey to Chungking in under a month by truck, rickshaw, train, a squat paddle-steamer and the last remaining civilian plane in China. On arrival she handed the British Ambassador her most precious possession: a roll of toilet paper. Wrapped inside it next to the cardboard core were thin strips of tissue paper on which were written the names of all the internees at Stanley. She received in return all the hospitality of the Embassy, including the luxury of a hot bath and a much-prized gift of soap. Several months later she flew to Calcutta where she persuaded a blond Captain of a Norwegian freighter bound for New York to carry her away from the horrors of war.

*   *   *

On 23 May, 1942, all prisoners were ordered by the Japanese to sign a guarantee that they would not escape. Among those who refused to do so was a Canadian, Lance-Corporal J. Porter. He was taken to the North Point POW Camp Commandant who for several hours begged him to sign the pledge. He was given two helpings of beef stew, cups of tea filled with sugar and invited to help himself from a silver cigarette case which was placed in front of him. The following day he was taken to a senior Japanese officer who appeared astonished to learn that Porter had volunteered for the war. The officer remarked on the Canadian's bravery in refusing to sign and added that he wished the Japanese behaved in such a way. 'I replied that I was not doing it because I was brave, but that I was doing it for my King. The interpreter then slapped my face hard,' recalls Porter.[4] He was taken to Stanley Prison with six others. The conditions there were foul, they were shaken awake every hour throughout each night, beaten with truncheons and urged to sign. 'On 31 May our food and water was stopped. Several of my fellow prisoners were suffering from dysentery, no toilet paper was supplied and the mess in the cells was frightful. Their sufferings became so acute that on 4 June we decided to sign the form.'

By July, 1942, Colonel Ride's British Army Aid Group was established in Waichow, ninety miles away in China, under two Majors in the Royal Artillery, J. D. Clague, and L. S. White, both of whom had themselves escaped from Hong Kong. Through the regular system of communication, described earlier, Clague urged the POWs to escape in parties of six which would be guided to safety. 'Such plans were considered carefully from every angle, and finally discarded,' wrote Major Price later. 'The risks were too great, and experience had taught us that mass punishment inevitably followed one single escape. 150 might die for the possible escape and safety of half a dozen. Instead we planned a mass escape to take place during an air raid.'[5] They hoped that about a thousand Chinese guerrillas, to be concealed in the ruined houses beyond the camp, would enable the POWs to break out.

General Maltby felt convinced that 'it was the correct decision in not attempting escapes by small parties or even individuals. In all three camps the general standard of health had reached a very low level, and any escape would have caused severe and immediate repercussions and further privations that would have been fatal to many. Therefore our aim, which unfortunately was never to materialise, was that a collection of food, arms and ammunition should be established in the nearby hills, a large diversion should be made by the guerillas accompanied perhaps by an air raid, and under cover of these there should be simultaneous breakouts from all three camps. One-third of our numbers, owing to their physical state, would have to be abandoned. Another third would have fallen in the subsequent fighting, but the remainder, we hoped, would be able to make their way to freedom and so continue to participate in the war. Ambitious perhaps, but that was our aim.'[6]

Colonel Ride realized that it was futile to rely upon the Chinese guerrillas for a mass escape into China. He proposed instead that the POWs should break out to Kai Tak airfield, where a *coup-de-main* airlift operation would carry them to safety. This plan was not accepted either by Ride's superiors. Nor was it accepted by the prisoners, for inadequate food had sapped their strength, and their will to do and to dare.

Nevertheless a few more small groups did try to escape. Lieutenant Proulx, HK RNVR, the former stockbroker, crawled through a drain from North Point Camp with two Dutch submarine officers. Fifty-nine days later he reached the HQ of General Chennault's American Flying Tigers in China.

Jan Marsman avoided internment by claiming Philippinian citizenship, and he fled to Chungking disguised as a Chinese. Private Russell of the Middlesex climbed over the wire and ran off for a two-day honeymoon with one of the girls from the Wanchai. He returned to camp with two black eyes, a broken rib and three missing teeth. C. Salter dyed his hair black and walked out with the Portuguese Red Cross. Four Winnipeg Grenadiers, J. H. Adams, G. Berzenski, P. J. Ellis and J. Payne escaped at night on 20 August, 1942, by climbing through the shell-damaged roof of the North Point Camp hospital. It is believed that they were captured and shot.

For over two years there was no successful escape from Shamshuipo camp. However a forty-one year old New Zealand naval officer of the RNZVR was determined to try. Lieutenant R. B. Goodwin wrote later: 'It would be so easy to sit back and wait for the war to end. Then visions of the future drifted into my thoughts and it seemed that an accusing spirit hovered on my shoulder, pointing a scornful finger. "You were afraid; your conscience was clear on every point, the way was open, and you were afraid to take the risk." Fear of my own soul was more powerful than any other. I was determined to go.'[7]

The night of Sunday 16 July, 1944, was miserable. Rain beat solidly down and squalls whistled around the camp as he wriggled under the concertina wire. An hour later he succeeded in climbing over a second fence without touching the electrified wires within it. Beyond was a third barbed wire fence which tore chunks from his flesh and clothing. The sentries were lazy, and the guard dogs were patrolling elsewhere. He waded into the sea and inflated the life jacket which he had kept hidden in a pillow for over two years. When he started to swim brilliant phosphorus marked every movement.

As he waded ashore he heard someone clumping along a road in wooden clogs. 'Suddenly a brilliant torch-beam streamed from right alongside me, and it held a Chinese coolie,' he recalls. 'Among mingled feelings of surprise and fright came the realisation that I was standing within two feet of a Japanese sentry, and also that some thirty yards to the right a narrow lane ran in towards the hills. There was my route.'

About a week later, his food exhausted and his feet a mass of bloody sores, Lieutenant Goodwin staggered into a Chinese village, Taimuisha, beyond the Border. He collapsed exhausted on a wooden bench. Everything seemed blurred, people appeared as black objects which danced in his vision. He realized that his sight was barely twenty-five percent effective, due to diet deficiency.

Goodwin learnt that the Communist guerrillas of Kwangtung were operating all through the Japanese-occupied territory, right into Kowloon City itself. They had blown up railway bridges and succeeded in a spectacular rescue of a United States pilot, D. W. Kerr, who had parachuted above Kai Tak. Goodwin was impressed by the strict discipline and high morale of the Communists, despite famine, disease and death which hovered close day by day. There was no love lost between them and Chiang Kai-Shek's Nationalists. Goodwin and others who escaped considered that the Nationalists were largely ineffective in their resistance to the Japanese, due to their incompetent leadership, pitiful equipment and the work of traitors. The Nationalist Army was run on lines that would not have been tolerated in any Western Country. Corruption was rife throughout its higher ranks, with the result that, in spite of their miserable pay, the officers waxed fat and wealthy, while the soldiers starved in rags.

As the naval officer was led further north for safety, the fame of the lone escaper preceded him. At one village he was presented with a bouquet of sweet-scented, white flowers and an umbrella. At the next a company of troops were lined up for his inspection, at the third bicycles were provided. On entering one village, Lieutenant Goodwin saw a chief waiting to greet him with a guard of honour, but his bicycle had gone berserk and he was out of control. Gathering speed as he went downhill, the naval officer charged between the headman and his troops while making frantic efforts to stop the bicycle, retain his balance, umbrella and bouquet, acknowledge the greetings of the Chief on one side and salute the troops on the other.

Goodwin reached Waichow three weeks after his escape, feeling very ill with malaria. There he met Colonel Ride's British Army Aid Group which was expecting him. The outpost included several officers with a secret radio. They were operating in considerable danger from traitors, and the very real possibility of being captured by the Japanese. The welcome of the British, and of the Americans who had their own radio stations, enabled the partially-blind New Zealander, who was tottering with fatigue, to feel that he could relax at last.

At Kweilin Colonel Ride introduced Goodwin to General Carton de Wiart, the formidable soldier with one arm, one eye and one Victoria Cross. The General was inspecting the forward area, which was overrun by the Japanese shortly afterwards. He listened attentively to the story of Goodwin's escape and gave orders that he was to be flown to safety by an RAF plane to Kunming that afternoon.

On 17 October, 1944, Goodwin flew to Calcutta and from there to Delhi, where he was able to tell Lord Louis Mountbatten, Supreme Allied Commander, South East Asia, of the conditions in Hong Kong. Goodwin finally reached his beloved New Zealand on 17 November, 1944, four months to the day after his escape from Shamshuipo. He was destined to return to Hong Kong with the relieving force in August, 1945, where he came face to face once more with Colonel Tokunaga, the cruel Commandant of the POW camps. Tokunaga failed to recognize Goodwin and started arrogantly to justify the execution of some prisoners. Suddenly the Japanese officer discovered Goodwin's identity, and blood drained from his face. He said no more.

There were only a few others who gambled with their lives in trying to escape the years of soul-destroying captivity and starvation. Several who succeeded modestly claimed no personal credit for surviving the 1,200 mile trek to Chungking. Perhaps they were right, for Luck played so great a part in every successful escape.

19
Occupation and Liberation

As a long term policy, the Japanese intended to subjugate the Chinese, to indoctrinate them and to absorb them fully into a Japanese Asia. In the meantime little was done to help or sustain them. Hong Kong's trade collapsed, and production from the thousand factories virtually ceased because raw materials became unobtainable, and markets had been cut off. The economy stagnated and food shortages soon developed, and worsened as the allied blockade of Japanese shipping later tightened into a noose round Hong Kong's sea lanes. Tens of thousands died from starvation, beri-beri and other deficiency diseases.

Hong Kong was occupied by 15,000 Japanese soldiers and 3,000 Japanese civilians, who cared little except to keep nominal control as caretakers until the war ended. Government departments closed, and many schools and other institutions also; Chinese 'white collar' workers therefore were not in demand, though some clerks, teachers and nurses remained at work under Japanese 'superiors'. In the schools that stayed open, Chinese children were taught Japanese and made to use it for their other lessons – not that there were many lessons, because history, geography and the English language all disappeared from the curriculum. By August, 1945, the number of children receiving education had shrunk from 120,000 in 1941 to 3,000, and this was reflected in the vast increase in juvenile delinquency.

Few Chinese received cash wages, and when the Japanese wanted them as coolies they worked for the traditional handful of rice a day. Chinese gangsterdom prospered. However the Japanese were shrewd enough to tolerate a small number of black marketeers, racketeers, gambling-den and brothel operators, and in return gained their assistance in reducing petty crime such as pilfering, and in exercising some control over potential trouble makers. The Japanese maintained a night curfew with the aid of dog patrols. Many Chinese were homeless, and so unable to keep off the streets at night. They were mauled to death if the dogs found them. Over twenty-two thousand dwellings were destroyed by bombing, shelling or neglect during the fighting and occupation.

There was little local guerrilla action against the Japanese, the exception being minor but persistent raiding and sabotage carried out by mainland Chinese bands from over and near the border.

In the face of starvation, unemployment, reduced educational and other social services, it is not surprising that the majority of the Chinese fled to their former homeland beyond the border.

A never-ending stream of hundreds of boats of every description flowed from the Colony from dawn to dusk. On the mainland the two roads that led north were often black with moving crowds. It was a journey not enlivened by hope, for every group knew that some of its number could not survive. They dropped out one by one, the very old and the very young going first, the weak tottering on as far as they could go and then lying down to die. The presence of robbers added new terror. They were quite merciless to their fellow countrymen; resistance meant death, and many were killed in an effort to save their few belongings.

By January, 1943, the population was below one million and by May, 1945, only 650,000 remained – one million Chinese had left Hong Kong during the occupation.

In the farming villages the enemy maintained a firm grip. They bled the countryside, almost every square inch of land being used for growing rice. The Japanese introduced Formosan rice to try to produce a heavier crop, but it attracted destructive insects. The soil was starved, fertilizers were unobtainable and manures very scarce since most of the domestic animals had been slaughtered.

At the time of the Japanese invasion there were over one hundred thousand fisherfolk living in about five thousand junks. During the occupation, the fishing industry was reduced to a chaotic condition, and the death rate from starvation among the fisherfolk was high. Their numbers were reduced to one-third of the pre-war total, and their vessels to less than half.

Public transport systems broke down through lack of spares, fuel and technicians. The handcart, bicycle and rickshaw came into their own to replace the 7,000 vehicles of 1941. Port facilities had suffered extensive damage as a result of the fighting, and subsequently through neglect. The harbour was littered with sunken wrecks, and only five hundred of the two thousand lighters operating in 1941 remained in service in 1945. Only two of the forty-eight commercial moorings survived, the remainder having been sunk or removed by the Japanese, while extensive damage had also been caused to ship-building and repair yards.

By the time the war with Japan ended, on 14 August, 1945, Hong Kong was down at heel, picked clean of her wealth. Prior to the Japanese surrender, huge tracts of Chinese territory around Hong Kong were in Japanese hands. The outlook for the POWs and internees was dismal, and many seriously doubted if any of them could survive. The Japanese 23rd Army holding the Hong Kong–Canton area by May, 1945, consisted of three divisions. There were no precise American or British plans to recapture the Colony. Instead Lieutenant-General Wedemeyer, the American Chief of Staff to General Chiang Kai-Shek, hoped to despatch Chinese divisions, which invariably were of dubious calibre, to force the Japanese troops and civilians in Hong Kong to surrender. A Japanese–Chinese war in the neighbourhood of the Colony would have been prolonged, the lives of the POWs and internees would have been jeopardized and it is doubtful if many of them would have survived. The decision by President Truman to use the atom bomb resulted in their release almost overnight. Seen in contrast with other possibilities, this was a wonderful outcome which was greeted with joyous disbelief.

But who was to claim Hong Kong? The Chinese Foreign Minister, Mr. T. V. Soong, in July, 1943, on a visit to London, had announced that it was a foregone conclusion that the entire Colony would be returned to China. However subsequent threats from the Chinese were less confident. The British Government adopted the policy of mentioning the question as seldom as possible and, whenever it was raised, treating it as a matter of course that there would be no change, and that the British possession needed no apology or justification. To the Americans, Britain took the line that Hong Kong's future was a question between Britain and China, and nobody else.

Gradually the British planned for the return to Hong Kong.

They were much assisted by the intelligence reports of Colonel Ride's British Army Aid Group. Even so, the abrupt Japanese surrender seemed to take the British by surprise. There was a delay of two weeks before units of the British Pacific Fleet, commanded by Rear-Admiral C. Harcourt, could reach the Colony.

During this period, with the Japanese only in token control, widespread looting by Chinese took place – of Japanese food stocks, of private houses and public property. The BBC was to refer to Hong Kong as 'the most thoroughly-looted place on earth'. Some control was exercised, illegally, by the mainland Chinese guerrillas. In the border areas and in some of the outer islands they firmly, but usually politely, established local administration alongside the Japanese. They thought, as did many others, that Hong Kong was to be taken over by China and not to be reoccupied by Britain. Almost every junk carried the Chinese flag, as did many of the buildings.

Meanwhile General Chiang Kai-Shek insisted on his right, as C-in-C China theatre, to accept Japan's surrender at Hong Kong, although he was prepared for Admiral Harcourt to act as his delegate. The British Foreign Office and Colonial Office were determined that Harcourt should receive Japan's surrender on behalf of Britain by virtue of her sovereignty over Hong Kong. A deadlock with China ensued. The American press, in particular, produced sensational stories of a race between Britain and China to receive the Japanese surrender at Hong Kong. Fortunately Prime Minister Attlee had obtained President Truman's agreement to the British policy, and Chiang Kai-Shek at last accepted the compromise that Admiral Harcourt should accept Japan's surrender on behalf of both Britain and China.

Paving the way for the reoccupation, much had been done by a temporary Administration of former British civil servants on their release from Stanley, headed by Mr. Grimson, the former Colonial Secretary. He had laboured far-sightedly throughout the internment to form a shadow administration, and was able to put it into effect immediately the surrender came. The only currency in circulation was the Japanese yen, and this was at best of doubtful value. But Mr. Grimson had been communicating, through underground channels, with London months before, asking that new Hong Kong dollars be printed in readiness for the liberation. They were in circulation less than a month after the surrender.

Agents were despatched to China to negotiate for supplies of essential food stuffs, to augment Japanese rice-stocks which were now confiscated and rationed out to the public.

The temporary Administration was badly handicapped by the lack of law-enforcement forces. They had to keep Japanese guards on duty. The looting was gradually checked, and an air of respectability began to creep back into the Colony.

The news of the Japanese surrender had reached the POW camps on 16 August, to be promptly denied by the Camp Commandant. But the Japanese guards were withdrawn on the following day, and the Union Jack was raised. On 29 August American planes dropped food, medical supplies and cigarettes from the air. The following day the Japanese delivered jam and eleven thousand packets of cigarettes for the ex-POWs, just as news reached everyone that British warships and aircraft carriers had been seen off Stanley.

Admiral Harcourt's fleet anchored in Hong Kong harbour, and at 5.00 pm he drove to Stanley Internment Camp. The National Anthem was sung and the flags of all nations represented in the camp were raised. A bugler sounded the Last Post in memory of the many who had died. The Hymn 'O God Our Help in Ages Past' was sung.

The hardships and indignities of life in the POW camps had been endured with a fortitude and stubborn good humour that won a very real, if intangible, honour to all. The morale and discipline of the prisoners of war, and of the civilians at Stanley, brought them through in triumphant fashion.

On 11 September, 1945, most of the prisoners sailed from Hong Kong in the *Empress of Australia*, on the long voyage via Manila, Singapore, Colombo, Aden and Suez to Liverpool. The accommodation in the ship was very crowded. Some of the ex-POWs reacted very unfavourably and the atmosphere on the troop decks became tense. While anchored in Colombo, Lady Mountbatten came on board, looking very smart in her Red Cross uniform. She went below to the troop decks, climbed on a mess table and spoke in simple and direct terms to the men. 'She drew their attention, probably for the first time, to the vastly different conditions in which life was being lived in ships and at home after six years of war,' recalls Lieutenant-

Colonel Bowie. 'Her talk showed her sympathy and her under-
standing and I have never known a speech to have a more direct
and immediate effect. The atmosphere on the troop decks
changed vastly for the better.'[1]

Empress of Australia reached Liverpool on 28 October, 1945,
having been delayed by storms and high winds. The difficult re-
adjustment for the POWs, after their lost years of captivity,
gradually started. Many died prematurely. A doctor treating a
Hong Kong survivor wrote later: 'It was an interesting experience, though heartbreaking, to learn that the elderly emaciated
gentleman before your eyes was a boy in his twenties.'

CAUSES OF THE DEFEAT

*Was it all worthwhile? What went wrong? Why were the allies defeated
in Hong Kong, on their own ground, after many years when the defences
could have been greatly improved?*

Students of the campaign can only be astonished by the
speed of the Japanese victory, bearing in mind that at no time
did they enjoy numerical superiority in infantry. Primarily this
was due to the advantage which in such circumstances must
always lie with the attacker. The defenders, too few in numbers
and too thinly spread, have no knowledge where the weight of
the attack is to be anticipated. So it can only be expected that
the assault, with the advantage of surprise, pressed forward in
great strength at a few points, will succeed in breaking through.
This the Japanese achieved, and then pushed forward to gain
possession of the commanding heights which dominate the
Island, and from that moment the campaign was lost.

The complete lack of air support, and inadequate sea power,
made the defeat of the Colony a foregone conclusion. The
absence of aircraft enabled eighty Japanese planes, based on
Canton, to observe and bomb where they wished. The Royal
Navy had insufficient ships decisively to interfere with the sea-
borne assault, or to determine where it would fall. General
Maltby tried to defend the whole perimeter of the Island for too
long, instead of relying on strongly defended localities which
could have destroyed or at least delayed the enemy. The allies
lacked sufficient troops to defend Hong Kong which, together
with deficiencies in equipment and training was due to the fundamental weakness of a democracy hoping above all things to

avoid war.

A first class division, in addition to what was available, was required, with full supporting arms and aircraft, for the successful defence of Hong Kong in the circumstances in which it was attacked. Whether, however, it would have done more than postpone ultimate defeat is a different matter, for there would have been no possibility of resupply and reinforcement of a larger force, and the Japanese would have had little difficulty in increasing the weight of their attack with additional formations from the Chinese mainland.

The Japanese 38th Division consisted of highly-trained troops with a wealth of battle experience from years of fighting in China. Their artillery was greatly reinforced beyond the normal establishment. By contrast, the British official history records that, 'The British forces consisted mainly of units employed overlong on garrison duties, indifferently equipped, lacking experience of warfare and even of battle training, and hastily formed into extempore formations.'

Lack of mules and pack equipment, and the shortage of ammunition, particularly for training before the war, prevented the allies from making good use of their mortars, whereas the Japanese handled theirs with commendable skill and devastating effect. As war with Japan was regarded as improbable, and to save money and avoid unpopular decisions, the machine-guns were usually sited, as in Singapore, in easily identifiable pillboxes, rather than concealed in reconstructed houses with good fields of fire. The Japanese machine-guns were well-supplied with armour-piercing ammunition which penetrated the steel shutters of concrete pillboxes and shelters.

Early in 1942, the British Military Adviser in Chungking, after interviewing the escapers from Hong Kong, tried to analyse the causes of the Colony's defeat. Their testimony greatly blamed a soft unhealthy atmosphere, lack of confidence in the local government, and the unreality of fighting on 'home ground'. Others emphasized that the Japanese soldiers had been grossly underestimated. Several spoke highly of the Chinese who, they said: 'Stood bombing excellently. Cooperated wholeheartedly if trusted, and were most useful against fifth column.' The Japanese use of impressed labour, the importance of fighting lightly equipped, and the need for mobile reserves were all emphasized.

There were other fundamental reasons for the allied defeat; prominent among which was bad intelligence. When the Japanese were described as having withdrawn to Canton 'distinctly nervous of being attacked',[2] they had 38th Division and a brigade, and over twelve battalions of artillery within forty miles of Hong Kong's border. General Maltby ignored information from inland China, preferring his own intelligence reports which proved futile. However he deserves considerable credit for having all his forces at their battle stations the day before the invasion – a contrast to Pearl Harbour. General Grasett, the previous GOC, deserves no gratitude for convincing in turn both the Canadian and British CGSs that additional battalions would make 'all the difference' to the defence of Hong Kong. Five hundred and fifty-seven Canadians never returned to their country due to this misplaced optimism, and the grossly-inadequate intelligence which so underrated Japanese fighting capabilities.

The lack of sufficient forces has already been mentioned. With the benefit of hindsight, it can be seen that the decision to fight on the Gin Drinkers' line when only three battalions were available, was a mistake. Air Chief Marshal Sir Robert Brooke-Popham stated in his despatch that at least two divisions would have been required to hold the Gin Drinkers' Line. The Shingmun Redoubt was insufficiently supported by fire, and was isolated with an open flank; no plans had been made, nor had formations rehearsed, for an immediate counter attack in the event of its fall. The Royal Scots were asked to achieve the impossible, and the redoubt fell in a few hours, although it was expected to hold for a week.

However valid all these criticisms may be, the overriding reason for the defeat lay in insufficient forces with adequate training for a rapid, highly-flexible defence against a first-class enemy. Tactically the allies were completely outclassed, as they were throughout the Malayan and Burma campaigns of 1941–43. The Maginot Line mentality induced by pillboxes and deep shelters gave way to utter bewilderment when quick counter attacks across country were called for. Objectives were seldom won, and if won seldom retained. Practically every allied move was made by road, whereas the Japanese came straight across country. They scrambled to the top of Tai Mo Shan, and straight from North Point to Mount Parker and

Jardine's Lookout. The allies moved along the road from Fan-ling, along the road to Kowloon, along the road from Sai Wan to Stanley, and from Repulse Bay and Victoria to Wong Nei Chong Gap. This obsession with road movement, due to inade-quate training to move fast across country, meant that the Japanese usually reached their objectives first, without meeting any serious opposition, although they were often moving by night and across unfamiliar territory.

Canada deserves infinite gratitude for sending rein-forcements to Hong Kong, when the international situation was so precarious. Nevertheless there was no justification for the Canadian CGS sending two battalions well-known to be untrained for anything other than mundane garrison guard duties. Trained and uncommitted battalions, impatient for action, were available, but were not chosen because the urgency was not understood. In any event it can be seen today that the decision to reinforce Hong Kong at the eleventh hour was a mistake. The arrival of two extra battalions was expected to be a strong deterrent, but had no such effect.

To what extent did the ruthless ferocity and fanatical cour-age of the Japanese soldier contribute to victory? Is there evi-dence that a more primitive nation, contemptuous of casualties, is more likely to fight better? Perhaps so, but victory usually lies with the better-trained, better-led and better-equipped. In the closing battle of the Burma campaign, in July, 1945, the Japan-ese Twenty-Eighth Army admitted twelve thousand killed and missing, while the allies suffered only ninety-five killed and three hundred and twenty-two wounded. General Slim's forces without lavish equipment, despite the monsoon and a reduc-tion in air support, were killing Japanese at a rate of more than a hundred to one. IV Corps had taken over seven hundred Japanese prisoners – an unheard of ratio, at least ten times as high as ever before. In the final analysis, therefore, the extra-ordinary fighting mentality of the Japanese must be considered with relativity. Many would argue that they did not prove better soldiers than the Germans.

General Maltby concluded his despatches: 'I submit that although I and my forces may have been a hostage to fortune, we were a detachment that deflected [the enemy] from more important objectives . . . Strategically we gambled and lost, but it was a worthwhile gamble.'³ Or was it? Few gambling men would bet on a hand so stacked against them, or subsequently have sought to justify the game when the losses were so grave, (although greater risks with more calamitous results were taken in Norway and Greece).

2,113 allies were killed, died of wounds or missing, and 1,332 were seriously wounded in Hong Kong. Nevertheless General Maltby was right. For political and moral reasons Hong Kong had to be defended. Many Chinese would have been seriously discouraged from continuing their weary and interminable struggle against Japan, if Britain had lacked the courage and determination to resist and had abandoned the Colony to the mercy of the Japanese before they had even declared war. Such a sordid act of appeasement would also have shaken the neutral Americans, who were then strengthening their forces in the Pacific while critically assessing Britain's determination to fight on.

The Japanese troops committed to the Colony were urgently needed elsewhere, for only eleven divisions could be spared for the sweep south. Within weeks of the Colony's surrender the regiments, seriously weakened from casualties, were despatched towards Timor, Java and Sumatra. The Japanese casualties were said to have numbered 2,654 and some evidence suggests that the figure was considerably higher.

AFTERMATH

Within one month of the Japanese surrender, trains, ferries, telephones, electric power, lighting, docks and wharves were all working once more, albeit on a reduced scale. The corpses found rotting in the streets were buried; the filthy hospitals cleaned up; rice, oil, fuel, wood and vegetables were imported, and trade rapidly recovered. Encouraged by this work of restoration, in the six months following the Japanese surrender two hundred and fifty thousand Chinese flocked into the Colony. Hong Kong had soon staged a remarkable recovery.

Meanwhile, evidence was being gathered about those responsible for the atrocities. Lieutenant-General Sakai, the Japanese Commander-in-Chief, was sentenced to death at the War Trials, and executed in Nanking. Colonel Tanaka, whose battalions had been responsible for many of the atrocities, received twenty years imprisonment. Major-General Sano, the

Divisional Commander, and Lieutenant Wada, who had the
hatches secured on the *Lisbon Maru*, both died before they could
be brought to trial. Two of the three Regimental Commanders
were returned to Hong Kong for lengthy investigations into
their conduct. The exception was Colonel Doi, the victor of the
Shingmun Redoubt. He took the name Keisho, became a
Buddhist priest and could not be traced until 1952 when he was
Chief Priest of the General Temple in Urakable.

Fate had eventually caught up with the 38th Japanese Division, for the greater part of it was destroyed at Guadalcanal in
early 1943. Major Kemotsu, whose 3rd Battalion had captured
Repulse Bay, was killed in New Guinea where his battalion was
annihilated.

Fortune smiled on most who had defended Hong Kong and
survived. Sir Mark Young was warmly welcomed back to Hong
Kong in 1946, to resume his duties as Governor. General
Maltby was honoured with the cb for his steadfast leadership in
appalling circumstances. 'He did not have a hope in hell of
undoing the lethargy and blindness of the past, nor of trying to
remedy and reorganise the Defence Scheme in a few months,'
wrote one survivor to the author. Chan Chak, the one-legged
Chinese Admiral, was decorated by the British Government,
and as Admiral Sir Chan-Chak kcb, he became the first post-
war Mayor of Canton.

Both Colonel Ride, of the British Army Aid Group, and
Doctor Selwyn Clarke were also later knighted, and many who
are named in these pages were decorated for their valour. Some
who soldiered on received high rank, while others distinguished
themselves in different walks of life.

THE LASTING HONOUR

Many of the actions in Hong Kong deserve to be legendary: the
gallantry of the Canadians at Wong Nei Chong Gap which
earned an extraordinary Japanese tribute to the survivors of the
Battalion, earlier considered to be 'not recommended for operational consideration'; the prolonged and heartening defence of
Leighton Hill by the 'odds and sods' of the Middlesex; the bitter counter attacks fought by the decimated Royal Scots
against two Japanese battalions at the Gap; the Rajputs with
100% British Officer casualties; the Volunteers whose proud

motto to this day is appropriately 'Second to None'; the truly epic defence of the Hughesiliers at their power station. They were heroes all.

'There was,' as the official history has it, 'no lack of good and gallant leadership.'[4] The deeds of such men as Lieutenant-Colonel Stewart DSO, Colonel Newnham GC, Captain Douglas Ford GC, Flight-Lieutenant Gray GC, Captain Ansari GC and CSM John Osborn VC, bear witness to this fact. Tragically, apart from their example, they had one other matter in common. None of them survived.

Five days before the last shot was fired in Hong Kong, Winston Churchill had signalled the Governor, on 21 December, 1941: 'The enemy should be compelled to expend the utmost life and equipment . . . Every day that you are able to maintain your resistance you and your men can win the lasting honour which we are sure will be your due.'[5]

He later wrote in his history of the war: 'These orders were obeyed in spirit and to the letter . . . The Colony had fought a good fight. They had won indeed "the lasting honour".'

Sources

The War Diaries, Regimental accounts and despatches were compiled months if not years after the surrender, in Japanese prison camps under the most difficult conditions, and often from memory. As a result several accounts are contradictory on some 'facts', and opinions invariably differ on important points. The author has reluctantly discarded some vivid but unsubstantiated accounts and preferred those which can be verified from different sources.

There are many files in National Defence HQ, Ottawa, and in the Public Records Office, London, which contain Hong Kong war time intelligence, summaries, signals, marked maps, appreciations, and Brigade, Regimental and subunit accounts. All have been consulted. The 'Mainland' and 'Island' war diaries quoted in *The Lasting Honour* were compiled by Brigadier C. Wallis MC in April-August 1942 in Argyle Street POW Camp, and were based on the diaries of the units under his command; the page numbers quoted below refer to the original manuscript pages of those diaries. Features shown on the maps are spelt as in 1941.

Abbreviations used are:
LTA: Letter to the author. (The writer is only named when he/ she is not obvious from the text.)
IWA: Interview with the author.
PRO: Public Records Office.
NDHQ: National Defence Headquarters, Directorate of History, Ottawa.
Desp: Despatches of Major-General C. M. Maltby, CB, MC

References

1 THE STRATEGIC LIABILITY

1 W. S. Churchill, *The Grand Alliance*, p. 157
2 File 106/2375 PRO
3 *Ibid*
4 W. Stevenson, *A Man Called Intrepid*, p. 158.
5 Memo Mr. Hollis to PM 10.9.41 PRO
6 File 593.013 (DS) NDHQ

2 THE CANADIANS ARE COMING

1 File S 8873 NDHQ
2 Report by the Royal Commission PC 1160 4.6.42 NDHQ
3 File 593 (D14) MOIO NDHQ
4 Skelton's Diary
5 LTA

3 HONG KONG

1 LTA from Iain MacGregor
2 LTA from J. A. Ford
3 A. Muir, *The First of Foot*, p. 85.
4 LTA
5 LTA from C. M. M. Man
6 P. K. Kemp, *The History of the Middlesex Regiment*, p.29
7 LTA from Iain MacGregor
8 LTA
9 File 106/2400 Signal 1488 19.11.41 PRO
10 Signal 54363 from WO to C-in-C Far East 27.11.41 PRO
11 File 106/2400 PRO
12 LTA
13 File 106/2400 PRO

4 THE ENEMY AT THE GATES

1 File 208/872 PRO
2 Statement taken by GHQ Far East Comd MI Sec GS NDHQ
3 *Ibid*

5   JUST THE USUAL CRISIS

1 IWA   5 LTA
2 Redwood's diary   6 Lewis Bush, *The Road to*
3 *Ibid*   *Inamura*, p.135
4 P. Harrop, *The Hong Kong Incident*

6   WITHDRAWAL TO THE GIN DRINKERS' LINE

1 LTA from H. G. Sullivan   3 LTA
2 IWA

7   THE BATTLE FOR THE MAINLAND

1 LTA   5 Desp para. 20
2 Progress report of 228 Regt   6 LTA
     written by Col Doi NDHQ   7 *Ibid*
3 A. Muir, *The First of Foot*,   8 Mainland War Diary, p. 37
     p. 102   9 *Ibid*, 41
4 Mainland War Diary, p. 22

8   NOTHING BUT DARKNESS AHEAD

1 A. Muir, *The First of Foot*,   2 File 982.013 (D3) NDHQ
     p. 108

9   CLAY PIGEONS IN A SHOOTING RANGE

1 Fuehrer conferences on   11 W. Brown, *Hong Kong*
     Naval Affairs   *Aftermath*, p. 22
2 Lawson's Diary   12 P. Harrop, *The Hong Kong*
3 Desp para 46   *Incident*
4 LTA   13 Newton's Diary
5 *Japan Times Weekly* 17.9.42   14 Lawson's Diary
6 LTA   15 Statement taken by GHQ
7 File 593 (D14) PRO   Far East Comd MI Sec GS
8 Redwood's Diary   NDHQ
9 LTA   16 *Ibid*
10 Island War Diary, p. 13   17 *Ibid*

10 THE JAPANESE LANDINGS

1 The Japanese plans and reports which are quoted in this and subsequent Chapters are taken from personal accounts and interrogation reports of Lieutenant-General Ito Takeo in July 1947; Major-General Shoji Toshishige in November 1946 to Captain E. C. Watson; Major-General Tanaka January–February 1947. All these accounts are in NDHQ as are Colonel Doi Teihichi's notes and statements.

2 Statement made to Mrs MacAuley in January 1943. File 593 (D22) NDHQ

3 Statement in NDHQ

4 *Ibid*

5 LTA

11 NUMB DESPAIR

1 Island War Diary, pp. 123–124

2 *Ibid*, p. 29

3 All statements concerning CSM Osborn VC, in NDHQ, were made to Lieutenant-Colonel G. Trist in Jan 1946

4 A. Muir, *The first of Foot*, p. 121

5 File 593 (DI) NDHQ and IWA

6 Island War Diary, p. 34

12 THE BATTLE FOR REPULSE BAY

1 Island War Diary, p. 42

2 *Ibid*, p. 54

3 File 593 (D5) NDHQ

4 LTA

13 THE JAPANESE ADVANCE WEST

1 Letter from Brigadier A. Peffers to Brigadier W. H. S. Macklin 22.9.45 NDHQ

2 Statement on board SS *Gripsholm* Nov 43 NDHQ

3 Statement to Major E. E. Dennison 28.2.46 NDHQ

4 Statement in NDHQ

5 Joyce's Diary

6 *Ibid*

7 Redwood's Diary

8 Island War Diary insert between pages 42 and 43

9 Desp para 109 (a)

10 Doi's account NDHQ

11 Winnipeg Grenadier account compiled in 30.4.42 NDHQ

12 IWA

13 Statement made 8.2.46 File
 593 (D5) NDHQ
14 Statement by Shoji 25.11.46
 NDHQ
15 Signal Admiralty to NDHQ

 27.11.41 NDHQ
16 G. Priestwood, *Through
 Japanese Barbed Wire*, p. 21
17 File 106/2420 A PRO
18 File 106/2412 PRO

14   THE ODDS AND SODS

1 LTA
2 *Ibid*
3 Statement made 28.2.46 File
 593 (D5) NDHQ

4 Statement made in January
 1947 prior to War Crimes
 Trial proceedings NDHQ
5 Redwood's Diary

15   CHRISTMAS DAY 1941

1 Campaigns in S. E. Asia 1941
 −2, 66
2 Desp para 142
3 *The War Against Japan*, Vol I,
 p. 142. Also C. P. Stacey,
 Six Years of War, p. 479
4 File 352.019 (DI) NDHQ
5 LTA. Also Island War Diary,
 pp. 124–126

6 Island War Diary, p. 112
7 *Ibid*, p. 82
8 LTA
9 Desp para 150
10 *Ibid* para 148
11 A. Muir, *The First of Foot*,
 p. 128
12 LTA

16   SURRENDER

1 A. Muir, *The First of Foot*,
 p. 126
2 Island War Diary, p. 88
3 Statement 10.8.45 NDHQ.
 (Barnett gave evidence at
 the War Crimes Trial in
 Tokyo in 1947 and 1948.)
4 *Ibid*
5 IWA
6 File 593 (D3) NDHQ

7 Statement in NDHQ
8 File 593 (D37) NDHQ
9 Newton's Diary
10 Lewis Bush, *The Road to
 Inamura*, p. 142
11 LTA
12 IWA
13 W. Brown, *Hong Kong
 Aftermath*, p. 46

17 IMPRISONMENT

1 LTA
2 File 106/2420 A PRO
3 G. C. Hamilton, *The Sinking of*
the Lisbon Maru, p. 1
4 LTA
5 *Ibid*

18 THEY ESCAPED

1 LTA
2 LTA from H. G. Sullivan
3 *Ibid*
4 *Townsville Sun*, November
1976, 43
5 LTA
6 R. B. Goodwin, *Passport to*
Eternity, p. 6
7 R. B. Goodwin, *Hong Kong*
Escape

19 OCCUPATION AND LIBERATION

1 D. C. Bowie, 'Captive
Surgeon in Hong Kong'
2 File 106/2400 PRO
3 Desp para 9
4 *The War against Japan*, Vol I,
150
5 W. S. Churchill, *The Grand*
Alliance, p. 634

Bibliography

W. Brown   *Hong Kong Aftermath*, 1943

Lewis Bush   *The Road to Inamura*, 1961

T. Carew   *Fall of Hong Kong*, 1960

F. A. E. Crew   *The Army Medical Services*, Vol. 2, *Hong Kong*, 1957

W. S. Churchill   *The Second World War*, Vol III, 1950

G. Dew   *Prisoner of the Japs*, 1943

W. A. B. Douglas, B. Greenhous   *Out of the Shadows*, 1977

L. P. Duff   *Report on the Canadian Expeditionary Force to the Crown Colony of Hong Kong*, 1942

E. Field   *Twilight in Hong Kong*, 1960

J. A. Ford   *The Brave White Flag*, 1961

R. B. Goodwin   *Hong Kong Escape*, 1953

R. B. Goodwin   *Passport to Eternity*, 1956

P. E. Guest   *Escape from the Bloodied Sun*, 1956

E. Hahn   *China to Me*, 1943

G. C. Hamilton   *The Sinking of the* Lisbon Maru, 1966

P. Harrop   *The Hong Kong Incident*, 1945

Hong Kong Volunteer Defence Corps,   *Record of the actions of the HKVDC in battle for Hong Kong*, 1954

D. H. James   *The Rise and Fall of the Japanese Empire*, 1951

P. K. Kemp   *The History of the Middlesex Regiment*

Woodburn S. Kirby   *The War Against Japan*, Vol. I 1958

J. Luff   *The Hidden Years*, 1967

J. H. Marsman   *I Escaped from Hong Kong*, 1942

A. Muir   *The First of Foot*, 1961

B. Prasad   *Official History of the Indian Armed Forces in World War II*, 1960

G. Priestwood   *Through Japanese Barbed Wire*, 1943

B. A. Proulx   *Underground from Hong Kong*, 1943

T. F. Ryan   *Jesuits under Fire*, 1951

C. P. Stacey   *Official History of the Canadian Army in the Second World War*, Vol. I, *Six Years of War*, 1957

Selected Articles

I. Adams   Macleans, Jul. 1968

D. C. Bowie   'Captive Surgeon in Hong Kong', *Journal of the Hong Kong Branch of the Royal Asiatic Society*, Mar. 1977, Vol. 15.

Canadian Veterans News Magazine, Spring 1977

J. N. Crawford   *The Canadian Medical Association*, 1947

J. N. Crawford   *Manitoba Medical Review*, Feb. 1946

K. Dobbs   *Star Weekly*, Aug. 1965

Hong Kong Volunteer Defence Corps   various articles

Journal of Imperial and Commonwealth History, Oct 1973, Vol I

W. K. Morrison   'Malaria in Hong Kong', *Journal Royal Army Medical Corps*, Vol 114, No 4, 1968

A. Muir   *The Scotsman*, 14 Nov. 1960

R. J. L. Penfold   'The Defence of Hong Kong', *The Gunner*, Dec. 1946

A. G. Penny   *A Short History of the Royal Rifles of Canada*

D. Pinkerton   *The Thistle*, Oct 1946, Jan 1947

C. P. Stacey   'The Defence of Hong Kong,' *Canadian Army Journal*, Dec. 1950

Despatches

1 Despatch by Air Chief
Marshal Sir Robert Brooke-
Popham, Commander-in-
Chief in the Far East, on
Operations in the Far East
from 17 Oct 1940 – 27 Dec
1941. (Published in the
supplement to the *London
Gazette*, 20 Jan 1948.)

2 Despatch by Major-General
C. M. Maltby, GOC
British Troops in China, on
Operations in Hong Kong
from 8 to 25 Dec 1941.
(Published in the
supplement to the *London
Gazette*, 27 Jan 1948.)

Diaries
(Excluding those still in private possession.)

Author	*Location* (in 1978)
B. C. Anslow (née Redwood)	Imperial War Museum
D. C. Bowie	Library of the Royal Army Medical Corps, Millbank
D. Joyce	Imperial War Museum
J. K. Lawson	Wolsey Barracks, London, Ontario
E. Levett	Royal and Gurkha Signals Squadron, Hong Kong
L. Newton	Imperial War Museum
M. Redwood	Imperial War Museum
S. Skelton	National Defence Headquarters, Ottawa

Glossary

Bren Gun Carrier	An open-topped, armour-plated, caterpillar tracked fighting vehicle armed with a light machine gun
CGS	Chief of the General Staff
C in C	Commander in Chief
C/Sgt	Colour Sergeant
CSM	Company Sergeant Major
GOC	General Officer Commanding
GSO1	General Staff Officer Grade 1
HQ	Headquarters
LMG	Light machine gun
Mortar	A large-bore, short-barrelled, muzzle loading gun designed to lob explosive projectiles at a high angle over obstacles
MTB	Motor Torpedo Boat
NAAFI	Navy, Army, Air Force Institutes
POW	Prisoner of War
RAOC	Royal Army Ordnance Corps
RNVR	Royal Navy Volunteer Reserve
VAD	Voluntary Aid Detachment
Volunteers	Members of the Hong Kong Volunteer Defence Corps

Index

(This Index gives the Grid Reference of places shown on Maps 2–3, pages 14, and 68–9.)